PERFORMANCE ROWING

THE ART AND SCIENCE OF MOVING YOUR BOAT FASTER

PAUL THOMPSON MBE and DR ANTHONY RICE

PERFORMANCE ROWING

THE ART AND SCIENCE OF MOVING YOUR BOAT FASTER

with a foreword by

SIR STEVE REDGRAVE CBE

THE CROWOOD PRESS

Contents

Foreword by Sir Steve Redgrave CBE

Rowing has been at the centre of my life for as long as I can remember. It's a sport that demands everything: physical strength, technical precision, mental resilience, unity of teamwork and unwavering commitment. But above all, it's a sport that thrives on the pursuit of excellence. No matter how fast you go, there is always something to improve. That's what keeps rowers and coaches coming back to the water, day after day.

During my career, I had the privilege of working with some of the finest coaches in the world – people who understood not only how to develop athletes, but how to unlock the tiny gains that ultimately decide races. Great coaching is more than instruction; it's insight, connection and the relentless pursuit of better. Training, too, is more than mileage. It's about knowing what to do, when to do it, and how to respond to what the body and the boat is telling you. When coaching and training are aligned, they form the foundation on which championship crews are built.

That's what makes *Performance Rowing: The Art and Science of Moving Your Boat Faster* such an important and timely contribution to the sport. This book dissects rowing and improves our collective understanding of what truly makes boats go faster. It is a blend of high-performance coaching insight, physiological expertise and biomechanical understanding, written by two people who know the sport inside out.

Paul Thompson is one of rowing's most respected and accomplished coaches. His career spans multiple Olympic cycles and world championships, and he has led crews to medal-winning performances across both men's and women's programmes. His technical mastery, strategic thinking, and relentless drive for performance have earned him international recognition and the trust of elite athletes worldwide.

Dr Tony Rice brings an equally vital perspective. With a strong academic background Tony is a Senior Sports Physiologist with decades of experience working in elite sport, including with national rowing teams. His expertise bridges the gap between high-performance sport science and practical coaching. He has contributed extensively to the advancement of physiological monitoring, training system design, and the effective application of data to enhance athlete development and performance outcomes. His work ensures that what happens in the lab translates to what matters on the water.

Together, Paul and Anthony have created a resource that is both deeply practical and grounded in evidence. This book is for anyone who is serious about performance. It's for athletes who want to train with purpose, for coaches who want to elevate their programmes, and for practitioners who want to bring clarity and structure to the complexities of elite-level preparation.

Sir Steve Redgrave CBE
Five-time Olympic Gold Medallist
Rowing Legend and Global Ambassador for the Sport

Introduction

There is a moment in rowing – fleeting but unforgettable – when everything clicks. The blade enters the water with precision, the boat glides effortlessly, and you feel an almost transcendent connection between power, rhythm and purpose. Whether you are a seasoned competitor, a coach fine-tuning your crew, or a dedicated club rower chasing personal bests, you know that making the boat go faster is about more than brute strength or endless metres of training. It relies on an intricate dance of physiology, technique, psychology and teamwork. This book is your guide to mastering that dance.

Between us, we have spent over 50 years immersed in the world of performance rowing. From racing on international waters to coaching and developing champions, we have studied and researched physiology and biomechanics, boat optimisation, and the techniques, training and psychology of the sport. We have learned that peak rowing performance comes from aligning science with intuition, data with experience, and effort with insight. Along the way, we have created the environment for rowers and coaches to collaborate and achieve World and Olympic success. We have worked within all levels of the sport and understand how to help rowers of all capabilities unlock speed they did not think was possible. This book is the culmination of that journey.

Why This Book Matters

Rowing is a paradoxically simple and complex sport. At its core, it is about moving a boat through water as quickly and as efficiently as possible. But anyone who has spent time on the water knows the complexity that hides behind that simplicity – matters of timing, technique, body mechanics, training load, boat feel, and crew cohesion, to name just a few. This book exists to decode those complexities and help you apply them practically, whether you are training solo in a single scull or managing the dynamics of an eight. The aim is to better understand rowing performance through exploring both the art and science of the sport.

You will not find one-size-fits-all solutions here. Instead, you will discover a tool kit of strategies, insights and frameworks designed to help you think critically about your rowing, assess where speed is gained or lost, and take control of your development. Think of it as both a coach in your pocket and a companion on your journey – one that speaks to the art *and* the science of making the boat go faster.

What You Will Learn

This book is structured around the key domains that contribute to elite-level rowing performance:

- Technique and efficiency: we will break down the stroke into its component parts – catch, drive, finish, and recovery – and explore how to optimise movement, minimise waste, and maximise boat speed. Through biomechanical insights and drills, you will learn how small adjustments can yield big gains.
- Training and physiology: we will delve into how to train smarter, not just harder. You will come to understand energy systems, periodisation, and how to tailor your training to your goals – whether that is a 2k erg test or Henley Royal Regatta. We will cover how to avoid over-training, track progress, and use science to your advantage.
- Mindset and psychology: performance does not come just from the body – it starts in the mind. We will explore strategies to build resilience, focus under pressure, and create a winning mindset. You will also learn how to cultivate trust and cohesion within a crew.
- Boat dynamics and technology: what really makes a boat fast? We will examine equipment, rigging, drag, and feedback tools that can help optimise your set-up and technique. Understanding the mechanics of boat movement will help you move with – not against – the water.
- The 'coach's eye': for coaches and self-coached athletes, we will offer frameworks for effective observation, feedback and progression. You will learn how to spot key performance markers, foster a learning environment, and translate training into race-day results.

Throughout the book, you will find stories from the water, case studies from top programmes, and practical exercises to put the concepts into action. Whether you are chasing tenths of a second or mastering the fundamentals, this book will help you think more clearly, train more effectively, and row more powerfully.

The journey to faster rowing is not linear, and it is never truly finished. But with the right tools, the right mindset, and a commitment to the craft, you can unlock more speed than you ever thought possible.

We hope you will find this book engaging and challenging, and that you will want to apply what you find here to your own rowing, crews or squads – and that they will be moving a little faster for it.

Will it make the boat go faster?

1 Contemporary Coaching

What does contemporary quality coaching look like? Success is measured today not only in medals but also in terms of athlete experience and holistic athlete development. This chapter explores the evolving areas and complexities of modern coaching and the leadership qualities, skills and programme components that the contemporary coach needs to consider.

What is a Great Coach?

Quality coaching is both fundamental and essential to the development of performance sport. Regardless of the level of rower – from an athlete in pursuit of an Olympic medal to someone who is taking to the water for the first time – the better the quality of coaching, the better the quality of their experience. A positive experience brings the aspiring Olympian one step closer to fulfilling their dream and the novice back to the boathouse. Coaching of a high quality engages people with the sport, promotes useful life skills, and grows friendships and opportunities.

A coach needs to be adaptable to stay relevant to the areas they oversee and the people they work with. Staying connected to youngsters or developing an understanding with a masters rower is all part of a coach's skill set. This should not mean that difficult discussions cannot be had when they need to be had, and that responsibility and accountability are diminished. A great coach is generally curious by nature.

A great coach puts the interest of the rower ahead of their own, builds relationships and challenges, and supports rowers by creating an environment in which they can develop, thrive and successfully achieve their goals. These principles are as relevant for novice rowers having fun and learning a new sport as they are for the rowers who are at the pinnacle of the sport – even though the complexities and details may be different.

A great coach coaches 'the person' and has a holistic approach to their development. A great coach is reflective – of themselves, of what they do, and how and why. They are accountable and take responsibility. A great coach is an observer, not just of the technical components, but of people. Observation and reflection, the coach's relationship with the athlete and the coaching solutions and interventions that are found are critical to the effectiveness of a coach's work.

A coach may be very close to the rower's performance, but they need to understand that ultimately it is the rower who is in the boat racing. Their role is to teach and instill responsibility and accountability and grow the rower's confidence to build their performance. Rowers equally need to understand and accept this too.

In order to get key messages across to athletes, it is vital for a coach to recognise their potential and to understand what they need. A rowing crew aims to be faster than the sum of its parts; similarly, the coach needs to be able to pull their understanding and vision together to create a programme that is more powerful than the sum of each coaching intervention.

Coaching Philosophy

A great coach understands themselves, what they personally stand for and what values they hold. A great coach lives their philosophies and beliefs every day and demonstrates these consistently through their actions, especially when under pressure. A coach's values should underpin their approach to coaching. Following personal reflection, a coach should be able to articulate what their coaching philosophy is, and how it influences their leadership style. If this philosophy is perceived to be true to their values and beliefs, this will engender trust in the rower, who will feel that the coach values them as an individual and will work hard to get the most out of

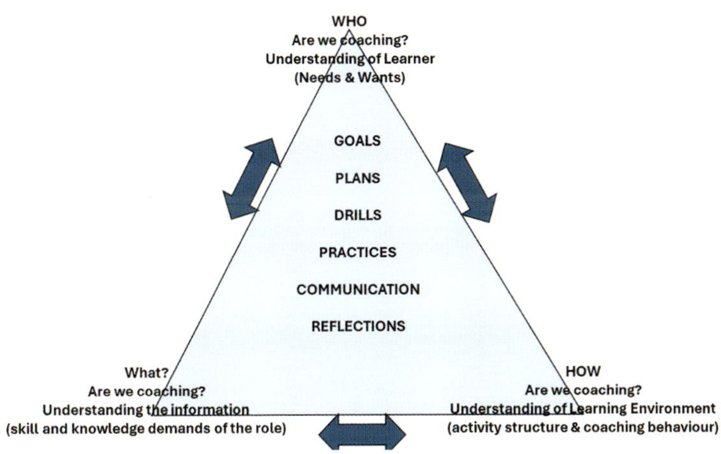

Figure 1.1
Adapted from Abraham and Collins (2011) and Muir et al. (2011), *The Coaching Matrix.*

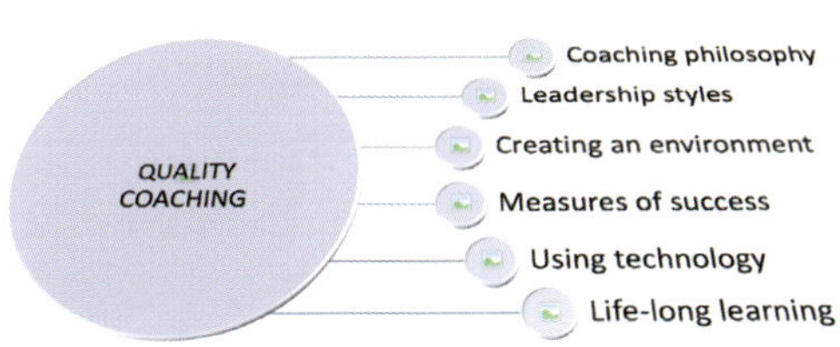

Figure 1.2
Understanding great coaching.

> *I am an authentic leader who treats each athlete as an individual. I get great satisfaction from helping people achieve their potential and aspirations. I value honesty, trusting relationships and hard work.*
>
> Paul Thompson

Post-training talk between rowers and coach. (Photo Peter Reed)

Keeping yearly coaching diaries is a valuable practice. (Photo Greg Hughes)

them. A strong relationship and a shared athletic journey will be created. Through this strong relationship, the highs and inevitable lows of sport will be jointly navigated, with the rower trusting that the coach is putting the rower's interest first. A high level of trust in the relationship will give the athlete greater belief and confidence in the coaching interventions that are being deployed, and the impact of those interventions will be increased.

A reflective coach must first understand themselves, to identify their own values and attributes, which will drive their strengths. Working through these, and using a coaching diary or personal journal to record them, will add clarity on how they want to be seen, how they want to influence, and what will underpin their own 'authentic' coaching style. Once their philosophy,

Reflecting on Your Coaching

Who do you coach? How well do you know your rowers?

How accurately do you read their body language, the way they move, their behaviour under stress or fatigue? Do you know what they really mean when they communicate? Do you understand their interaction with clubmates, teammates, or support staff?

How well do you appreciate the differences in communication styles between different people and generations?

Observational skills and experience underpin a coach's intuition and their way of interacting with people. Credibility and trust are pillars of a great coach. Being transparent, doing what you say you are going to do, acknowledging your own mistakes, and being authentic are all traits of a successful coach. Communication and messaging have always been critical to coaching, both on and off the water.

How do you identify and deliver the key messages, and when? What takes priority?

A great coach can take complex concepts or skills and communicate them in a simple and straightforward way. A good coach also needs to ensure there is alignment between what they observe or say and what the rower actually hears and understands.

style or values have been captured, it will be instructive to touch base with some trusted colleagues to determine whether they are actually living it.

Coaching Leadership Styles

There has been much written about different coaching styles – autocratic, democratic and laissez-faire are just a few that have been described. The following definitions date from 1939 (Lewin et al., 1939), but they have stood the test of time:

- the 'autocratic' coach decides what is to be done, when, where and how. The athlete has minimal input and discipline is high;
- the 'democratic' coach leads by setting the scene and deciding what is to be done, but seeks feedback from the athletes on how best to move forward. This style can also be described as a collaborative or partnership coaching style;
- the 'laissez-faire' coach takes a less active role and allows the athlete to guide the programme, development and responsibility. This type of coaching leadership is usually more prevalent in individual sports; in rowing, this would be single sculling.

In practice, a contemporary coach will need dexterity and flexibility in their approach and will often move between the various leadership styles to suit the situation in which they find themselves. In other words, they will need to be a 'multi-dimensional' coach. This is often referred to as 'situational leadership theory' (SLT), a model described originally by Paul Hersey and Ken Blanchard (Hersey & Blanchard, 1969) in *Management of Organizational Behaviour – Utilizing Human Resources* (New York, USA, Prentice Hall).

A coach also needs to be adaptable enough to move between being a trainer or instructor and mentor. A coach is an educator, who supports and guides a person to unlock their potential. Coaches need to give instructions, but the concept of coaching is about more than just barking orders and teaching. Coaching facilitates learning and growth. In rowing this is as critical as the training programme itself. The coach needs to be able to explain their programme so that the rowers understand what the training objectives are, and how to achieve them, in order to grow and develop both on and off the water. Coaching interventions can be adversely affected by the mental and physical demands being placed on an athlete, and this is particularly relevant in rowing. It takes considerable

The word 'coach' originated at universities in England in the eighteenth century to describe a tutor. As a horse-drawn coach carried the passenger to their destination, so the tutor or coach carried their students towards learning and passing their exams. The term was first used in a sporting context in the Victorian age, to describe someone who would 'carry' their charges to their sporting goals.

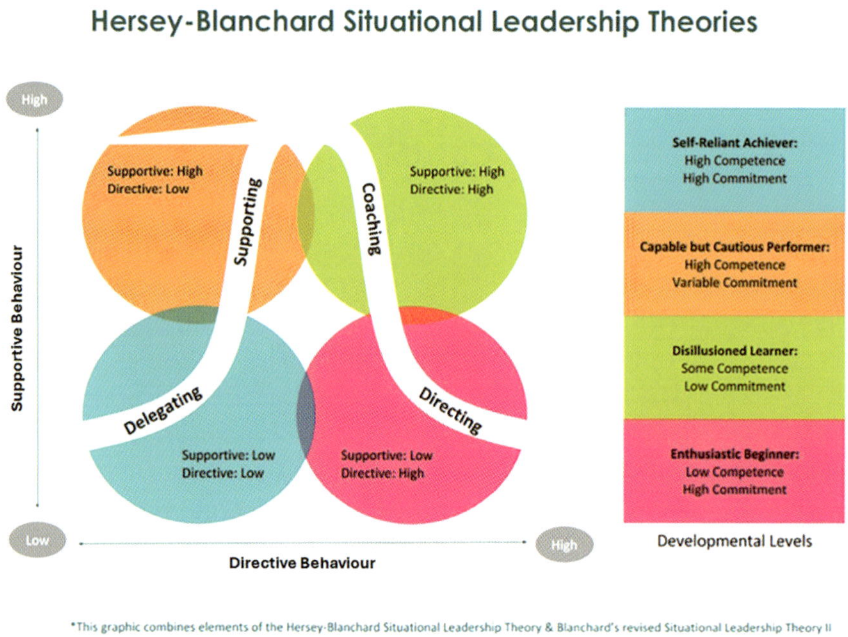

Figure 1.4
'Situational leadership theory' (SLT) model, originally created by Paul Hersey and Ken Blanchard.

effort to focus and concentrate over a two-hour training session whilst the body is operating at a high level of energy output and technical proficiency – often three times a day.

The nature of rowing coaching, especially on the water and predominantly in crew boats, means that the coach needs to be able to both instruct and coach. They will inevitably need to move between different leadership styles. Most on-water coaching is delivered from a distance, either from a coaching launch or from a bicycle on a path alongside the water. While the rowers are rowing, the coach will be using a megaphone, radio or simply shouting to get a point across. The nature of this dynamic means that the pre-training briefing is critical, outlining the training and technical objectives, session structure and targets. Everyone needs to know what they are going to do and what is expected of them. The coaching and instructing are done while the rowers are rowing, and any further follow-up or more in-depth coaching happens after the boat has stopped. There is, however, a tricky balance to be struck between the time needed to communicate feedback on the water, and the competing need to keep moving and achieve a physiological training load. Once off the water, it is important to debrief the training session by asking, 'Did we achieve what we set out to do? What is our objective next session?'

Rowers need constructive feedback and goals if they are to progress, so coaches need to cycle through 'Plan-Do-Review' on a daily basis. Understanding the athlete and the demands of the training programme, and being able to match the rower's level to those demands are critical skills for a rowing coach.

Creating the Right Environment

The Self-Determination Model (Deci & Ryan, 1985) has become increasingly popular in sport in recent years. The theory centres on three basic psychological needs of people: autonomy, competence and relatedness. Intrinsic motivation stems from an athlete's growing independence and autonomy, developing their competency and skills as well as connecting and relating to their goals and team. Coaches play a big part in creating an environment where motivation and performance can shine.

'Culture' is a much-used word in the arena of international high-performance sport, defined by UK Sport in 2020 as 'the lived experience of people in the [UK Sport] World Class Programme (WCP)'. UK Sport has invested time and resources into measuring the climate of the high-performance system through 'cultural health checks'. Its September 2020 'Update on Culture' reinforced the key characteristics of positive sports culture, which were developed from collaborative work done in 2017 with Lane 4, a management consultancy company focused on people development. Those characteristics were 'integrity, value and respect people, inspiration, and pursuit of excellence'.

This work is a very helpful lead for a coach to reflect on the environment they provide and facilitate for their athletes. They can do this by asking themselves the following questions:

- What characteristics describe the environment I facilitate?
- Would the characteristics I describe be the same as what the rowers would describe?
- What are their lived experiences? Is there both challenge and support?
- Would my rowers recommend their peers to join my squad?

For high-performing teams or individual athletes, high levels of challenge are required to achieve continuous improvement and to fulfil their potential. This needs to be combined with a significant level of support to make the most of their capabilities, lay down foundations for their post-sport life, and ensure a positive experience during their training career.

The coach cannot enable the right culture completely alone. It must also come from an athlete's own support structures – both sporting and personal. These should co-exist to unlock potential, with important performance values such as responsibility, accountability and, of course, winning.

A coach needs to be able to create a vision that their rowers can get behind, and they need to create an environment of challenge and support in order to achieve it. In practice, this means that the athlete's input is integral to the process. They must be connected to the journey and able to imagine the outcome. Facilitating and developing co-created goals will create connection between coach and rower, and better engagement in the mission on the part of the rower. Goals can be identified by asking the following questions:

- What are the team values and rules?
- What is important?
- What makes a difference?

The details should be fleshed out and communicated so that rowers, crews, squad, club, coaches and support staff ('the rowing team') can all engage in and commit to the goals. Culture and maintaining alignment between the agreed values, actions and lived experiences is a shifting entity, requiring regular check-ups, honest discussions and constant re-evaluation in a safe environment. When functioning at its highest capacity the rowing team will regulate itself and ensure it remains accountable to the agreed philosophies, openness, transparency and goals – essentially, it will keep itself 'on track'.

Rowing is a team sport, and, in any club or squad, there will also be 'teams within teams', as well as crews of varying levels, categories and genders. It is also a competitive environment in terms of boat, club and squad resources. Developing the right kind of culture will allow those teams within teams to function effectively. Good coaches will encourage and facilitate all members of every team to be the best versions of themselves, in an environment that offers both challenge *and* support.

Relationships

Relationships are critical for coaches. Coaching relationships are complex and exist on a variety of levels: coach–athlete, coach–coach, coach–support staff, coach–equipment/material supplier, coach–management, coach–official, coach–sponsor, to name just a few. In addition to all these relationships, the coach will need to balance their own private life and personal commitments.

Coach–athlete relationships are critical for unlocking potential. The ability for athletes and coaches to connect, engage and inspire, creates a foundation for performance. The performance journey becomes a shared and productive path – a partnership – which is a key component of the culture developed between both athletes and coaches.
The stronger the relationship, the better prepared the athlete and coach will be for the inevitable bumps in the road. A coach will be building these vital relationships with a wide variety of personalities and personality types. Being considered and considerate, and reflective, and developing an ability to establish mutual respect are qualities a coach can call on to develop a stronger relationship with all those types.

Professor Sophia Jowett from Loughborough University in the UK has been studying this subject since the 1990s. She describes the coach–athlete

Many of the successful long-term coaches would recommend to young upcoming coaches to find a mentor coach they look up to and trust.

relationship as being 'at the heart of coaching'. Jowett's research (Jowett, 2020) is widely published in psychology and sporting journals and some of her presentations can be found on YouTube (https://youtu.be/GtuFHMrhoDQ). She has also produced online tools to assist coaches and athletes in this area (www.tandemperformance.com) (Jowett, 2022). Coaches can easily engage with this work, reflect on their own relationships and practices, and pursue a competitive edge by improving their relationships.

Coaching is an international craft, and a coach may find themselves working outside of their own culture and not in their native language. In this case, the coaching messages may need to become simpler and more focused on what will make the biggest impact. This type of coaching will challenge a coach to reflect again on what is important and how they will deliver their vision. They may want to bring about change, but they may need to be sensitive to a variety of cultural and social factors. It is a good way to gain trust and understanding and to steer the rower or crew in a particular direction. People are people and coaching is a people game.

Diversity and Inclusion in Coaching

Diversity in the coaching space in terms of gender, sexual orientation, ethnicity, race, socio-economic background and disability enables the sport to reach out and create an environment where people feel they belong and can be the best version of themselves. It enriches the processes and experience for both coaching teams and their athletes, fostering better relationships, and leading to more effective and meaningful engagement. Diversity brings a varied perspective, leading to innovative problem-solving and strategies. It helps bring a deeper understanding of and respect for differences in athlete groups, which assists in strengthening relationships. It also brings a variety of role models, who can motivate more broadly, and inspire a deeper level of trust. Diverse coach groups can also tackle a wider range of athlete and coach performance issues, as well as general life challenges.

In summary, diversity has a long list of benefits:

- enriches coaching processes and experiences;
- fosters better communication, relationships and trust between athletes and coaches;
- brings varied perspectives for innovative problem-solving;
- encourages continuous learning and adaptability;
- provides diverse role models and broader inspiration;
- enhances performance and engagement through deeper understanding of the needs of athletes.

Diversity can be enabled by:

- creating environments that foster inclusion and belonging;
- creating a positive, supportive culture to attract and retain coaches from diverse communities;

- celebrating diverse community role models;
- instigating mentoring and networking initiatives;
- offering flexible working and family support;
- providing leadership development and opportunities for diverse communities.

Diversity can be blocked by:

- a lack of representation and voice; diverse community role models; mentoring and networking opportunities;
- inequality in pay;
- experiences of bias, bullying and poor treatment during recruitment and beyond;
- harmful assumptions and behaviours that marginalise minorities;
- unconscious bias towards certain communities.

The benefits of diversity are clear, and everyone involved in sport should be working towards being as inclusive as possible at all levels.

A Coaching Teams vs A Team of Coaches

Rarely is a coach operating on their own. In most boathouses, clubs, schools, universities, teams and squads, there will be more than one coach working and interacting. These are great learning opportunities. Often, coaches learn and develop experientially, through observation and trial and error. Curiosity is an important attribute in a coach. Every coach's eye is different, as is their interpretation of what they learn and experience.

Coaching is an art, and there are many ways in which a rower can develop into a high-performance athlete, just as there are many ways in which a coach can develop into a master. Similarly, there are many ways of crafting performances. A confident coach will use any opportunity to ask other coaches and experts for opinions on their crews, thus developing their ideas and building communities of good practice, which can be either formal or informal. This is very valuable in 'sense checking' a coach's ideas and experiences. The communities of practice can come from the coaches within a club or squad. When they work well together, a team of coaches can become a coaching team, where coaches know their role, but can bring out their own individual expertise to comment on and assist with other crews at any time, without fear of resentment. Shadowing of other coaches represents a very good learning opportunity. An experienced retired coach can also provide a good perspective and act as a mentor to current coaches.

Professional development is the responsibility of the individual and can be informal or formal. A coach's curiosity needs to extend to themselves, beyond what they do. Rowers need to be always progressing and developing, and the coach needs to do that too.

Performance Support Teams

No one person can embody all the expertise required in modern performance sport. The requirements of the event, whether it is a 2000m or head race, sit at the centre of a performance programme. The rowers, the crew and boat are the focal point, and the coach is one step removed, although it is the coach who needs to offer leadership and guidance in a multi-disciplinary performance support team to achieve the peak performance of the crew or squad. For all the coaching interventions and support around them, however, high-performance success is still built on outstanding athletes.

The coach needs the skills and knowledge to develop a cohesive training and performance plan that underpins and delivers the performance when it is required. Likewise, monitoring and testing protocols to assess performance, demonstrate improvement and build confidence are required to address each individual rower's needs and prioritise the input from the sport and medicine sciences and allied fields. A coach should utilise the skills of a variety of practitioners, if accessible, and make the most of the capabilities of the support team around them, to create the most effective training environment possible. Collaborating with rowers and support staff in the training plan creates better understanding and engagement. A performance support team effectively led by the coach can be a performance advantage.

A well-written performance plan, with visual references and cues, offers clarity to the support staff on how they can support the coach and rower. It can also identify what the priorities are and when they occur. Reviewing performance and training blocks with the multi-disciplinary team builds momentum in the programme and gives the opportunity to assess and challenge whether progress (visible and quantitative) is being made in the most important areas.

In creating a performance support team, a coach is seeking to develop trust in those around them, be they athletes (the performers), other coaches (the supporting cast), performance peers (the production crew), and other critical parties.

Measures of Success

How you train is how you race!

Rowing is clear cut when it comes to the outcome of a race: there is a winner, and all the other participants are placed behind them. The competition can be fierce and the margins small, so the daily training environment must prepare the rower for a challenging environment. However, every rower's experience of competition and what they feel as a measure of success varies, according to their past experiences and internal and external expectations. Making sense of and processing their aspirations and expectations against their outcome and experiences is an important and often underrated part of the post-race process. One person's 'success' can be perceived by another person as failure.

The coach plays a significant role in framing what success looks like for each of their rowers, crews or squads. Building on small successes in training, celebrating personal bests and consistency, overcoming adversity and turning around setbacks all feed into a rower's expectation and confidence in their performance.

'More than medals' is a concept in sport today that emphasises the importance of *how* medals are won over the winning itself. The ability to create a safe and nurturing environment, and to balance challenge and support, is a critical factor in a contemporary coach's tool kit. For an insight into what success can look like, have a look at Olympic medallist, former World Champion rower and diplomat Dr Cath Bishop's book *The Long Win: The search for a better way to succeed* (Bishop, 2020).

Coaching Technology

Technology can assist, not *replace the art of coaching!*

When it comes to the question of what a coach does and how they do it, technology and data have provided a daily 'objective eye'. A fast-growing and increasingly accessible and affordable technology market now offers a wide range of miniaturised user-friendly tracking and feedback devices, wearables and applications for capturing off- and on-water rowing characteristics and performance. These tools make it simpler for coaches and athletes at any level to gather, monitor, analyse and database training and rowing-specific information, either in real time or post-session, on or off the water.

Modern sport today is trending towards greater specificity and individualisation, and the design and materials of equipment (boats, oars, riggers, stretchers and seats) are also becoming increasingly technical. Seat shapes, handle grips and footstretchers are more individualised and gender- or weight-specific, to suit various body types or leg lengths, or accommodate various particular requirements for Para Rowing.

While the 'coach's eye' has special significance in instruction and training, because of the speed of feedback, it can lack precision. The coach may have a personal opinion about the rower's understanding of the training programme or about the efficiency of their rowing motion, or may interpret technical faults differently, so the feedback can be subjective. Technology, additional biomechanical equipment and applied analyses can add another layer, acting as an objective 'coach's eye'. They can quantify and monitor the training process, the well-being of the athlete and, ultimately, the racing. As data is measurable, this can provide the precision that might otherwise be lacking. As long as the information is correctly measured, analysed and presented, as well as being meaningful and applicable, feedback can be used to monitor the rower's technique and control the development of their performance. These objective messaging tools can be an extremely effective way to support a coach's objectives.

Although coaching is fundamentally about people, technology and data play an important objective role in supporting the modern coach. Coaches and rowers

Any information gathered and provided (in real time or post-session) needs to be

- applicable (rowing-specific);
- coachable (complements the coaching terminology); and
- trainable (athletes can relate to the information to make technical changes).

now have effective and efficient ways to monitor, test and track performance assessment and improvement over time, during training and in competition. Gathering, understanding and prioritising data and sport intelligence can provide a competitive advantage, identifying performance trends and breakthroughs. Technology can facilitate a deep dive into a rower's performance to understand their stroke and racing profiles and what underpins and creates their performance. From the perspective of most rowers, the key focus is most easily understood by the 'feel' in the boat. When rowers and technology collide and a technical change is required in the boat, the feel is, naturally, different. Often, the rower will simply say that the boat feels 'better' or, sometimes, 'worse'. Properly calibrated technology on the boat can measure the facts – the stroke length is x degrees, the shape of the acceleration trace is y, and the Watts the rower is producing is z – but the interpretation of the data will be down to the coach and rower. Both the subjective feel and the hard data are valuable pieces of feedback. The coach and rower need to take both into account when assessing the change.

If an element can be measured, it can be better understood and improved. Technology allows this to be done in greater detail and the more information a coach has the more areas they can coach. The skill of the coach is to identify and focus on the parameters that are key in tracking and developing performance, and to present that information in a meaningful way to the rower. A rower today may have more sophisticated technology skills and understanding than the coach and will be able to consume information in an evolving way. However, it is important to ensure that when an athlete is presented with data feedback on their performance, it is given and received in an objective constructive manner and not taken personally. Many modern athletes have a thirst for data and the coach can expect high quality questions, understanding and discussions. The more a rower understands and is engaged in the coaching focus, the more committed they will be to the coaching intervention.

The timing of feedback is important too. Should it be given immediately on the water, after the training session or demonstrating on the ergo, or on the bank before they go out for the next training session? In each of these scenarios the rower will have a varying degree of bandwidth available to take in the information, process it and achieve the desired coaching intervention. Too much information can overwhelm the rower and confuse the coach's message.

The coach needs to be cognisant of this and strategic in the delivery of feedback if it is to have maximal impact.

The combination of the 'art and science of coaching information' allows coaches and rowers to examine the different aspects of executing the rowing movement more precisely whilst allowing for individual differences and comparing it to a 'technical rowing model'. This model should be evidence-based and respect the physical and physiological principles that apply to rowing and racing. For more on this, *see* Chapters 2 and 3. A rowing model provides a basis for the development of other physical and psychological requirements.

Coaching Tips: A Summary

- Coaching is about people.
- Be reflective, and work to be the best version of you.
- Create and understand your own philosophy.
- Co-create a performance environment.
- Build relationships.
- Don't be an island, be collaborative; build a network of coaches to help develop your ideas.
- Utilise support staff expertise.
- Embrace technology.
- Use coaching and sport-specific terminology.
- Find a mentor (someone you look up to – not necessarily a rowing coach).
- View yourself as a facilitator and coordinator of others.

Tips from the Expert

Tom Dyson MBE, Great Britain Multiple World and Paralympic Gold Medal-winning coach has the following advice to offer:

- Always have clarity in your objective.
- Be ruthless about not focusing on things that will not add speed to the boat.
- Learn the craft properly; there are no short cuts.
- Always be progressing the person you coach.
- Undertake holistic development of the people you coach.
- Trust the rowers; you do not need to see everything.
- Individualise each rower's set-up.

2 Key Principles of Good Technique

This chapter explores the physics and biomechanical principles of effective technique in classic, Para and indoor rowing, and explains how to apply these principles. It will also present a Principles-Led Technical Model.

Understanding the physical principles of how a boat moves will enable you to develop your coaching and to articulate the most effective means by which to achieve that movement. A boat moves at three levels: first, there is the interaction of the whole system (boat, rowers and oars) with the water; second, the interaction of the crew as a collective with the boat; and, third, the interaction of the individual crew members with each other. These three interactions need to be considered alongside the unique way in which a rowing boat moves compared with other watercraft. The nature of rowing – which has a propulsive phase followed by a run or recovery phase – is distinctive and differs from the propulsion of other crafts, which is consistent.

Biomechanics

Before considering the key principles of good technique, it is important to have an understanding of some of the basic physical and biomechanical terms and principles that govern rowing. This section is not meant to be an academic treatise on biomechanics, which extends into many technical areas of physiology and sports science, but it will cover rowing technique as seen from a mechanical perspective, measurement techniques and equipment, and offer a refresher of the basic principles of force and power.

One source of information is Peach Innovations (http://www.peachinnovations.com/), established in 2002 by founder and engineer Paul Haines, and now the world-leading supplier of biomechanical instrumentation for rowing. Haines defines biomechanics as the study of biological systems using the methods of mechanics. Since the essence of rowing is a highly controlled and repetitive power stroke, it is a sport that is well suited to such analysis. Furthermore, the equipment involved readily lends itself to a variety of measurement techniques, enabling data to be collected and analysed relatively easily.

The science of biomechanics is used in many areas of rowing, including:

- development of technique
- equipment optimisation
- monitoring of training
- race strategy analysis
- injury prevention management

A good coach is an instinctive biomechanist who does not necessarily need costly equipment to make useful observations on their crew. However, data can often throw up surprises – even something as simple as 'you can actually row harder' – enabling improvements and allowing targets to be quantified. Crucially, it also provides a good point of interaction between coach and athlete, to reinforce discussion of technique and performance.

Biomechanical Measurement and Analysis of Rowing Technique

The following information uses typical force and motion data taken from a boat and relates it to rowing technique. It takes

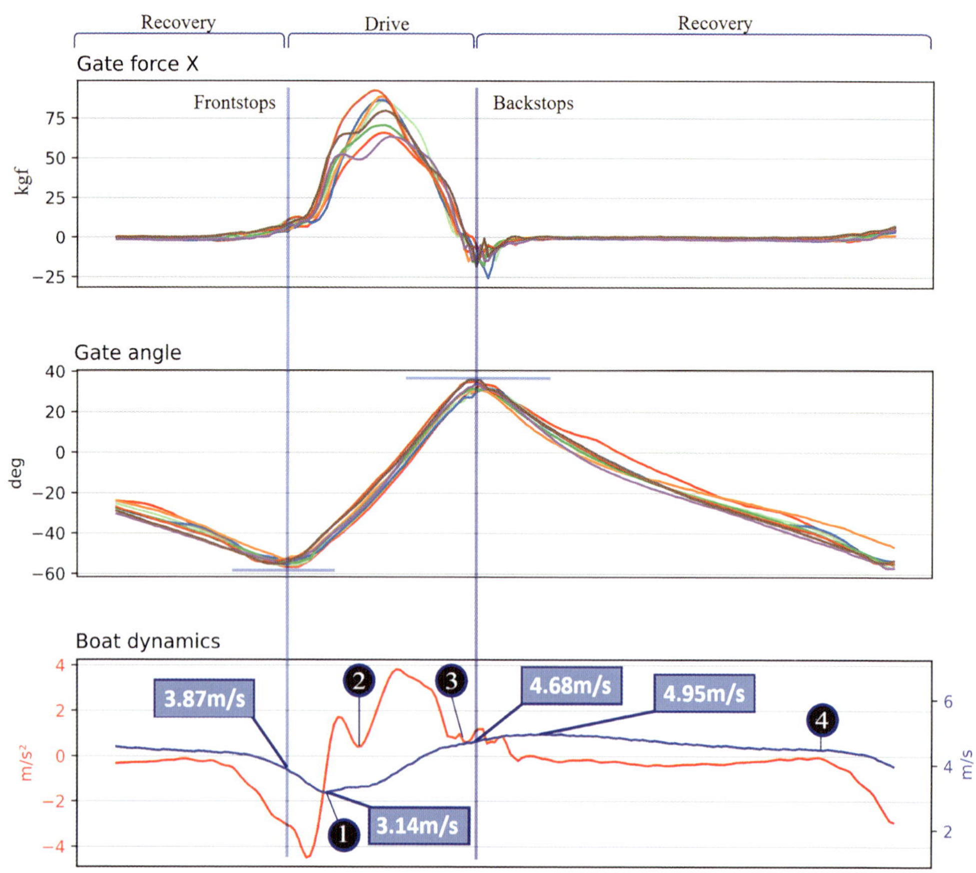

Figure 2.1

The oarlock force, angle and boat motion for a single stroke, using data taken from an eight rating 18spm.

a simplistic approach, concentrating on the dominant factors in the interactions between rower, boat/oars and water. All the comments apply equally to sculling as to sweep oar rowing. The graph (Fig 2.1) shows data taken from an instrumented eight rating 18spm, plotted against time. The data has not been selected as a model of perfection – far from it – but simply to illustrate various points.

The graphs at the top display the force applied at the oarlock in the direction of travel of the hull. There is one trace per rower, each colour-coded. The graphs in the middle show the angles of the oarlocks, and the graphs at the bottom show the acceleration of the hull (in red) and the speed of the hull (in blue). From the angles, it is possible to see where the rowers reach their furthest position forwards (front stops) and the furthest position backwards (back stops). This cannot be determined precisely, as the eight rowers are not quite together, but it is possible to take a rough average. Reading off the graphs, the hull speed at these two points is 3.87 metres per second and 4.68 metres per second.

The graphs between these two points represent the drive phase. At front stops, the rowers still have their blades in the air. Their task is to place the blades in the water and push their feet backwards. However, blade placement cannot possibly be instantaneous, and, as the rowers start to push backwards without full blade engagement, the reaction of the hull is to kick towards the stern. This is conservation of momentum at work. In this particular dataset, the hull reaches a minimum speed of 3.14 metres per second at point 1 in the graph above. As the blades progressively cover, their grip in the water leads to a coupling between hull speed and handle speed. If the blade does not slip rearwards, then the pin position, and therefore the hull position, is determined solely by oar angle. This is illustrated in the second graph (Fig 2.2), below. As the rowers move the handles, the boat moves; the ratio of the movements is determined by the geometry of the rigging.

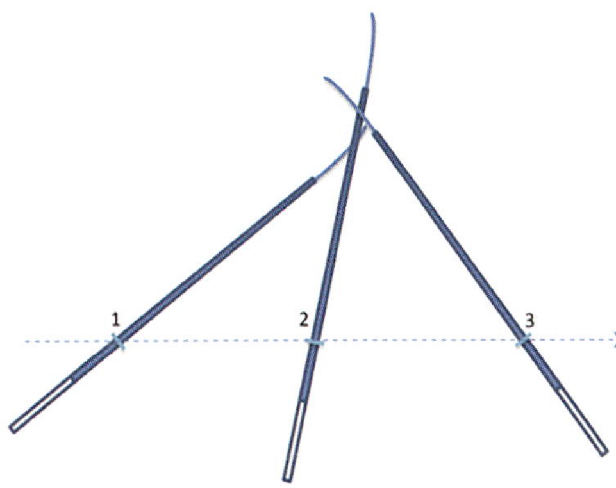

Figure 2.2
The sweep of the oar through three angles, and the corresponding forward progress of the pin, with no slippage of the blade in the water.

Before the blade enters the water, the hull speed is determined by the rowers' catch of the boat through their feet as they change direction. Once the blade is engaged with the water, the hull speed is directly related to handle speed. The hull therefore has to accelerate rapidly to make the transition between these two modes. This can be seen in the red acceleration trace between front stops and point 2 in the first graph (Fig 2.1). If the rower has the coordination and strength to make this transition happen quickly, then the acceleration of the hull will be very rapid, even reaching a local peak before point 2. Such a peak is a useful indicator of a fast catch placement and application of work.

From point 2 onwards, the hull speed will track oar speed, and the acceleration of the two is a function of the applied force.

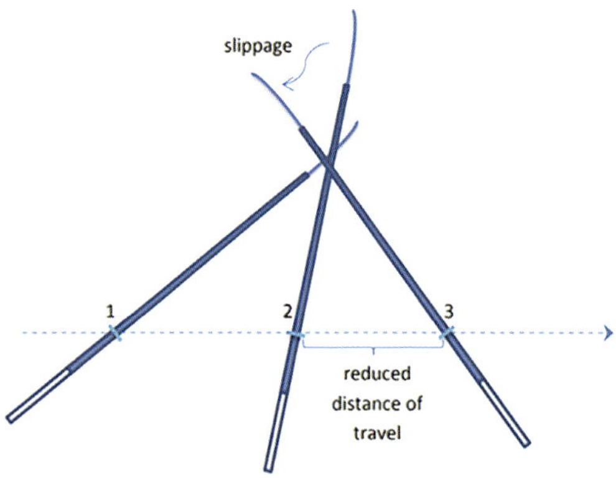

Figure 2.3

The sweep of the oar where there is some slippage of the blade in the water: although the change in oar angle is the same as above, there is a reduced distance of travel between points 2 and 3.

In the first graph, the hull acceleration can be seen to mirror the forces, peaking at around the same time. Of course, the relationship between hull and oar is compromised by the amount that the blade slips through the water, and part of the skill of a rower is in managing that slippage through efficient bladework. The progress of the pin is lessened if the blade is gripped with the water.

Looking at the curve of oar angle velocity for two rowers reveals various features related to this (Fig. 2.4). The initial peak in oar angle velocity (A) is mainly due to the bending of the oar during the early loading phase, giving rise to an apparent excess of oar velocity over boat speed. This will be further heightened if the blade is being rowed into the water, as is slightly the case in the left-hand graph (B). Once the blade is buried and engaged with the water, the expectation is that it will track boat speed. The graph on the left shows this well (C), but the graph on the right shows a surge in oar velocity halfway through the stroke (D),

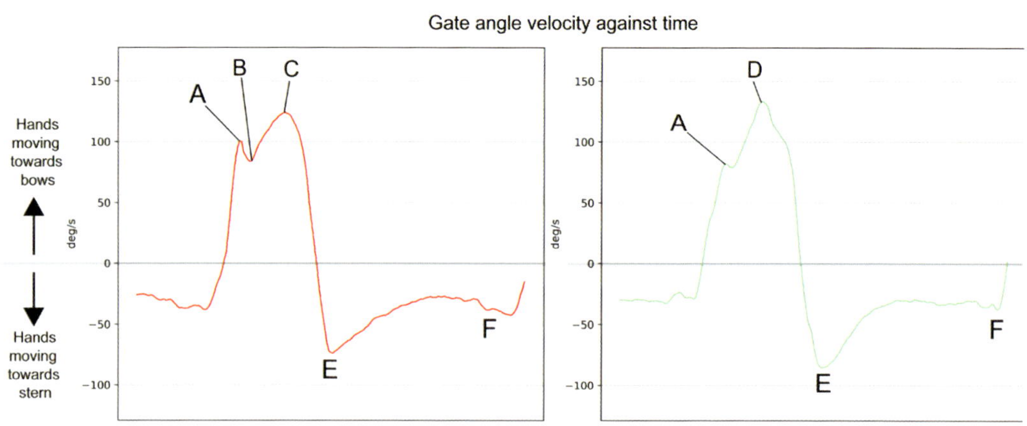

Figure 2.4

Gate angle velocity (degrees per second) for two rowers plotted versus time, through a single stroke. Positive angle velocity means the handle is moving towards the bow of the boat.

unrelated to force, as the blade is pressed through the water. Both graphs show a style of rowing that emphasises an exaggerated handle speed at the recovery (E), and a slight increase in handle speed towards the catch (F).

At the end of the drive, coming towards the release, some of the energy put into the stroke will have been absorbed into the bend of the oar. Towards the end of the stroke, the rower needs to be able to hold a strong position so that, as pressure falls off, the whip of the oar back into shape can effectively move the boat. There is a lot of 'noise' on the acceleration and force curves shown at point 3 in the first graph [Fig 2.1], as the rowers extract the blades and change the direction on the stretcher, some more efficiently than others.

Once the blades are out of the water, the acceleration of the hull will be dictated by the motion of the rowers and by water drag. The effect of water drag can be eliminated by considering a frictionless lake. Conservation of momentum dictates that, as the rowers accelerate their weight towards the stern, the hull will respond by accelerating forwards. The early part of the recovery sees a motion of the arms, which weigh relatively little, and the hull is therefore not much affected. As the rowers bring in body swing and movement up the slide, their full weight is moving and the hull will shoot forwards. If the rower completes this change in direction early on and moves at constant speed up the slide, then the hull will see no further acceleration forwards. The decline in speed due to water drag, which is proportional to the square of hull speed, is then superimposed on to this pattern. The example data, however, show that the speed of the hull is not really decreasing through the latter part of the recovery 4 (*see* the first graph [Fig 2.1]). This is because this crew is increasing their momentum transfer late on in the recovery, either by speeding up on the slide or by lunging forwards with the trunk. This is apparent from the increase in negative oar velocity coming into the catch, as seen earlier. With additional data from seat position, it will be possible to discern the extent to which this can be attributed to trunk or seat movement. As the rowers come into front stops, they decelerate to rest on the slide, and the hull, dutiful as ever to the conservation of momentum, responds by kicking backwards. The cycle is complete and another stroke commences.

The analysis of the stroke has so far been quite simple, concentrating on the dominant features of the interaction between rower and boat. With some detailed refinement of this model, it will be possible to learn how changes in technique will affect performance, and how factors such as sweep versus scull, blade slippage, centre of mass, rigging geometry and physiology modify the model.

Force Curve Shape

The most commonly asked question in rowing biomechanics is, 'What is the shape of the perfect force curve?'. Unfortunately, there is no single answer, as it depends on the physiology and anatomy of the athlete as well as the seat and the boat class.

However, it is underpinned by some general principles. It is generally accepted that work ought to be applied early on in the stroke, for several reasons: the athlete is using their largest muscle groups; the handle is moving at its slowest, which is easier to work against; and the blade is working at its most efficient as it comes through square to the hull. It is therefore very important that the catch technique enables an early application of work. However, it is possible to work too early and to row the blade into the water, typically by lifting on with the body. This results in a loss of energy to water turbulence as the blade makes an impact. This can appear in a force curve as an initial hump – the result of the blade impact (*see* below [Fig 2.5]). Ideally, the oar should be placed quickly and 'quietly', carved edge on into the water, and the work should be picked up quickly.

Much has been written on the subject of the sequencing of the legs, trunk and arms in rowing. A simple view is that, once the blade has gripped the water, then any work put down, up to the point at which the blade loses efficiency in the water, should be useful work. Given this, the task is simply to maximise the work, and the choice of sequencing will come down primarily to the physique and conditioning of the rowers. The sequencing does determine the motion of the centre of mass of the rower, and with it has various effects on the hull dynamics. However, these considerations are secondary to choosing a technique that enables an athlete to unleash their energy in a manner that is natural and that they are able to sustain over a 2000m race.

When measuring force curves on the boat, smoothness indicates that the rower is opening up and driving in a

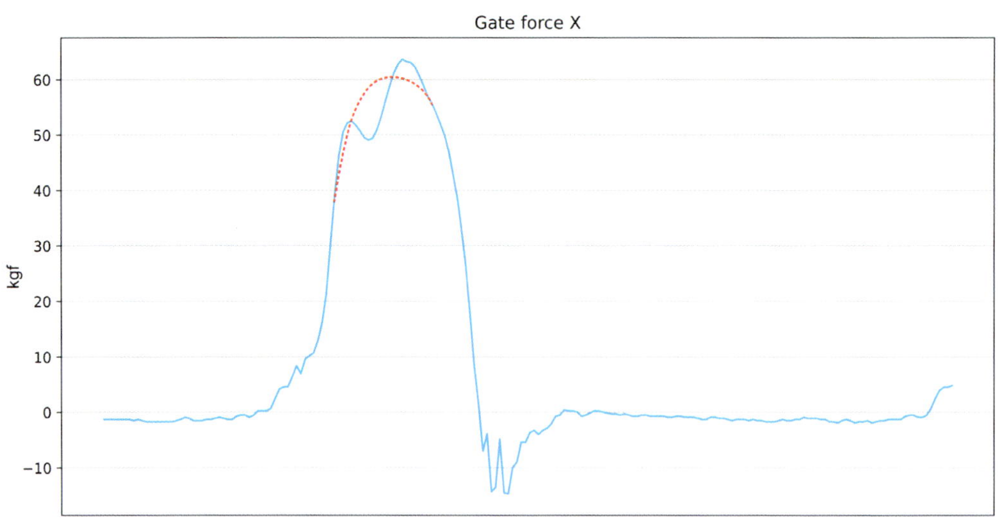

Figure 2.5

The force curve displays an initial hump due to rowing the blade into the water. The red dotted line represents a more idealised curve shape, with proper grip on the water.

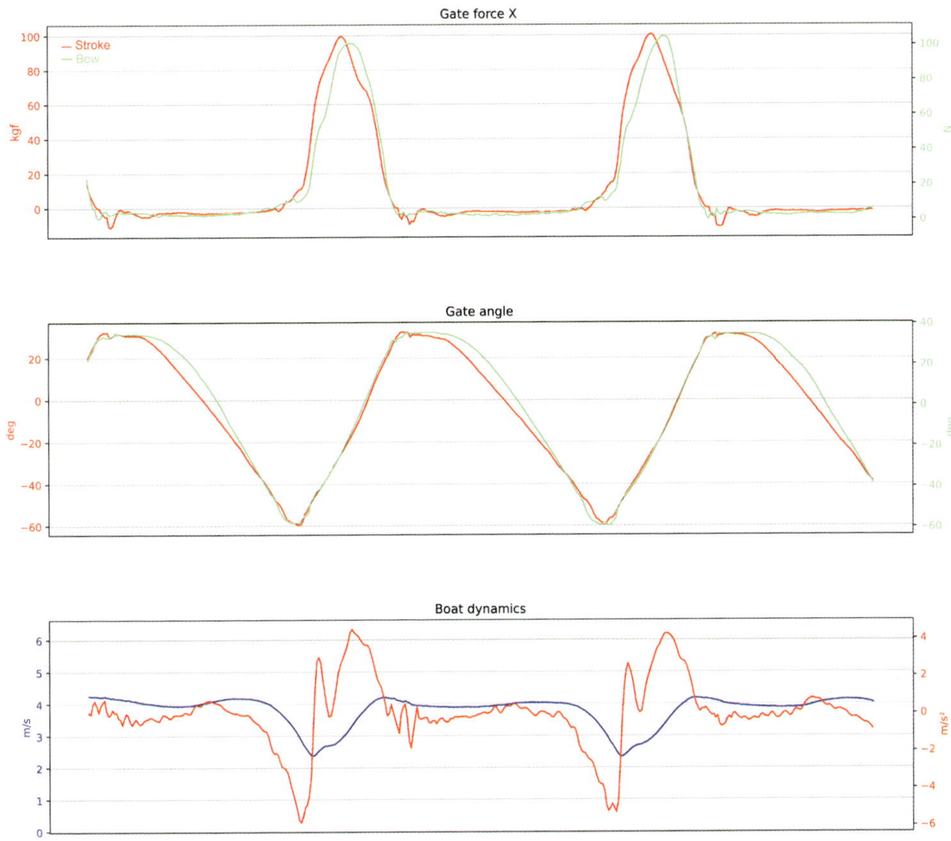

Figure 2.6
Elite pair rowing: note the slight dominance of the stroke force (red) in the first half of the stroke, switching to dominance of the bow (green) in the second.

fluid, relaxed manner. Assessing the seat and trunk position can help clarify the sequencing and identify any disjointed motion. Of course, the application of technique cannot be made entirely without reference to boat type. In large boats, such as eights and quads, the speed of motion determines an especially fast movement of the athlete at the front end of the stroke, otherwise they will not catch up with the water speed. In small boats, the extra time spent in the water determines an emphasis on the endurance rather than speed properties of the muscle. In pairs in particular, the force curves of the bow and stroke seat will need to differ for optimal performance – if they apply the force equally, then the reach of bow's blade round at the catch will have more turning effect on the hull than stroke's and the hull will not run straight. It is therefore necessary for bow and stroke to emphasise the loading at the back and front end of the drive respectively. A good pair will achieve this instinctively (*see* below [Fig 2.6], for an elite pair rating 20spm).

Uniformity of Style

The instinct of a coach is to achieve uniformity of movement and timing in a crew boat. Why is this the case? Might athletes of differing physiques rowingtogether benefit from pursuing their own individual style? At an extreme, various theories have emerged over the years promoting the theoretical advantages of time-delayed rowing, in which crew members take it in turns to pick up the work. The reality is that, under the duress of working hard, the body performs best when encountering predictable and smoothly applied loads. If athletes are emphasising different parts of the drive, then the platform presented to each rower under their feet and in their hands will undergo erratic motion driven by the others in the crew. Achieving some uniformity is not only technically beneficial but also offers an immense psychological advantage, as the rowers work together and feel their rhythm reinforced by the others. Uniformity of style can be identified by how well overlaid the force curves are at both the pin and the stretcher. However, an averaged indicator of how well a crew is moving together can be picked out from the graph of hull acceleration (*see* Fig. 2.7).

Crew members who do not arrive together at the front turn, or who adjust or hesitate to place the blade, will characteristically have a broad minimum on the acceleration (*see* Fig. 2.8).

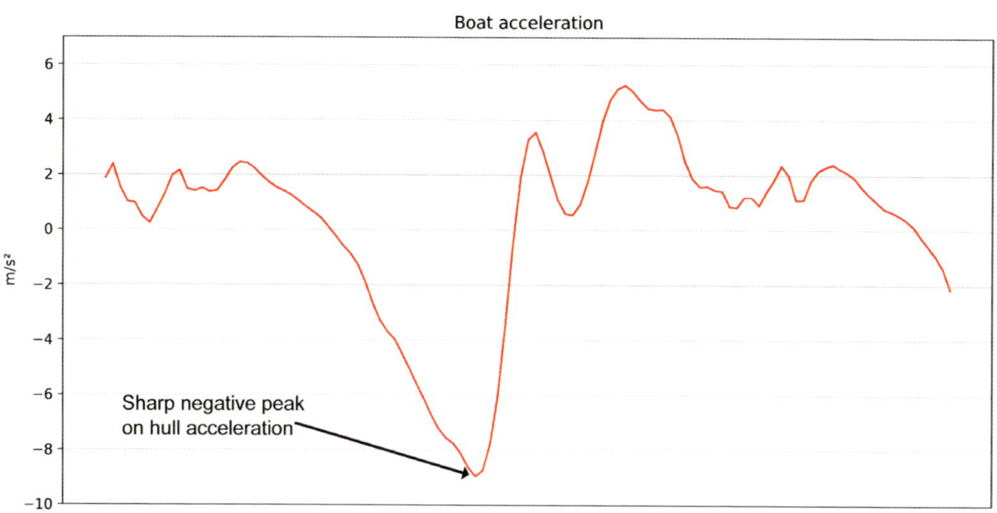

Figure 2.7

The acceleration curve shows a strong downward shape followed by a sharp pick-up, reflecting a crew that is moving together into front stops and driving off together.

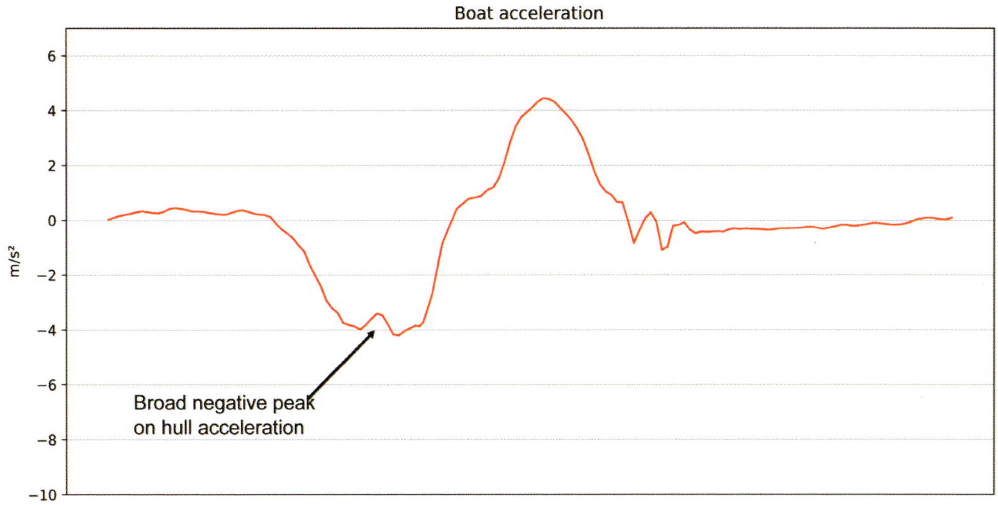

Figure 2.8
The broad negative trough in the acceleration before the catch shows a lack of crew coordination and some hesitancy at the catch. Note also that the acceleration subsequently rises quite slowly and fails to reach an initial peak unlike in figure 2.7.

Force, Energy, Work, Power and Momentum

Force

Everyone has an instinctive appreciation of force: it is the application of a pressure or attraction that can cause the motion of an object. If force is applied to an ergo handle, the flywheel moves in response. The unit of measurement of force is Newton (N) in recognition of the scientist who first observed the relationship between applied force and the acceleration of an object: a 1N force accelerates a 1kg mass at 1 metre per second per second. A mass of 1kg hanging on a wire (and therefore resisting acceleration due to gravity of 9.8 metres per second) will be restrained from falling by a tension of 9.8N in the wire.

Energy

Some examples illustrating the instinctive notion of energy are a moving object, which has kinetic energy, a rising object that acquires potential energy, and a compressed spring that stores energy in the shear of its molecular structure. The unit of energy is the Joule (J), and there are equations to compute the magnitude of the energy in all its forms. The kinetic energy of a mass m moving at speed v is $\frac{1}{2}mv^2$, so a 70kg rower moving at 5 metres per second has kinetic energy of $\frac{1}{2} \times 70 \times 52 = 875$J.

Work

Work is done when one object transfers energy to another. By combining the equations of force and energy, we end up with a very simple relationship: when an object is pushed, the energy transferred to it is equal to the magnitude of the force applied multiplied by the distance moved – this is independent of how long it takes and what the energy is converted into. With an ergo, if a rower applies a constant force of 300N (approximately 30kg 'feel' in the hands) through a 1.5m range of movement, they will have done 450J of work. This energy is converted into the kinetic energy of the flywheel, which will subsequently dissipate into the airflow around the fan and ultimately into sound and heat. Of course, if the ergo handle has not moved because the chain was jammed, no work will have been done, even though a force has been applied.

Power

Power is the rate of doing work and is measured in Joules per second, also known as Watts (W). If the rower is taking a stroke every two seconds (in other words, rating 30), their averaged power output is 225W (expending 450J over 2s). The instantaneous power output is the force applied multiplied by the speed: the power required to apply a constant force to an accelerating handle therefore increases as the handle speed increases – it takes more power to apply a force at the back end of the stroke than at the front end.

Momentum

The final factor is momentum. Imagine that the boat is sitting on a perfectly frictionless lake. Without any external forces, the centre of mass of 'the system' – the hull plus rowers – will not move. If the rowers pull themselves towards the stern, the hull will slide forwards in reaction; as they push off the stretcher, the hull will kick backwards. This is known as the conservation of

Energy Exchange

There are various forms of stored energy in a rowing boat system:

- The hull, rower and oars all have the kinetic energy of motion.
- Oars can store energy by virtue of deflection.
- The rower changes their potential energy through vertical motion (the ability to do work by falling back down again).

All these energies are exchanged by mechanical linkage, and one form of energy can be recouped to increase another. Ultimately, all energy is dissipated through friction, primarily into the flow of water and air around the boat, but also within the boat and the rower. It is only the continued injection of energy into the system by the rower (courtesy of their breakfast, metabolism and muscular activity) that keeps the boat moving. One interpretation of 'efficient rowing' is the adoption of a style that minimises the losses, so that a greater part of the energy injected by the rower remains stored as kinetic energy – in other words, motion towards the finish line.

momentum. The mathematics dictate that if, for example, the rowers weigh six times as much as the hull, then, relative to the lake, the hull will move six times further than the rowers. If the rowers traverse 700mm on the slide, someone looking at the boat from the lake will see the hull move 600mm in one direction, and the rowers move 100mm in the opposite direction.

Applying Biomechanical Principles to High-Performance Rowing

Level 1: The Whole Rowing System

In the first interaction of the whole system, the boat is accelerating (during and after the propulsive phase) and decelerating (during the recovery phase). This cycle of acceleration and deceleration means that the velocity of the boat increases and decreases during the stroke cycle. During the front turn and the initial drive the boat can change quickly from deceleration to acceleration, therefore keeping the minimum velocity higher creating a faster average boat velocity. In terms of technique, this means that the rower needs to have a fast and well-timed entry and catch and to apply their force quickly at the catch. This is where the boat is at its slowest and therefore there is the greatest requirement to apply force to accelerate quickly and turn the boat's minimum velocity around at a higher level.

Research into rowing performance on the ergometer from Imperial College, London (Buckeridge et al., 2015) describes the importance of the catch to maximal handle force, which is described as the critical drive. The best rowers were able to maintain their lumbar/pelvic position in place between the catch and maximal handle force. The hypothesis is that this solid trunk position is most effective in allowing the force produced by the legs to be transmitted through the trunk and arms to the handle. A collapse in the trunk risks leaking power. This strong trunk position and engagement of the gluteal muscles also provide protection for the rower's back when the load on the rower is at its highest during the drive.

To maximise the boat's acceleration the rower needs to accelerate the boat all the way from the catch to the finish, which means technically that the rower has to sequence their drive phase well. This requires them to maintain their bodyweight suspension between the handle and the foot stretcher, producing power ahead of the boat speed to keep the boat accelerating for the whole of the drive. This maximises the drive phase, keeping the average velocity higher for longer and a higher velocity of the boat into the recovery phase. Rowers who have a poor sequence tend to lose connection with the oar's blade on the water, resulting in reduced force and therefore reduced acceleration. Two technical faults leading to this are poor sequences resulting in poor suspension and rowers who draw their arms too low at the finish and wash out their blades. This leads to reduced force available to accelerate the boat.

The recovery phase during the interaction of the whole system with the fastest crews sees them maximise the boat's run between the strokes. This demonstrates a crew's efficiency. Hydrodynamic drag (the drag of the hull on the water) is the predominant resistance that works against

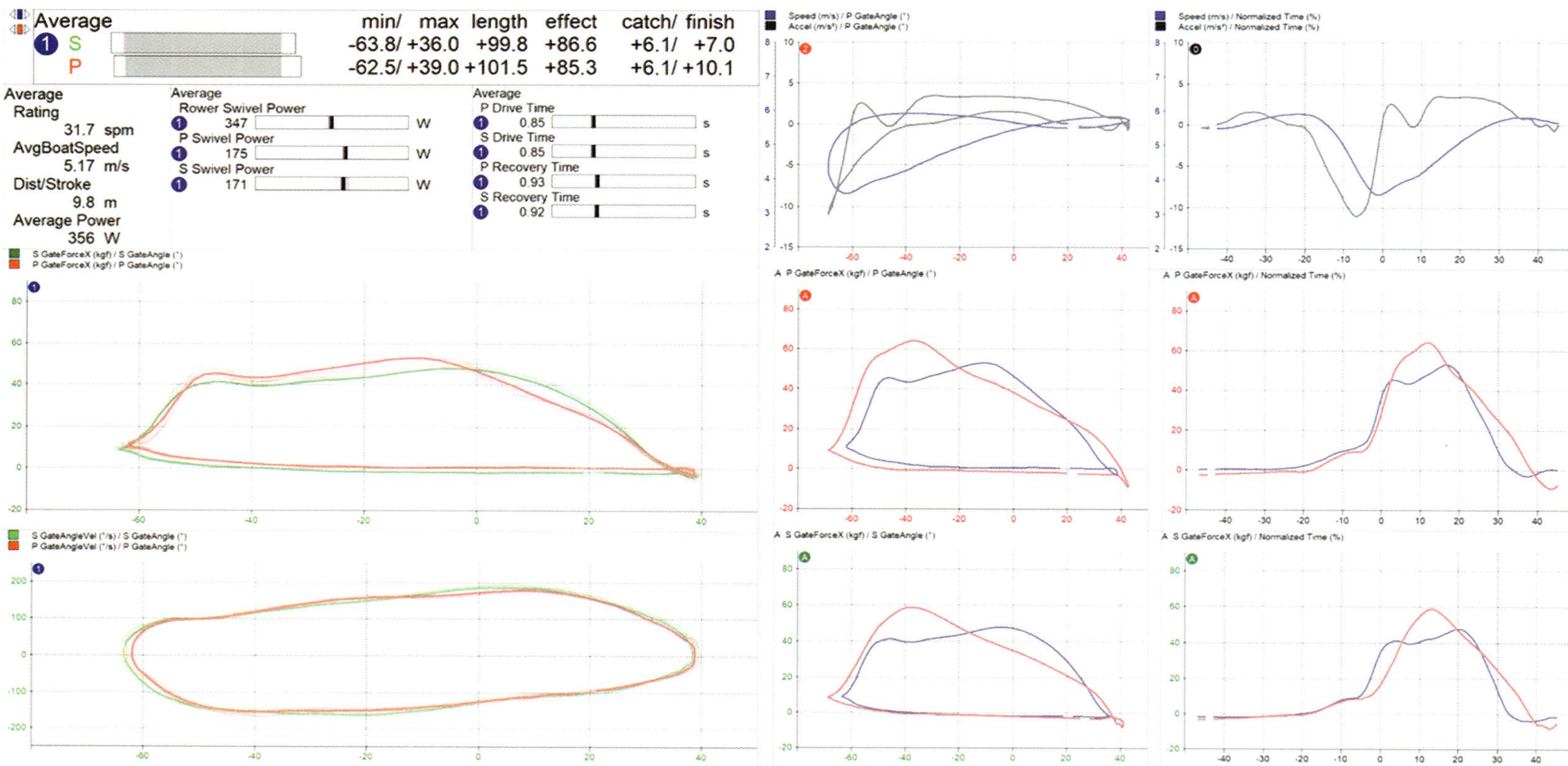
Average
1 S
P
min/ max length effect catch/ finish
-63.8/ +36.0 +99.8 +86.6 +6.1/ +7.0
-62.5/ +39.0 +101.5 +85.3 +6.1/ +10.1
Average
Rating
31.7 spm
AvgBoatSpeed
5.17 m/s
Dist/Stroke
9.8 m
Average Power
356 W
Average
Rower Swivel Power
347 W
P Swivel Power
175 W
S Swivel Power
171 W
Average
P Drive Time
0.85 s
S Drive Time
0.85 s
P Recovery Time
0.93 s
S Recovery Time
0.92 s
S GateForceX (kgf) / S GateAngle (°)
P GateForceX (kgf) / P GateAngle (°)
S GateAngleVel (°/s) / S GateAngle (°)
P GateAngleVel (°/s) / P GateAngle (°)
Speed (m/s) / P GateAngle (°)
Accel (m/s²) / P GateAngle (°)
Speed (m/s) / Normalized Time (%)
Accel (m/s²) / Normalized Time (%)
A P GateForceX (kgf) / P GateAngle (°)
A P GateForceX (kgf) / Normalized Time (%)
A S GateForceX (kgf) / S GateAngle (°)
A S GateForceX (kgf) / Normalized Time (%)

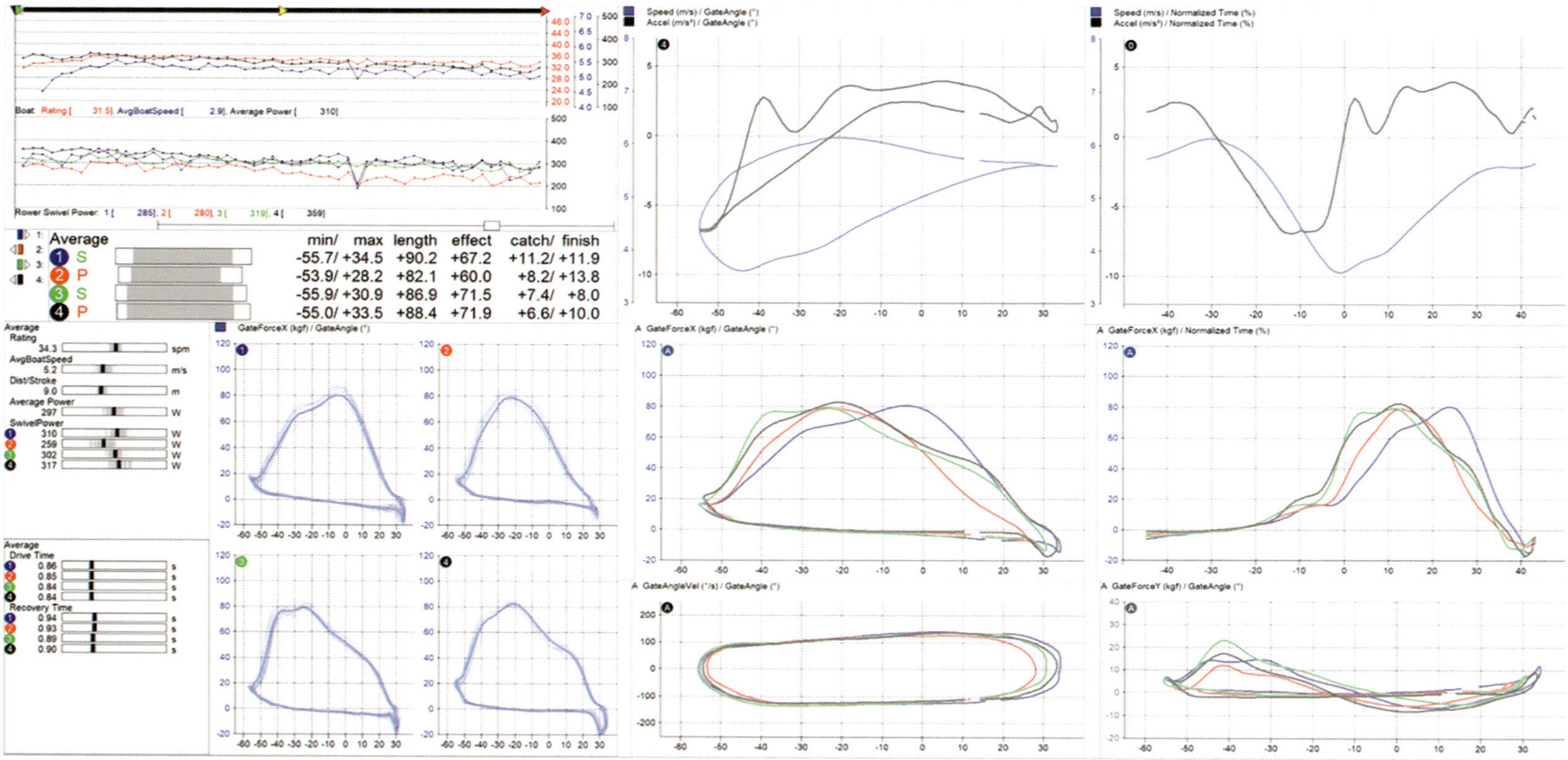

Figure 2.9 [left] and Figure 2.10 [right]

Comparison between a stroke with a well-timed recovery and force application (left) and a poorly timed recovery and application of force (right). The top right-hand graph expresses the boat acceleration and the graph below the timing of the force application. The V-shaped boat starts its deceleration at 20% of the stroke duration and the U-shaped boat at 30%, meaning that the latter is in deceleration for 10% longer than the former. The first image also shows a steep, fast initial drive, in which the crew's effort is well timed and together; this contrasts with the variation in the way power is applied in the second. The crew with the V-shaped curve has won World Championships and Olympic medals.

the boat during the stroke cycle. A skilful crew can master the control and timing of the boat during the recovery phase to reduce the negative effects of the boat's pitch (up and down movement), roll (keeping it balanced) and yaw (sideways movement). To achieve this, the rowers need to be in 'balance' with themselves and the rest of the crew, and take their timing from the boat. A skilful crew can keep their boat in acceleration for a longer percentage of the recovery and have the boat in deceleration for the shortest time possible (*see* Fig. 2.9).

A men's eight demonstrating good connection with the water in a horizontal, suspended sequenced drive phase.

An efficient recovery sees the rowers relaxing and moving in sync with the motion of the boat. They are well organised in their sequences and prepared for the catch.

Level 2: Interaction of the Crew on the Boat

Kleshnev's research (2006) on the body components of the rowing stroke found that the legs contribute 46% of the power during the drive, the trunk 32% and the arms 22%. One interesting finding is that the legs increase their contribution as the stroke rate increases as they can express 95% of their potential, whereas the trunk can only express 55% of its potential and the arms 75%. For the boat to turn the deceleration into acceleration through force applied to the oar at the catch, the most effective technique for the rowers to deploy is a front-loaded, leg-driven stroke that is well suspended to maximise the boat's acceleration during the drive phase. This has implications for technique and for rower selection.

The rowers' recovery sequences are key to controlling the boat during the recovery phase and preparing them for an effective change of direction at the catch. If the crew can sequence the reverse of the drive sequence – arms, trunk, then legs – the crew can control their mass coming down the slide. This will allow them to glide freely, keep moving and accelerate through the front turn to efficiently and effectively connect the recovery phase with the drive phase, having maximised the boat's acceleration and decreased the time the boat is in deceleration during the recovery.

Level 3: Interaction of the Individuals with Each Other

Looking at the three levels of interactions, it is possible to see how each one affects the higher order. The summation of each rower's forces directly influences the acceleration profile of the boat, which in turn influences the velocity of the boat. A slow rate of force development at the catch means lower acceleration peak and a lower minimum velocity for the boat. Rowers who hit the catch with a high rate of force but do not hold on to the load reduce the acceleration of the boat over the whole stroke. The comparison graphs above (Figs 2.9 and 2.10) demonstrate how the force application of individuals can affect the interactions with the boat acceleration and boat speed. They also illustrate the difference between a V-shaped boat and a U-shaped one.

Effective Work Per Stroke

One technical principle that needs to be considered in prescribing both rowing technique and training is distance and work per stroke. The crew that rates the highest most of the time is not the winner of the race. This has been understood for some time and has been confirmed via race analysis over the years. Although race rates may creep up, stroke length, effectiveness and efficiency are key. Dr Valery Kleshnev's findings of the 2019 World Rowing Championships, presented at the 2020 World Rowing Virtual Coaches Conference, were enlightening in this respect:

More than half of the winners in Olympic Events (8 out of 14) won with a lower stroke rate than their competitors. This means they got an advantage because of higher effective

Ideal interaction of stroke length, stroke rate and power with increasing speed					
Stroke Rate (per minute)	**Boat Speed (metres per second)**	**Average Power (watts)**	**Catch Angle (degrees)**	**Finish Angle (degrees)**	**Total Length (degrees)**
22	4.6	265	67.5 66 69 69.5	39.1 40.9 39.3 40.2	106.6 106.9 108.3 109.7
25	4.8	295	66.5 64.5 68.6 67.6	37.7 40.6 39.1 40	104.3 105.1 107.8 107.6
28	5	346	65 62.9 67.9 66.9	37.8 40.2 38.7 40.7	102.8 103.2 106.6 107.6
32	5.1	367	63.9 62.6 66.5 66	37.7 38.9 39.2 40.2	101.6 101.6 105.7 106.2
34	5.3	412	63.4 61.8 65.7 65.6	37.6 38.5 38.8 39.6	101 100.3 104.6 105.2

Figure 2.13

The ideal interaction of stroke length, stroke rate and power with increasing speed.

ROWING MEN	Internat. Level	Crew Power (W)			Length Total (deg)			Length Effective (deg)			Catch Angle (Min) (deg)			Finish Angle (Max) (deg)			Catch Slip (deg)			Finish Slip (deg)			Timing diff. between oars (s)***		
INTENSITY	Boat Category	Seniors	U23	U19	Seniors	U23	U19	Seniors	U23	U19	Seniors	U23	U19	Seniors	U23	U19	Seniors	U23	U19	Seniors	U23	U19	Seniors	U23	U19
		>	>(-30W)	>(-60W)	>	>(-2deg)	>(-4deg)	>	>(-4deg)	>(-10deg)	>(-)	>(-1deg)	>(-2deg)		>(-1deg)	>(-2deg)	<	<(+1deg)	<(+3deg)	<	<(+1deg)	<(+3deg)	<	<(+0.01s)	<(+0.02s)
	M2-	290	260	230	90	88	86	78	74	68	-60	-59	-58	+32 -34	+31 -34	+30 -34	5	6	8	7	8	10	0.04	0.05	0.06
	M4-	290	260	230	90	88	86	78	74	68	-60	-59	-58	+32 -34	+31 -34	+30 -34	5	6	8	7	8	10	0.04	0.05	0.06
	M8+	300	270	240	90	88	86	78	74	68	-60	-59	-58	+32 -34	+31 -34	+30 -34	5	6	8	7	8	10	0.04	0.05	0.06
	M1x	300	270	240	110	108	106	96	92	86	-68	-67	-66	+42 -45	+41 -45	+40 -45	6	7	9	8	9	11	0.04	0.05	0.06
2km (SR20)	M2x	280	250	220	110	108	106	96	92	86	-68	-67	-66	+42 -45	+41 -45	+40 -45	6	7	9	8	9	11	0.04	0.05	0.06
	M4x	280	250	220	110	108	106	96	92	86	-68	-67	-66	+42 -45	+41 -45	+40 -45	6	7	9	8	9	11	0.04	0.05	0.06
	LM1x	250	220	190	108	106	104	92	88	82	-66	-65	-64	+42 -45	+41 -45	+40 -45	7	8	10	9	10	12	0.04	0.05	0.06
	LM2x	250	220	190	108	106	104	92	88	82	-66	-65	-64	+42 -45	+41 -45	+40 -45	7	8	10	9	10	12	0.04	0.05	0.06
	LM4x	230	200	170	108	106	104	92	88	82	-66	-65	-64	+42 -45	+41 -45	+40 -45	7	8	10	9	10	12	0.04	0.05	0.06
	M2-	450	420	390	88	86	84	80	76	70	-58	-57	-56	+32 -34	+31 -34	+30 -34	3	4	6	5	6	8	0.04	0.05	0.06
	M4-	450	420	390	88	86	84	80	76	70	-58	-57	-56	+32 -34	+31 -34	+30 -34	3	4	6	5	6	8	0.04	0.05	0.06
	M8+	450	420	390	88	86	84	80	76	70	-58	-57	-56	+31 -33	+30 -33	+30 -33	3	4	6	5	6	8	0.04	0.05	0.06
2km race/	M1x	460	430	400	108	106	104	98	94	88	-66	-65	-64	+42 -45	+41 -45	+40 -45	4	5	7	6	7	9	0.04	0.05	0.06
Mid-race SR*/**	M2x	440	410	380	107	105	103	97	93	87	-65	-64	-63	+42 -45	+41 -45	+40 -45	4	5	7	6	7	9	0.04	0.05	0.06
	M4x	440	410	380	108	106	104	98	94	88	-66	-65	-64	+42 -45	+41 -45	+40 -45	4	5	7	6	7	9	0.04	0.05	0.06
	LM1x	380	350	320	106	104	102	92	88	82	-64	-63	-62	+42 -45	+41 -45	+40 -45	6	7	9	8	9	11	0.04	0.05	0.06
	LM2x	380	350	320	105	103	101	91	87	81	-63	-62	-61	+42 -45	+41 -45	+40 -45	6	7	9	8	9	11	0.04	0.05	0.06
	LM4x	360	330	300	106	104	102	92	88	82	-64	-63	-62	+42 -45	+41 -45	+40 -45	6	7	9	8	9	11	0.04	0.05	0.06

* Rowing Race Pace (based on mid-race SR)

** estimated required Target Power values over a 2000m race distance to reach prog. Boat speed (WBT)

*** Timing difference betw. oars (s)/ crew: rel. timing diffence betw. rowers/ oars throughout drive time/ recovery time

ROWING WOMEN	Internat. Level	Crew Power (W)			Length Total (deg)			Length Effective (deg)			Catch Angle (Min) (deg)			Finish Angle (Max) (deg)			Catch Slip (deg)			Finish Slip (deg)			Timing diff. between oars (s)***		
INTENSITY	Boat Category	Seniors	U23	U19	Seniors	U23	U19	Seniors	U23	U19	Seniors	U23	U19	Seniors	U23	U19	Seniors	U23	U19	Seniors	U23	U19	Seniors	U23	U19
		>	>(-30W)	>(-60W)	>	>(-2deg)	>(-4deg)	>	>(-4deg)	>(-10deg)	>(-)	>(-1deg)	>(-2deg)		>(-1deg)	>(-2deg)	<	<(+1deg)	<(+3deg)	<	<(+1deg)	<(+3deg)	<	<(+0.01s)	<(+0.02s)
	W2-	200	170	140	88	86	84	72	68	62	-58	-57	-56	+32 -34	+31 -34	+30 -34	7	8	10	9	10	12	0.04	0.05	0.06
	W4-	200	170	140	88	86	84	72	68	62	-58	-57	-56	+32 -34	+31 -34	+30 -34	7	8	10	9	10	12	0.04	0.05	0.06
	W8+	210	180	150	88	86	84	72	68	62	-58	-57	-56	+31 -33	+30 -33	+30 -33	7	8	10	9	10	12	0.04	0.05	0.06
	W1x	210	180	150	108	106	104	90	86	80	-66	-65	-64	+42 -45	+41 -45	+40 -45	8	9	11	10	11	13	0.04	0.05	0.06
2km (SR20)	W2x	190	160	130	108	106	104	90	86	80	-66	-65	-64	+42 -45	+41 -45	+40 -45	8	9	11	10	11	13	0.04	0.05	0.06
	W4x	190	160	130	108	106	104	90	86	80	-66	-65	-64	+42 -45	+41 -45	+40 -45	8	9	11	10	11	13	0.04	0.05	0.06
	LW1x	150	120	90	106	104	102	86	82	76	-64	-63	-62	+42 -45	+41 -45	+40 -45	9	10	12	11	12	14	0.04	0.05	0.06
	LW2x	150	120	90	106	104	102	86	82	76	-64	-63	-62	+42 -45	+41 -45	+40 -45	9	10	12	11	12	14	0.04	0.05	0.06
	LW4x	140	110	80	106	104	102	86	82	76	-64	-63	-62	+42 -45	+41 -45	+40 -45	9	10	12	11	12	14	0.04	0.05	0.06
	W2-	300	270	240	86	84	82	72	68	62	-56	-55	-54	+32 -34	+31 -34	+30 -34	6	7	9	8	9	11	0.04	0.05	0.05
	W4-	300	270	240	86	84	82	72	68	62	-56	-55	-54	+32 -34	+31 -34	+30 -34	6	7	9	8	9	11	0.04	0.05	0.05
	W8+	300	270	240	86	84	82	72	68	62	-56	-55	-54	+31 -33	+30 -33	+30 -33	6	7	9	8	9	11	0.04	0.05	0.05
2km race/	W1x	310	280	250	106	104	102	90	86	80	-64	-63	-62	+42 -45	+41 -45	+40 -45	7	8	10	9	10	12	0.04	0.05	0.05
Mid-race SR*/**	W2x	290	260	230	105	103	101	89	85	79	-63	-62	-61	+42 -45	+41 -45	+40 -45	7	8	10	9	10	12	0.04	0.05	0.05
	W4x	290	260	230	106	104	102	90	86	80	-64	-63	-62	+42 -45	+41 -45	+40 -45	7	8	10	9	10	12	0.04	0.05	0.05
	LW1x	250	220	190	104	102	100	86	82	76	-62	-61	-60	+42 -45	+41 -45	+40 -45	8	9	11	10	11	13	0.04	0.05	0.05
	LW2x	250	220	190	103	101	99	85	81	75	-61	-60	-59	+42 -45	+41 -45	+40 -45	8	9	11	10	11	13	0.04	0.05	0.05
	LW4x	240	210	180	104	102	100	86	82	76	-62	-61	-60	+42 -45	+41 -45	+40 -45	8	9	11	10	11	13	0.04	0.05	0.05

* Rowing Race Pace (based on mid-race SR)

** estimated required Target Power values over a 2km training/ race distance to reach prog. WBT Boat speed

*** Timing difference betw. oars (s)/ crew: rel. timing diffence betw. rowers/ oars throughout drive time/ recovery time

Figure 2.14

This biomechanical set of norms developed from the database of Dr Conny Draper, a world-renowned rowing biomechanist, is a wonderful resource for coaches. Her analysis supports international, university, school and club crews across the globe. The values have been derived off the Peach Biomechanical system. The values relate to the estimated crew power and angle to achieve a world best time.

work per stroke. In some boats (M2x, W2x,M4-, M8+,W8+), the winners rated 1.2–2 strokes per minute less than the silver medallists, so they took 8–14 less strokes over 2000m to overcome their competitors.

His conclusion was that 'the advantage of a higher stroke rate is quite doubtful and higher effective work per stroke may have a better potential for speed improvement'.

Effective work per stroke is underpinned by overall stroke length, effective stroke length and power. Rowing is a leverage sport, and there is a balance in racing between stroke length and stroke rate, both to produce speed and to pace the 2000m race physiologically. The more strokes the rower undertakes, the greater the physiological cost to them.

Not only does the rower require a long stroke, they also need to make that length effective. Peach Innovations (UK) produces a sturdy, reliable and accurate biomechanical and coaching tool that can measure gate force and stroke length, amongst other parameters. They have set a catch slip of the degrees it takes from the minimum angle (catch angle) to reaching a threshold of above 30kg of gate force in sweep boats and 20kg in sculling. The finish slip is degrees from when the gate force falls below 15kg in the sweep and 10kg in the sculling to the maximum angle (finish angle).

The crew that rates the highest most of the time is not the winner of the race.

Paul Thompson

The degrees between these two thresholds are described as the effective length.

The rower needs to find a way with rhythm and through training to 'scale up' their power, effective stroke length and stroke rate. This in turn increases boat speed, from steady state and low stroke rate training to racing pace and above. There is little point in increasing stroke rate and reducing power through shorter strokes and ultimately limiting boat speed or even reducing pace in the boat. The table below (Fig 2.13) gives an overview of increments that rowers should be looking to attain.

Principles-Based Technical Model

In presenting the principles-based technical model, the differences between sculling and sweep boats and Para rowing, and between different boat classes and the different seats in the boats, will be described. However, the basic principles of how a boat moves remain the same. In coaching, a coach is always wise to focus their attention on how well their rowers and crews can deliver the basic evidence-based parameters that underpin boat speed.

This extremely effective rowing technical model is demonstrated by Olympic medallist Huang Wenyi.

The Drive Phase

The entry of the blade to the water is **the last thing done during the recovery**. This needs to be in harmony with the boat so that the rower is at full length on the slide as the spoon grips the water.

The entry of the blade to the water.

The rower **catches the water and the boat** by driving down through the feet into the foot stretcher, applying force to the spoon. The shoulders and arms are relaxed and loose.

The **catch to maximal handle force** is the **critical** part of the stroke. The rower needs to have **suspended** themselves well and drive through their big muscle groups – gluteal and quadricep – in a leg-driven and -dominated stroke. The rower hangs off the oar handle with relaxed shoulders and arms during this phase.

The late drive sees the rower's **trunk open** aggressively away from the driving legs to add **acceleration to the oar handle and more power into the rower system**. This further accelerates and drives the boat.

The rower **maintains their suspension** to the natural finish point of the drive. They release the pressure on the handles and tap the handles down to step the oar's blade out of the water cleanly in the vacuum that has built behind the blade during the drive.

The catch.

The late drive.

The critical part of the stroke.

Maintaining the suspension to the finish of the drive.

The Recovery Phase

The sequencing of the recovery.

The second half of the recovery.

The **sequencing of the recovery** from the finish is crucial for the rower to both maximise the run of the hull during the recovery and prepare for the timing of the blade entry and catch at the end of the recovery. The hands lead the arms, then the shoulders and hips over from the finish. The hand speed away should be timed with the speed of the hull.

The **rockover is led by the hands and arms from the finish** while the rower presses against the footstretcher with their gluteal muscles at the finish. By drawing the lower abdominal muscles in towards them, the rower will **rock over their sitting bones** (ischial tuberosity) on the seat. This brings the rower's weight to the front of the seat and their feet.

During the second half of the recovery the rower should be feeling that the **boat is running naturally**, and that they have **freedom to glide** with the seat. They need to **relax their hamstrings** to feel this. It should feel that the feet are moving to the seat and that no extra weight is being pushed by the rower into the stern. The rower should be sitting with good trunk control and not allowing the trunk to fall on to the thighs. Squaring of the oar is done in this phase as part of the rhythm of the front turn.

The blade entry to the water is in harmony with the boat at the end of the recovery so the blade buries before force is applied through the footstretcher to catch the water and boat. The rower needs to relax before the catch as they let the boat bring

The rockover.

The blade entry to the water.

them up on to their toes to maximise the full length of the slide.

Sculling vs Sweep Rowing

There are obvious differences between sculling boats, which are symmetrical, and sweep boats, which are asymmetrical. For example, a sculling boat demands a longer stroke length at both the catch and finish.

There are three points of connection between the rower and their equipment: hands, feet and seat. The biggest and most obvious difference between sculling and sweep in this respect is the grip on the handles of the oars and the rotation that occurs with the shoulders in sweep rowing. The grip on the handles clearly differs between sculling and sweep, but there are some strong similarities. The rower's grip on the handle is a key contact point on the oars and sculls if they are to achieve effective power application and skilful blade work.

Sweep Grip

For the most effective position to lever the sweep boat, the outside hand needs to be on the end of the handle. This is the starting point for a correct grip. The inside hand should be placed down the loom in a position that is comfortable for the rower, almost shoulder width apart. During the drive the rower should have flat wrists and their first set of knuckles (the metacarpophalangeal joint) at almost 90 degrees. This is a strong hanging position for the drive of the stroke. As the rower approaches the finish during the drive they need have sequenced drawing through their latissimus dorsi muscles (lats), then the biceps to keep their suspension and therefore force on the spoon. This will help to maintain effective length through the stroke. Timing the relaxation and force coming off the blade, the rower should apply downward pressure with the outside hand to release the oar cleanly from the air pocket that is created behind the blade during the drive. During the downward movement of the oar handle, the rower uses their inside hand to feather the oar by rolling the handle with the thumb and drawing the fingers over the top of the handle as well as using some wrist flexion. The outside hand guides the handle around the back turn connecting the drive phase with the recovery phase.

The grip stays the same during the recovery until the outside hand leads and loops the handle through the front turn connecting the recovery phase with the drive phase. As the rower approaches

World Championship medallist Ben Canham displaying an effective grip. His wrists are flat during the drive phase, and his outside arm is at the end of the handle, maximising his leverage.

the front turn the blade is squared in preparation for the catch. The inside hand works in a mirror image of what it did in feathering the blade by drawing the thumb up, rolling the fingers down and extending the wrist to square the blade.

Rotation

The semi-circular path of the handle created by the oar moving around the rigger pin sets the line in which the rower rotates. To maximise relaxation and simplify the movement, the rower's rotation should be through the thoracic spine (the upper part of the spine). The outside arm leads the rotation both during the recovery and the drive, and the rower's shoulders should rotate at the same angle as the handle. To maximise the leverage of the oars, the outside hand needs to be on the end of the handle, and the rower needs to use it to suspend off the oar. The inside knee comes straight up and down through the stroke and room for rotation is made by the outside knee coming slightly outside the outside arm.

World Championship medallist Joe O'Brien and Olympic Champion Spencer Turrin maximising their length through rotating around the rigger pin.

Sculling Grip

The sculling grip is similar in both hands to the role of the inside arm in sweep rowing. Keeping the thumbs at the end of the handle will maximise the leverage the sculler has during the drive. For an effective grip the sculler needs to hang off the handles, with a slightly arched wrist and the first set of knuckles (the metacarpophalangeal joint) almost at 90 degrees. As in sweep rowing, the sculler hangs and draws through the lats then uses their biceps to keep the force on both oar blades to maximise their effective length. Relaxing to relieve the pressure on the spoon, the sculler rolls the tip of the handles with their thumbs, draws the fingers over the top of the handle and uses some wrist flexion to feather the blade. This connects the drive phase with the recovery phase.

The same grip is held during the recovery and, as the sculler approaches the front turn, they flick the thumbs, draw the fingers over the handles and straighten the wrist to square the blade and prepare for its entry. This connects the recovery phase with the drive phase. As the sculling handles are smaller, the thumbs have a bigger role to play. An experienced and skilful sculler can leave their squaring late, taking advantage of the aerodynamic benefit of the flat recovery profile of the blade.

Sculling Rotation and Crossover

Whilst the sweep rower rotates around their rigger, the sculler rotates around both their pins. To do this effectively the sculler needs to have a small amount of lateral pressure from their thumbs into the ends of the handles against the rigger's gate. This creates a position where the sculler looks to have wide distance between their two hands at the catch. When an experienced sculler times the entry and catch well, they feel their hands stay wide longer during the initial drive. Poorly timed connections from scullers see the handles come back to a narrow position too quickly. At the finish it is important for the sculler to hold their suspension rotating around the rigger's gate to maintain their force on the spoon and their effective length.

The sculler's hands and handles will cross over each other during both the drive and recovery phases of the stroke. There is an internationally accepted convention that, during the recovery, the left hand leads the right hand and is slightly astern and above it, and that the hands cross in the same way during the drive phase. This simplifies working the rotation around both riggers and saves the hands getting tangled up. Single scullers have the option to develop their own pattern and go their own way, but scullers who are to row in crew boats need to have standardised patterns, to keep a balanced boat and achieve a more matched and effective drive. Sculling boats are usually rigged with the left rigger

World Championship single sculling multi-medallist Tara Rigney at the crossover with her left hand slightly astern and above her right hand.

Tara Rigney displaying outstanding technique with wide arms and a perfectly timed catch.

1–2cm higher than the right to enable the standardised pattern.

Para Rowing

Classes

There are three different sport classes in Para Rowing: PR1, PR2 and PR3. All Para rowers go through a classification process that includes both a medical and technical review to ascertain the class in which they are allowed to compete. The 2022 World Rowing Para Classifiers manual (available at worldrowing.com) provides the following definitions for each sport class:

> *PR1*
>
> *The PR1 class is for athletes who have joint, strength, or coordination restrictions that lead to a significant impairment in performing the trunk swing and leg drive of the rowing stroke. The PR1 class includes athletes who predominantly apply force using the arms and shoulders for rowing.*
>
> *PR2*
>
> *The PR2 class is for athletes who have joint, strength, or coordination restrictions that do*

not allow sufficient compression during the recovery part of the stroke and results to an inefficient leg drive. PR2 class athletes have functional trunk swing during the rowing stroke and require a fixed seat for rowing.

PR3-PI [Physical Impairment]
The PR3-PI class is for athletes with joint, strength, or coordination restrictions that impact the overall force production of the rowing stroke. These athletes can perform sufficient compression during the recovery and force production during the leg drive of the stroke. PR3-PI athletes have functional use of their legs, trunk and arms for rowing and can utilise the sliding seat to propel the boat.

In summary, this means that athletes with compromised sit balance and/or trunk function usually fall into the PR1 class and predominantly move the boat using their upper back, shoulders and arms. PR3 Visual Impairment (VI) is classified through the International Blind Sports Association and athletes with a B1, B2 or B3 visual impairment are eligible to row in the PR3 classification.

There are five Para rowing events raced at the Paralympic Games and World Rowing Championships:

1. PR3 Mixed Coxed Four (PR3 Mix4+)
2. PR3 Mixed Double Sculls (PR3 Mix2x)
3. PR2 Mixed Double Sculls (PR2 Mix 2x)
4. PR1 Men's Single Sculls (PR1 M1x)
5. PR1 Women's Single Sculls (PR1 W1x)

An additional four boat classes appear during some of the World Cup series events:

6. PR3 Men's Pair (PR3 M2-)
7. PR3 Women's (PR3 W2-)
8. PR2 Men's Single Scull (PR2 M1x)
9. PR2 Women's Single Scull (PR2 W1x)

Boats

At World Rowing events the PR3 Mix 4+, PR3 2- and PR3 Mix 2x boats are subject to the same restrictions as coxed fours (4+), pairs (2-) and double sculls (2x) under the International Rowing Federations Rules of Racing. The rules of racing outline a mandatory international standard for boats in the PR1 1x, PR2 1x and PR2 2x classes. They are wider and shorter than conventional sculling boats, with a fixed seat and strapping.

Boats in Para rowing are governed by the same biomechanical principles as Olympic boats, with boat speed primarily determined by stroke length, effective stroke length and power. Despite the different techniques required by the three boat classes with fixed seats, they all adhere to the core principles. Fixed-seat rowers typically use a shorter overall stroke length, often led by smaller muscle groups, but still focus on utilising the largest muscle groups available. For instance, PR2 rowers generate most of their stroke length and initial power from the hip joint. Coaches of fixed-seat rowers often take an iterative approach to rigging, adjusting spans, blade length, and inboards to achieve optimal catch force and ideal length (*see* Chapter 5 for more details).

Additionally, the placement of safety and support strapping is crucial. For PR1 rowers, a safety strap across the waist is mandatory, while in the PR2 event, strapping is optional. This provides an opportunity to use approved equipment to adjust a rower's position in the boat, optimising their functionality during the rowing stroke cycle. For instance, some PR1 rowers might choose to position their waist strap higher to support them in the recovery and provide a brace during the drive phase. This approach requires a deep understanding of the individual rower and their impairment, identifying areas for improvement and adjusting equipment to fit their needs. Given the diversity of the rowers involved in Para events, it is essential that the boat, technique and training are all tailored to the individual.

The biomechanical profiles of a fixed-seat PR1 men's single sculler and a sliding-seat men's single sculler are different. The magnitude of force that can be applied by the sliding-seat sculler (due to utilising a sliding seat and their lower body) increases the magnitude of the boat acceleration and in turn velocity, in comparison with the fixed-seat PR1M1x. The fixed-seat boat is also considerably heavier than the M1x. World Rowing minimum weight for the PR1M1x is 24kg whereas the M1x is 14kg. All these factors contribute to a reduced magnitude of acceleration and lower velocity in fixed-seat boat classes.

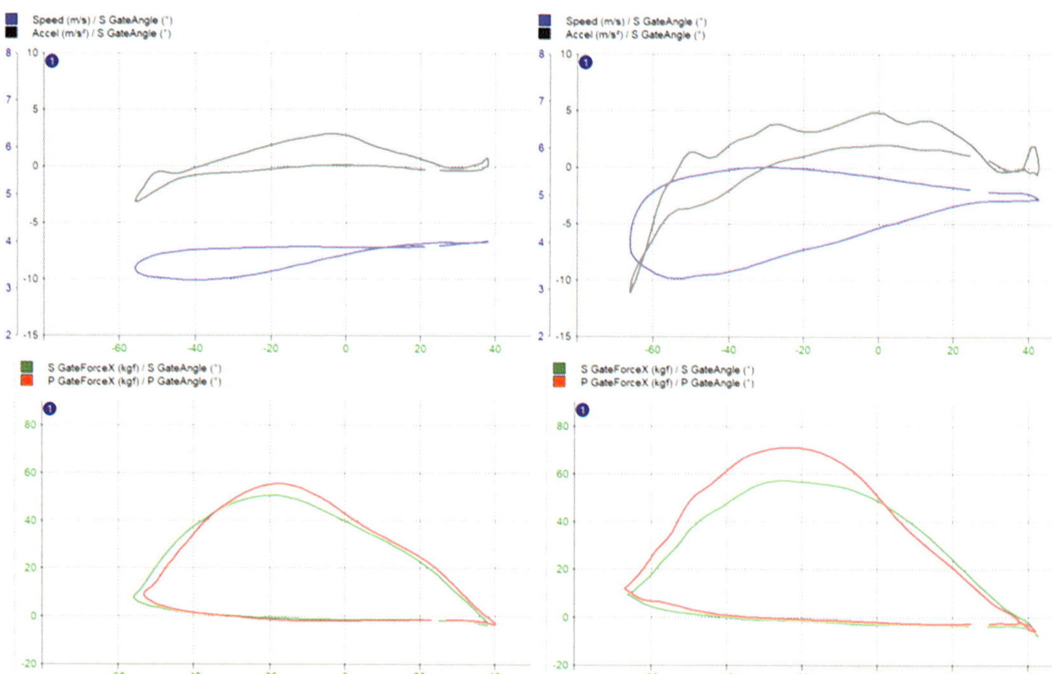

Figure 2.28

Comparison between the biomechanical profiles of a fixed-seat PR1 men's single sculler (on the left) and a sliding-seat men's single sculler (on the right).

Comparison between the biomechanical profiles of a fixed-seat PR1 men's single sculler and a sliding-seat men's single sculler.

The PR3 Mix 4+ is the biggest boat that Para rowers race internationally. Great Britain has been undefeated in this boat class for more than a decade at World level.

Paralympic champions Jed Altschwager and Nikki Ayers with a well-timed drive phase during training in Italy prior to the Paris Paralympics. The Paralympic events include two mixed double sculls in the PR3 and PR2 categories.

Five-time World Champion and four-time Paralympic medallist Erik Horrie in the PR1 Men's Single Scull. The Paralympic programme's single sculls are in the male and female PR1 category.

Different Boats - Different Techniques?

Although there are differences between the various boat classes, fundamentally the way in which the boat moves is similar across all categories. From 1999 to 2004, Kleshnev (2010) explored the differences between boat types, genders, sculling and sweep and increasing stroke rates acceleration traces. Testing 294 elite crews – males and females, lightweight and open-weight rowers – from the Australian Institute of Sport and the Australian Rowing Team, he divided the stroke cycle into nine micro cycles to identify and locate where the differences occurred. He found that blade burial at the catch, the initial rower's acceleration and initial boat acceleration were slightly longer in sweep boats than in sculling boats. Conversely, second rower and boat acceleration was slightly shorter in the sweep boats than in the sculling boats. Kleshnev hypothesised that the longer duration of the blade burial in sweep could be due to the larger surface area of the sweep blades in comparison with the sculling blades. The shorter initial rower and boat acceleration in sculling boats may be due to the length of the catch angles that scullers get compared with sweep crews, which makes the gearing heavier at the catch.

Male crews had a longer initial boat acceleration, possibly due to their being able to generate forces more rapidly. Outside the initial boat acceleration, Kleshnev found no statistical difference between males and females. There were no significant differences in the duration of blade burial, initial rower and boat acceleration and blade extraction in different boat categories. Second rower acceleration was longer in duration in quads and eights than in smaller single sculls and pairs. Singles and pairs had longer second boat acceleration compared with quads and eights. Except for the initial boat acceleration, absolute duration of all stroke micro phases tended to decrease at higher stroke rates. This decrease was in strong correlation with the reduced total drive time at higher stroke rates. The relative share of the stroke micro cycle of the blade burial tended to decrease at higher stroke rates where the blade extraction took longer.

Interestingly, the initial boat acceleration exhibited a maximum level at stroke rate 30 for sculling crews and stroke rate 36 for sweep crews. It is not understood why there is this difference. In looking to find the relationship between the acceleration trace and the force curve profile, Kleshnev found that the blade burial period had the strongest positive correlation for achieving 30% of the rowers' maximal force.
The second boat acceleration had the strongest negative correlation with the time for achieving 70% of maximum force. The blade extraction period also had a negative correlation with the time taken to achieve 30% of the maximal force curve.

Kleshnev's research reinforces the importance of a front-loaded leg-driven stroke. In comparing an Olympic champion crew with an A Final crew from the World Rowing Championships, he found that the Olympic champion crew produced a much quicker rise in handle force, achieving 70% of their force at 23% of the drive time. The A finalist had a slower rate of force development, achieving 70% of their maximum force at 29.1% of their drive time. The faster rise in force in the Olympic champion boat coincides with a faster increase in velocity. The maximum leg velocity of this crew was achieved at 22.4% of the drive time. Conversely, the A Final crew had a slower leg speed early in the drive phase, reaching maximum leg velocity at 32.2% of the drive time. Consequently, the handle velocity of the Olympic champion crew increased more rapidly during the first half of the drive.

Each boat category has a different dynamic and a rower's abilities will tend to be more suited to a particular type of boat and seat.

There is an enormous disparity in race times over 2000m in rowing, ranging from a men's eight world's best of 5:18.68 to a lightweight women's single scull world's best of 7:24.46. The total mass of a men's eight system weighs in at approximately 934kg, with eight rowers averaging 95kg, a coxswain at a minimum weight of 55kg, a minimum boat weight of 96kg and eight oars at 2.9kg each. The mass of a lightweight women's sculling set-up is approximately 76kg, made up of around 59kg for the rower, 14kg for the boat and the sculls at 1.5kg. The dynamics of the two events are quite different. At the start of the race, the eight requires a huge amount of force to get up to its race pace, but the large mass involved keeps the momentum in the hull and the race is over quickly. There is very little opportunity to change speed during the race and it is exceedingly difficult to overcome a poor start in a top-flight eights event. Conversely, a single scull race lasts longer, it is easier to get the mass of the boat moving, and there is a greater opportunity for speed variation and changes in position over the 2000m race distance.

These factors have implications for training, selection and coaching. The attributes of the rower in an eight will be quite different from those in the smaller boats. An eights crew requires explosive, powerful and strong athletes. The size of the boat also means these rowers can have a lower level of skill than those who excel in the smaller boats. The rowing attributes required for each boat class could be summarised as follows:

- The single scull (1x) is the slowest of the boat classes, meaning a long powerful stroke is essential. The force curve of the sculler is a well filled-out bell shape.
- In the double scull (2x), timing the force application together is critical. Skill and communication between the two rowers are needed in order to move the boat effectively and efficiently.
- The quadruple scull (4x) has the greatest ratio of surface area of oars to rowers of any of the boat classes and operates like a fast-moving eight. The rowers need to be skilful and explosive to pick up and move with the fast pace of the boat.
- The coxless pair (2-) class is unique in its asymmetrical nature. The stroke person has the biomechanical advantage at the catch and the bow person at the finish. Timing is critical in this small boat to ensure that the strokes match evenly up on either side and the boat is made to go fast and straight.
- The coxless four (4-) is a rhythm and power boat. Rowers need to combine well together in applying power to the oars and moving well on the recovery to maximise the boat's run.
- The coxed eight (8+) is a power boat and the fastest of all the boat classes. Due to the combined weight of the set-up, the rowers have to be powerful in order to drive the boat up to its maximum speed out of the start. Due to the boat's momentum, they need to be able to quickly apply power to keep it running at its optimal race pace. This requires a leg-driven front-loaded stroke.

Indoor Rowing Technique

The indoor rowing machine, or ergometer, has become increasingly popular, both as a cross-training tool for water rowers and as an essential piece of equipment for gym users. It is perfect for training, monitoring and testing of training status and progress, and developing gross motor technical patterns. There are also ergometer competitions, with continental, virtual and world championship events as well as world records established over distances from 100 to 42,195m, and the ultra-distance of 100,000m, and over durations from 1 to 60 minutes, in both individual and team formats. Over the last 30 years the rowing machine has become a core part of the sport. These days, one of the first questions a rower gets asked is, 'What's your ergo score?'

There are a variety of machines available on the market, with different ways to provide braking resistance. Some are static, some have moving heads and seats, and some can be put on sliders.

There are kinematic differences between a static and dynamic ergometer due to the way the rower has to change direction, load and drive at the front turn. There is less load to turn around on a dynamic ergometer than the static ergometer. This means that there is the opportunity for the rower to rate higher on the RP3. As Hislop et al. (2010) commented, 'There is speculation among rowers that it is hard to maintain a low rating on a Rowperfect and much easier to maintain a high rating. This has been attributed to the additional work that the rower has to perform on a static ergometer with respect to the acceleration and deceleration of their body mass at the catch and finish, as opposed to the Rowperfect, where the body moves less relative to the centre of mass of the whole system.' The findings in this study imply that in terms of kinematics the Concept2 encourages a better body position along with much higher forces and a shorter stroke than the Rowperfect.

Due to this loading differential between static and dynamic ergometers, it has

Brand	**Resistance**	**Comments**
Concept2	Air	Accurate, robust, reliable and easy to store. The most widely used machine. Can be used with sliders and connected so they can be used statically or dynamically, individually and collectively.
RP3 (formerly Rowperfect)	Air	A dynamic ergometer where the head and feet move along the rail, with a moving seat. The seats and/or the handles can be connected together so they can be rowed individually or collectively.
Oartec	Air	Offers an advantage because it can mirror sweep or sculling rotation.
Water rower	Water	Provides a different feel in the resistance as the rower is working against the water

been suggested for some time that the injury risk on the former is higher than on the latter. Bernstein (2002) hypothesised that 'the mean forces are higher on fixed compared with floating power head ergometers. This could increase the risk of injury.'

Both types of ergometer have their place in a well-planned and balanced training programme. An ergometer is a cross-training tool and on its own not a substitute for training on the water. However, it can help develop water performance and build confidence in a rower.

The Concept2 is easily transported, robust and accurate. It is a good tool for training, monitoring and testing, rowing-specific functional training and gross motor technical development.

The Concept 2 ergometer is a reliable tool for testing and monitoring of a rower's physiological level and training adaptation improvement.

Training on the dynamic RP3 ergometer is a good way to promote leg drive. Ergometers can be connected together so that rowers can develop the timing between themselves.

Ergometers are excellent tools for teaching a rower gross movement patterns, sequencing and body suspension. A coach can manipulate the ergometer with straps to emphasise technical points and also encourage the rower to activate the right muscles at the correct part of the stroke.

It allows coaches to measure the standard of the rower's physiological capacity and standard. As it is the most widely used machine, rowers can also compare themselves with and challenge rowers from all over the world.

The RP3 experience is closer in terms of load and feel to that of the real boat, which makes it ideal for off-water technical and rhythm development. It also has good software to track force curves and stroke length, is reliable and is good for monitoring and testing rowers. Connecting the seats and handles together can help rowers learn to find their timing and rhythm with each other.

Coaching Top Tips

- Have a technical model that is evidence-based.
- Concentrate your efforts on improving the physical components that underpin boat movement.
- Include physical technical training in the programme.
- Understand the differences between boat classes.
- Coach the individual, understand the differences and look to set the boat up to maximise the rowers' force development together.

3 Exercises for Improving Technique

This chapter will explore common technical faults and the reasons behind them, and provide a range of drills, exercises and cues to remedy them. It will delve into coaching feedback and the tools that are available to help the coach, including a wide range of technology that can receive feedback, and identify and monitor technical parameters.

Improving Rowing Technique

Once the principles and the technical model of good rowing technique have been understood (Chapter 2), the next step is to deal with stroke correction and explore some exercises to improve that technique.

Technical faults and a lack of crew synchronisation are easy to see but difficult to rectify. The art of a skilful coach is to find a remedy – a way to help change a habit, describe a feel or demonstrate an action – and then show a way to improve. A rower cannot change their height, leg length or arm span, and fitness or effective mental skills can take years to develop. However, technical changes can be made quickly, as long as the athlete is resilient and motivated, and supported by good feedback and coaching. A rower's racing standard is developed in training – the more they achieve and repeat strokes of gold-medal quality daily in training, the higher their chance of a gold-medal-winning opportunity in racing. A rower with good technique will be better able to work to a higher standard and improve the quality of daily training. Becoming technically effective and efficient will allow a rower to move ahead with race development and execution training.

There are no short cuts in training for performance rowing. Technique alone will not win the race. In performance racing, a rower's physicality and fitness are paramount. However, technique could just as easily as any other factor – for example, endurance or strength – be a limiting factor to performance. The margins are tight at the highest level and rowing

Do not just see the mistakes – a good coach needs to know how to fix them.

(Gianni Postilione)

performance is about optimising the capacity of the rowers. The race does not go to the strongest, the fittest or the technically best. The race is won by the rower or rowers who can most effectively and efficiently apply their power, either as an individual or together as part of a crew. The coach needs to use their eye and experience to make sure that rowers do not get distracted by what is not essential to performance. The first priority is physical principles: stroke length, body sequences, power and timing of force application. Rowers who have had a good technical coach from the outset of their career and who have been taught the correct stroke sequencing are able to keep developing those skills in a more sophisticated manner. Rowers who have been taught poorly at the beginning of their involvement – if at all – can be limited by having to undo unproductive learned movement patterns in order to combine or synchronise with other rowers. During their formative rowing years, a rower will develop a signature stroke pattern that is unique.

Regardless of the type of training session – rowing in the boat on the water, ergometer rowing or tank rowing – every stroke completed is an opportunity for a rower to improve their technique. Every training session should have a technical component alongside one or two training objectives.

Using Exercises to Develop and Perfect the Stroke

The accuracy and consistency with which exercises are performed in their discrete motor patterns and sequences will influence an athlete's ability to execute technical skills such as suspension, balance and rhythm. Developing the qualities that underpin motor actions is the primary objective of sport-specific training. Coaches and athletes employ a variety of exercises and drills during training to develop qualities that improve technical consistency and influence the likelihood of success. The rower will derive technical benefit from an

Setting a Technical Objective

Every session should have a technical objective:

Type of training	Prime aim	Other objectives	Method
Ergometer	Load regulation, physiological training	Gross motor skills and ergometer technique training	Individual and team drills
On-water	Technique and performance development and assessment	On-water technique training	Individual and crew drills
Rowing tank	Movement regulation	Additional technique training	Individual and crew drills

exercise only if they apply a high level of concentration and discipline in its execution.

The following exercises can be divided into two distinct groups: exercises to improve technical skills (motor performance) and exercises to improve physical capacities (athleticism). The series of exercises described below can help coaches and rowers improve skills and correct faults, resulting in better and faster rowing. Technical exercises allow the rower to hone their focus on to a particular part of the stroke, improve it and feel it, and then incorporate it into their rowing on an ongoing basis.

Focusing on the Connection Points

There are three points where the rower is in real contact with the boat system: the footstretcher, the handle and the seat. The rower's interaction with each of these points will determine how effective and efficient they can be with their rowing technique.

Footstretcher: Technique

The footstretcher set-up is one of the most overlooked parts of the boat system, yet it can make a major difference to a comfortable and effective drive position, which in turn will make the drive phase more effective. For more on the set-up of the footstretcher, *see* Chapter 5 on rigging.

Technically, the rower should approach the work on the footstretcher board as follows:

1. Approaching the upcoming catch, they come up on to the balls of the feet as they approach the front turn towards the end of the recovery.
2. Once the blade has entered the water, they drive the feet down through the heels into the footstretcher, using as much of the sole of the foot as possible, engaging their strong quadriceps and gluteal muscles.
3. They push through the footboard throughout the whole drive phase as the trunk opens back and the arms finish the stroke off.
4. The pressure through the feet should stay with the footboard at the finish of the stroke as well as when the weight of the rower is transferred from the drive to the recovery during the rockover.

Footstretcher Exercise: Feet Out

This exercise improves:

- contact with the footstretcher
- optimal body swing
- bodyweight transference
- timing of the release of the water
- crew timing at the finish

Rowing with the feet out of the shoes teaches the rower to maintain contact with the footstretcher as maximum force is applied. It also helps with the timing of initiating the trunk opening and completing the stroke with the arm draw. It provides good feedback on keeping contact with the footstretcher through the finish of the stroke and rockover into the recovery.
If the rower loses connection with their feet on the footstretcher, they will fall back into the boat and have difficulty rocking over.

World and Olympic champion Jack Hargreaves demonstrates rowing 'feet out' with eyes closed.

Exercise: Top Tips

When practising footstretcher exercises:

- Keep foot connection with the footstretcher at the finish – use the toes to help.
- Maintain rockover and rhythm.
- Keep pressure on the spoon and speed on the hull.
- Keep both full slide length and body swing.
- Combine feet out with quarter-slide pauses.
- For more advanced athletes, combine this sometimes with 'wide grip' rowing (*see* below), or higher ratings.

'Feet out' is also a good exercise to improve balance. By taking the feet out of the shoes, rowers need to find the connection through the finish and their hand heights and handle speed into and around the finish together.

The rower will also learn that, when they lean too far away from the centreline of the boat (in any direction), they will not be able to keep connection between the feet and the footstretcher during the rockover.

Handle: Grip and Technique

The rower's grip on the oar or the sculler's grip on their sculls is a highly important part of effective rowing technique. Rowing is a leverage sport and it is important that the rower maximises that leverage via the position of their hands on the handles. This is done by gripping the oars and sculls as far away from the fulcrum as comfortably possible. Having the hands on the end of the handle provides the most effective leverage, and it also optimises the rigging and gearing of the boat. The grip needs to be relaxed so that the rower can feel that they are suspending and hanging off the handle, driving through the footstretcher and being light on the seat during the drive phase. Relaxation of the grip during the recovery phase assists with moving with the boat and enabling the blade to fully roll on to the feather. Relaxing the hands before the front turn promotes speed and accuracy of the blade entry – relaxed muscles are able to make faster movements and quicker reactions.

In sweep rowing, the little finger on the outside hand (the hand closest to the end of the handle) ideally needs to be on the end of the handle. The two hands should be approximately three thumb-widths apart; for rowers with wide shoulders, this may be four or five thumb widths. The outside

Olympic medallists Mian Tian and Zhang Min demonstrating good sweep grip positions.

hand provides the most leverage, as it is the leading hand. During the drive phase, the handle sits in the palm at the base of the fingers, with a flat wrist, the fingers hooked around the handle and the thumb on the bottom of the handle. The inside hand is in a similar position further down the handle, with the wrist slightly arched to assist with feathering the oar at the finish of the stroke. At the finish, the outside hand is high up on the trunk at approximately the level of the rower's second-lowest rib, and the rower is holding their blade fully in the water. For coaches this is a good opportunity to check the rower's seat to gate height and then adjust the gate height until the rower is set up in this position.

The principles regarding the grip in sculling are the same as for sweep rowing. The handles sit in the base of the fingers (the proximal phalange) and the palm. When the blade is square during the drive phase, the proximal phalange sits at 90 degrees to the palm with the index finger sitting next to the thumb at the end of the handle. This ensures that the inboard does not lose contact with the oarlock whilst moving the sculls during the recovery. Keeping the inboard locked with the oarlock during the drive and finish also supports firmer posture and a more controlled movement around the back turn, resulting in a more effective power application.

The thumb also plays an important role in both squaring and feathering along with the wrist. At the finish the wrists are flat and the pressure of the water on the spoon is felt in the base of the fingers. The pressure on the water is released by the rower and they tap the handle down, pivoting from the elbow, rolling the thumbs down and slightly arching the wrist downwards. Importantly, this sequence of movements needs to be executed with a speed that matches the boat. An effective movement will extract the blade from the water cleanly and roll the blade from being square in the water to feathered during the recovery phase of the stroke.

As the sculler approaches the front turn, they roll the thumbs up whilst arching the wrist up to square the blades – experiencing the feeling of throwing their hands away from the centreline of the boat to bury the blade in the water at the front turn. Due to the smaller handle size, a sculler can use the thumbs skilfully to keep their blades on the feather for longer during the recovery. This reduces the aerodynamic drag when compared with an earlier squared blade. Flicking the thumb at the front turn will make the blade faster to bury in the water, creating a longer effective connected stroke length at the catch.

The left hand is slightly astern and above the right hand at the crossover during the drive.

Handle Exercise: Wide Grip

This exercise improves:

- suspension and hang during the drive;
- rower's appreciation of the optimal role of each hand;
- handle height during the recovery;
- appreciation of the role the weight of the blade plays in developing 'passive' boat balance;
- in sweep, the exercise develops an appreciation that the outside hand is the leading (and dominant) hand in balance and handle height.

Leaving the outside hand on the end of the handle, the rower places their inside hand down the loom of the oar, approximately 10cm from the start of the handle. This enables them to feel how the outside hand is the leading hand. With the wide grip, the rower gains a better feeling for the role of the outside hand in following the arc and path of the handle around the rigger's gate. Maximising the path of the handle with the outside arm enables the rower to get to length during the recovery and achieve a better leverage during the drive, as the outside hand is furthest away from the fulcrum. Fundamental to this is how the rower 'organises' their sequences from the finish of the stroke. The lumbar region does not rotate but the thoracic region does. The rower needs to lead with the outside arm while holding the inside shoulder back as the hands lead away. This ensures that the shoulders stay aligned with the angle of the handles. That means that the inside shoulder does not rise higher and forward of the outside shoulder, and will therefore not block thoracic rotation and stroke length, or create tension before the catch. The wide grip exercise is excellent for correcting this mistake and promoting good rotation and relaxation.

Wide grip also enables the rower to get a better feel for horizontal hang through the latissimus dorsi muscles; in sweep, this is felt particularly in the 'outside' latissimus. Through the catch, a rower can slightly internally rotate their elbows to activate and feel the hang and suspension.

In sculling, rowing with a wide grip means the hands move down the loom of the oar to where the handle meets the carbon shaft. This wider grip enables the sculler to feel the hang and load through the latissimus dorsi muscles. The sculler can also internally rotate the elbows through the catch to feel the engagement of the lats and improve the feelings of hanging and suspension.

Handle Exercise: Inside and Outside Hand Only

This exercise is similar to the wide grip exercise in its effects. It improves:

- suspension and hang during the drive;
- understanding of the optimal role of each hand;
- handle height during the recovery;
- appreciation of the role the weight of the blade plays in developing 'passive' boat balance;
- rower's self-belief in their skill level (and boat balance).

Rowing with the inside hand only, with the outside hand on the waist, helps the rower feel the weight of the oar in the handle,

Wide grip is a good exercise for both sculling and sweep rowers.

Australian rowers Joe O'Brien and World and Olympic champion Spencer Turrin rowing inside arm only.

and understand the control they can have with the inside hand. The inside hand is used for squaring and feathering. Rowing in this way enables the rower to make sure they have the optimal grip and blade depth. Placing the outside hand back on to the handle teaches the importance of the outside hand in controlling the handle height. It also helps the rower appreciate the extra leverage and hang the outside hand and latissimus dorsi can bring.

Rowing with the outside hand only, with the inside hand on the waist, teaches rotation and working 'around' the rigger, and optimising the hang and suspension with the outside arm. The outside arm utilises its biomechanical advantage over the inside arm being furthest away from the fulcrum.

Handle Exercise: Legs Only

One variation to inside arm only is to do legs only – with inside arm only. This is a good way to teach the rower how to hang and suspend with long arms and not to grab and bend the arms at the catch. Connecting with the water and hanging with long arms means that the rower can learn to utilise their strong leg muscles to move the boat. By increasing the pressure on the blade to 50–60%, the rowers can feel how weak their arms are compared with their legs and trunk.

Seat Exercise: Rockover

This exercise improves:

- rhythm
- rockover and bodyweight transfer
- moving with the boat
- stroke sequences
- relaxation
- rower's appreciation of using body swing for boat speed
- maintaining contact with the footstretcher

The rockover exercise is good for learning sequencing, and teaching the rower the role that it and weight transference play in the movement of the boat. Sitting in the finish position, with their arms straight and the blades resting lightly on the water, shoulders and arms relaxed, the rower

Exercise: Top Tips

When practising handle exercises:

- Make sure the rower's drive grip is correct as a starting point for stroke correction.
- Emphasise the role each hand plays during the stroke cycle: the leading of the outside hand and the supporting and squaring of the inside hand.
- Maintain good bladework with the blade coming down to the water. Poor bladework is often a grip issue.
- Ensure good front turn timing.
- Check that the handle and rower's shoulders are parallel as the rower rotates around the rigger.
- Encourage the rower to engage the latissimus dorsi muscles to hang off the handle.
- Encourage the rower to try to feel the weight of the blade in the outside hand.

activates their gluteal muscles and draws in their lower abdominal muscles to initiate the trunk swinging towards the stern, and the pelvis rocking over the rower's sitting bones (ischial tuberosity). This rockover needs to be done in a rhythm, and the rower should swing as far back as they swing forwards and as far forwards as they swing back. In a crew setting, this must be done with perfect timing.

The next progression is to release the hamstrings and swing out to quarter-slide. Once this length has been stabilised, the arms can be introduced. Going through this sequence produces a rhythm through the hips and a rockover of the pelvis and a correct sequencing of the late drive and early recovery. The rower can then progress up to half-, three-quarter and full slide, all with the blades on the water. This will reinforce optimal sequencing and give an understanding of how the weight transfers on the seat from the back of the sitting bones to the front and then on to the feet during the recovery. It then transfers from the front of the sitting bones to the back and from the feet to the seat during the drive phase.

Tokyo Olympic medallist Caleb Antill demonstrating the rockover exercise.

In a further progression in this exercise, the oars are taken off the water, so that they are doing 'fresh air' rowing. If they are timing this exercise well, the rowers will see and feel the boat continue to move forwards. A good test is to see how many hundreds of metres the boat can go doing the 'swing and swing' exercise.

As a further progression, the stroke rate can be increased, to see how high the rowers can rate with the boat moving forwards and not being kicked back.

Seat Exercise: Double Finishes

This exercise improves:

- rhythm
- rockover and bodyweight transfer
- moving with the boat
- stroke sequences
- relaxation and confidence

Exercise: Top Tips

When practising the rockover seat exercise:

- Relaxed arms and shoulders, blade softly running across the water.
- This exercise can be used for a hamstring stretch.
- Emphasise the rockover.
- To increase stroke rate, open the elbows faster leading the hips over.
- Try to feel the rhythm in doing this together as a crew.

The double finishes exercise is similar to the rockover exercise in that it is effective in optimising a rower's sequences and rhythm through the finish. By utilising 'fresh air' or unloaded strokes (with feathered blades), it improves relaxation and enables the rower to develop their sequences, pattern and rhythm. By using a sequence of one normal stroke to two 'fresh air' strokes, the boat is moving and the 'fresh air' strokes are done in synchronisation with the speed of the boat. The exercise progresses from hands away and quarter-slide. The rower needs to feel the same sequences, pattern and rhythm in both the loaded and normal strokes.

Rhythm and Acceleration

The essence of rhythm is the contrast between fast and slow movements.
Good rhythm in rowing is created by the rower's feel and the contrast between the drive and recovery phases. When it is well executed, the motion looks smooth, continuous and unhurried. Rhythm is essential in winning rowing races. A crew or single sculler's rhythm is what allows them to maintain their speed throughout the 2000m. Rowing races can be won on the last stroke, so the ability to find, feel and maintain a high average boat speed is critical. Rowers can change their drive acceleration to promote their rhythm. One way of doing this is to focus on a 30% catch to a 70% pressure finish with good drive sequences – and to feel the rhythm. The crew can then vary the ratio and see what works for them.

World and London Olympic champions Katherine Grainger and Anna Watkins work on their rhythm with the double finish exercise.

Exercise: Top Tips

When practising the double finishes seat exercise:

- Emphasise sequences and relaxation.
- Emphasise timing of 'both' finishes in a crew boat.
- Emphasise keeping the relaxation and sequences of the 'fresh air' strokes in the normal strokes. The rhythm should be the same in the 'fresh air' and the normal strokes.
- Connect the sequences and swing with the speed of the boat.
- Emphasise the rockover of the rower's sitting bones (ischial tuberosity). They should feel the seat move to the bow as they rock over at the finish.
- The recovery should be free and smooth.
- Time the blade placement and catch the boat through the feet.

In training, the recovery rhythm can be promoted through pauses and by controlling the recovery speed. Rowers need to move freely and easily during the recovery phase, to feel that the boat is running high and fast under them and that they are on top of it. By manipulating the speed of the recovery, they can teach themselves the feeling of controlling it. For example, by moving freely and smoothly twice as fast as the drive phase they are exaggerating the speed and reducing the contrast. In essence, this is flipping what normally happens in a crew rhythm, in which the drive phase is quicker than the recovery (depending on the stroke rate). When the crew comes back to normal speed and rhythm, the rowers will have a better sense of how to control the speed. Coaches throughout the twentieth century also referred to this feeling as 'swing'. In both definitions, the skill of the crew to 'synch' with each other and with their boat movement is a valuable one to train.

Rhythm is teachable, although there is no doubt that some athletes are born with greater kinaesthetic awareness ('feel') and find it easier to create rhythm than other members of the crew. The less instinctive rowers will bring other strengths to the crew combination, however, such as longer length or higher power. 'Feel' athletes have superior neurological systems that provide them with a greater awareness of where their body parts are in space and time. This enables them to flow through the drive and recovery phase with well-sequenced movements that others can easily follow. They generally connect with and release the water effectively and know where the impulse should be applied during the drive. Athletes demonstrating a natural awareness of rhythm usually find their way to the stroke seat of a boat due to the consistency in their movement patterns.

It is worth noting that in small boats rhythm can be *recovery*-based, while in the 8+ it is *drive*-based – everyone driving together then finding some patience. As Curtis Jordan (the 'winningest' coach at Princeton University) noted: 'The "mass" has to move together. In the 8+ the bodies may not look exactly the same, but if the *entire mass* can move in/out of catch together and in/out of finish together, it will develop a rhythm on its own.'

'Adding Pairs' Exercise

'Adding pairs' is a great way to teach eights to understand and feel the way a fast boat accelerates. This is done by asking stroke and seven to row together, with the rest of the crew balancing the boat with their blades on the water. The two who are rowing should feel how heavy the boat is, and how quickly it decelerates between strokes. After about 20–25 strokes, rowers six and five are asked to join in. Seven and eight should feel an immediate increase in boat speed, and will need to adjust their own acceleration in the water, and their speed and rhythm to suit this. Three and four then join in and, finally, bow and two. Each pair coming in will increase the boat speed, and all rowers, whether continuing or joining in, will need to adjust their acceleration in the water and their rhythm to keep up. The most significant change will be noticed when the boat moves from four to six rowers.

In a smaller boat, the acceleration and rhythm can be felt by using a 'brake' or towing a 'drag' and then removing it.

In all cases, when a crew finally comes back together, or a brake is removed, it is a great idea to let the crew go immediately into 20–30 strokes of good powerful rowing at three-quarter race rate with 80% catch and 100% finish.

Roll Ups – The Ultimate in Exercises

This exercise improves:

- feel and timing
- recovery and drive sequencing
- understanding of weight transference and handle heights
- moving with the boat
- rhythm
- 'passive' balance

The roll up is an excellent exercise for both rowing and sculling. It allows the rower to organise their recovery sequences early, sit tall and feel the boat move towards them. Done properly, it promotes good timing for the placement of the blade, having encouraged optimal hand height during the recovery, and allows 'passive' body and boat balance. Starting from a stationary position, the rower places the blade at the end of the recovery and catches through the feet, so that they can feel the load of the stationary boat. This promotes a 'place and a push' timing, which is required while the boat is moving and, ultimately, at full race speed and in good rhythm.

Sitting at the finish with the blades square and buried in the water, the rower taps the handle down and executes the finish and recovery sequences. They straighten the elbows, draw the lower abdominal muscles inwards, rock over from the pelvis, relaxing the hamstrings (if this is done properly, the rower will feel their seat move back to the bow), and then bring the knees up. The handle heights need to be even amongst the rowers for the boat to stay balanced. The boat will give excellent feedback to the rowers, rolling to one side or the other if the weight is not central in the boat and the handle heights and speeds are not evenly together.

As a first step, the rowers roll out to one-quarter of the recovery slide length and hold the boat stationary for five seconds. Once this has been mastered, the crew can roll and pause further down the slide lengths, at half-slide and three-quarter-slide. They will find that it is more difficult to balance the boat the further down the slide they pause. Once the crew have mastered these stepping stones, they roll from the finish to the blade placing at the front turn and pause

Caleb Antill displaying total boat control during roll ups.

Variations on roll ups: Georgie Gleeson, Rowena Meredith, Harriet Hudson and Kate Rowan skilfully using only one finger to control the handle.

with the blade buried, taking a continuous recovery sequence. It is important that they roll continually forwards, finishing the recovery sequence with a buried blade. Rolling forwards and stopping at the front slide and then trying to place the blade is a mistake. Generally, what crews do at this point in the exercise is a reflection of how they row continuously. Stopping at the catch then placing the blade means that the crew's bodyweight is pushing the boat down deeper into the water, which is of course less effective. It produces a shorter stroke length, as the timing point has been missed, and the blade comes back towards the stern instead of placing the blade as it sweeps to the bow during the recovery.

Once the timing of the placement has been mastered, the rower can 'catch' the boat through the footstretcher and take one stroke finishing in the one-quarter-slide position. If this is timed correctly, the stern of the boat will lift up, and the boat will travel forwards. If the timing is poor, the stern will be kicked backwards. Once one stroke has been mastered, the crew can move on to two, three and more strokes.

Drive Phase: Legs Only Exercise

As described in Chapter 2, early force application in the initial drive leads the boat to move from decelerating to accelerating earlier. The boat therefore runs at a higher minimum velocity. A soft catch and slow rate of increase of force application means the boat takes longer to accelerate, which results in a lower minimum velocity.

The legs only exercise improves:

- drive phase coordination, sequencing and timing;
- horizontal force application;
- pushing through the feet instead of pulling the handle;
- blade entry and catch timing;
- suspension.

The legs only exercise focuses on the first part of the stroke and needs to be done in rhythm and with good timing. The rower sits in the catch position on the front of their sitting bones (ischial tuberosity), glides on the slide and times the blade to enter the water at the last point of the recovery before catching the boat through the footstretcher. They need to feel the power application simultaneously through the hands on the handle and the feet on the footstretcher. This gives them a connection to the water and suspends their bodyweight between the handle and the footstretcher.

The legs only exercise can be done at varying slide lengths. Short slide (up to 5cm) sees the initial connection and driving just 5cm on the slide. If the

Exercise: Top Tips

When practising roll ups:

- Correct recovery sequences: hands, trunk, slide.
- Correct drive sequences: legs, trunk, arms.
- Central weight distribution and even handle heights result in a balanced boat.
- Try to 'dominate' the tap down with the outside hand.
- Focus on placing the blade as the last part of the recovery.
- Move with the boat's speed, feeling the place and push of the boat.
- Start slow, then try roll ups at a higher speed.

timing is correct, the boat's stern rises quickly and runs continuously. The rower should feel that, and the coach should be able to see it. If the boat's stern kicks backwards then the rower has been late with the blade entry. This can be remedied by focusing on an earlier entry and improving the timing between the hands and the feet.

Once this short catch with the legs has been mastered to a satisfactory level, the rower can go to using half the slide's length (40cm). This enables the rower to move the boat when it is slowest, utilising the legs – primarily the large quadricep and gluteal muscles. The rower should be hanging off the handle and feeling this hang through their latissimus dorsi muscles. Their hips should be forward, and they should still be sitting on the front of their sitting bones (ischial tuberosity). Rowers and crews should not rush through the back turn on this exercise. Instead, they should take the time to finish each stroke and feel the boat run – even though their body and hands are forward of their hips.

When done effectively, the correct stroke will have early force application and a corresponding steep initial boat acceleration.

The aim of any stroke correction exercise is to improve the rower's technical ability whilst rowing normally. It is therefore important that the rowers continue to concentrate fully after completing the exercise to ensure that they incorporate the gains made into their normal rowing. To build from legs only to normal rowing, the rowers and crew should gradually add in half the body swing with straight arms, then the full body swing with straight arms. The final step is to add the arm draw for the last 30cm of the stroke. These sequences will see the improved drive sequences underpin the rower's normal rowing.

Suspension

The ability of a rower to connect the blade with the water and suspend their bodyweight between their feet and the handle is a critical element of fast rowing. The more effectively this is done, the greater the effective stroke length,

The aim of the legs only exercise is to focus on the first part of the stroke, moving the boat only with the legs.

and the more effectively they can apply their bodyweight and power to propelling the boat.

The principles and basic feel of good suspension can be taught in the boat and on the ergometer. It is something that the best rowers have grasped well, because they are able to connect and suspend at full race pressure and race rate.

Push Back Strokes

This exercise improves:

- change of direction, optimising the rower's body-weight suspension at the front turn
- drive sequencing
- effective drive length
- focus on pushing through the feet and not pulling through the handle

Starting at three-quarter-slide on the recovery with the blade square and buried under the water, the rower pushes the handle forwards towards the stern, and the boat moves backwards. The rower can feel the water gather on the spoon and as the water pulls them into the catch position, they drop into their heels, pushing against the footstretcher. This moves the force on from the back of the blade to the front. The load on the blade will be enough for the rower to suspend up above the seat – at the extreme, the rower will be able to stand up. In the optimal suspension, the rower is very light on the seat but does not come off it.

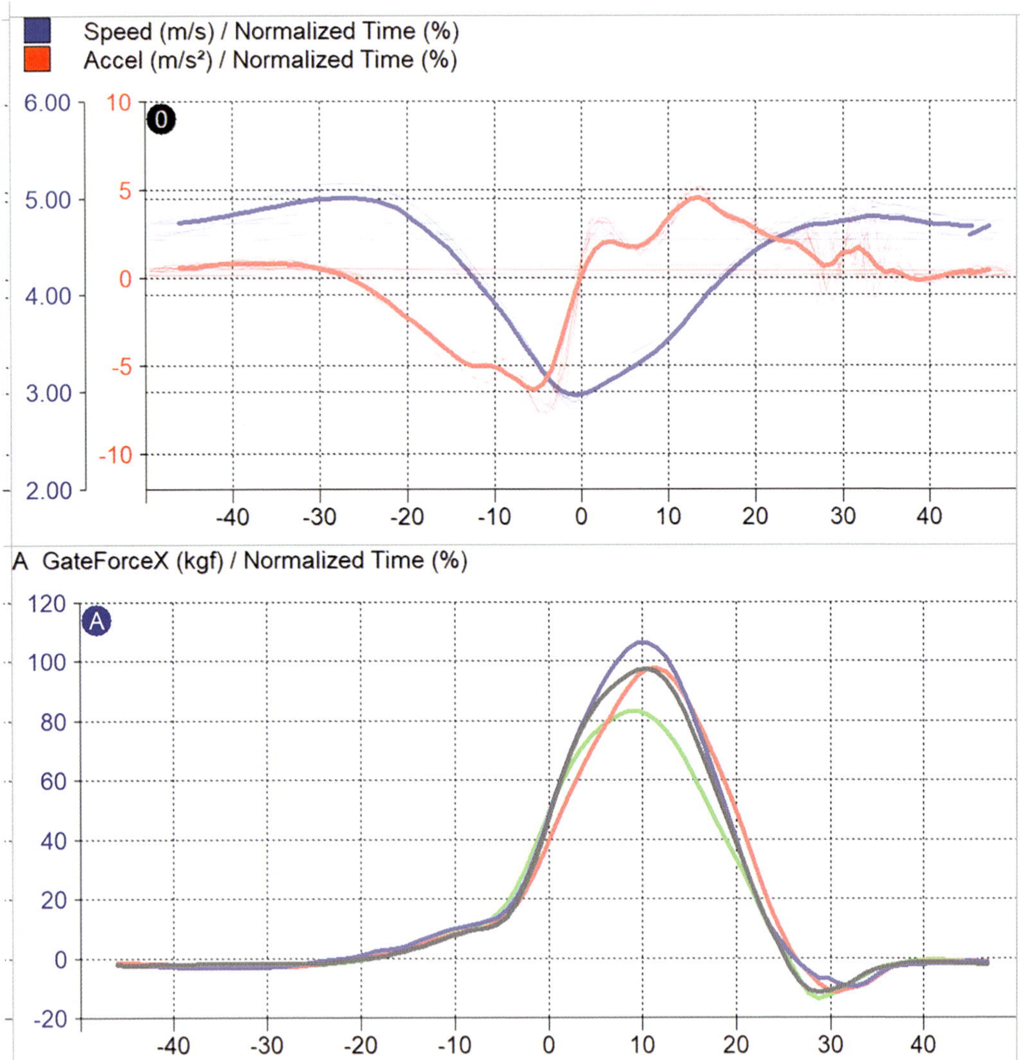

The force curve from a women's coxless four, demonstrating the effect of a correct stroke with early force application on initial boat acceleration.

Initially, just use the first 30cm of the drive, so legs only, then build out to legs and trunk with straight arms and full stroke. When doing the full stroke, the rower needs to learn that it is important not to come crashing down, or to slump (dropping the hips) on to the seat at the finish. The suspension needs to be held while the blade is in the water. There needs to be a connection between the recovery and drive through the finish sequences and rockover so that the bow of the boat remains running as high and horizontal as it can. If the rower suspends and then 'dumps' their bodyweight aggressively on to the seat, the boat will be pushed deeply into the water.

Starting the push back sequence.

Exercise: Top Tips

When practising the legs only exercise:

- When using just the legs, keep the hips forward and the shoulders in front of the seat.
- Heels drop down to engage the gluteal and quadricep muscles.
- Arms and shoulders are relaxed.
- Take time at the finish to relax and feel for the run of the boat.
- Sliding is smooth, free and relaxed.
- The blade should enter the water as part of the recovery – catch the boat through the feet as the first part of the drive.

Suspended Ergometer

This exercise improves:

- optimisation of the rower's bodyweight suspension throughout the drive phase
- drive sequencing
- effective drive length
- focus on pushing through the feet and not pulling through the handle
- horizontal force

The ergometer is a good tool for teaching technique and especially suspension. It has the added advantage that the coach is closer for instruction and for careful manipulation of incorrect grip and knee angles, and also to explain the engagement of certain muscles.

By tying the ergometer handle to the ergometer at different lengths with a boat tie, the coach can have the rower suspend in different positions and explain where vertical and horizontal force can be applied and which parts of the body need to hang to relax. The most common suspension points are at the catch, and the mid drive.

The ergometer can be used to assist the rower in understanding the muscle groups and sequence of firing to produce an effective stroke.

Exercise: Top Tips

When practising the push back exercise:

- Have even blade depth across the boat when pushing back.
- Be set and activated with abdominal muscles coming into the front turn so that the trunk is not pulled out of position during the front turn.
- A crew should all suspend to the same level.
- Shoulders and arms are relaxed, legs loaded.

Key coaching points of the suspended ergometer in the catch position.

Key coaching points of the suspended ergometer in the mid-drive position.

Bladework

The most effective boat-moving force on the blade is in the horizontal plane and the force on the water is opposite to the desired direction of the boat. It is important that the entry of the blade to the water is well timed and that the blade is quickly buried. This provides stroke length and 'bite' on the water at the catch. If the rower sequences their drive correctly – with legs, then trunk, then arms – they will be able to draw the handle up and keep the blade buried for longer. This will increase effective stroke length. When the blade is under force in the horizontal plane, the rower is maximising their power and bodyweight to move the boat. When the blade is at an ideal depth, the water will be covering the spoon and not more than 10cm of the oar's shaft (in a sculling boat), or 20cm in a sweep boat. It can be useful to place coloured tape on the shaft of the oar, giving the coach (or coxswain) a good reference point for what the oar is doing and how well each rower's oar is timed with the rest of the crew.

Good bladework promotes effective stroke length.

During the recovery phase the blade needs to feather to clear the water during the recovery and also to offer a more aerodynamic blade profile. Feathering the oar at the finish and squaring the blade as they approach the front turn both play a part in a crew's rhythm. Another notable factor – which is difficult to quantify even with modern biomechanical equipment – is the effect of touching the blades on the water in

Exercise: Top Tips

When practising mid drive:

- Choose a sturdy tie for the ergo and adjust its length to get the right position.
- Put a small gym weight or object on the rail to hold the seat in place.
- Emphasise horizontal foot force.
- Suspend by pushing into the heels and activating the gluteal muscles.
- Activate and draw the lower abs inwards to hold the trunk position. If the tummy bellows out, the hold should end.

the recovery. Clearly, this will add drag and reduce the speed of the boat to some extent. For these reasons, the importance of good technique and timing in bladework should never be underestimated.

Square Blades

This exercise improves:

- handle shape
- effective stroke length
- optimisation of bladework and crew timing
- correct weight in the hand during the recovery

Rowing with square blades without feathering is a basic but important exercise for both rowers and scullers, as it promotes the correct shape of the handle through the stroke cycle. During the recovery, the rower has to tap the handle down far enough to get the whole spoon out of the water cleanly. They need to have deep hands during the recovery if the square blade is to clear the water. The rower should keep this shape (and height from the water) when rowing with feathered blades. During the drive phase, the coach should be looking for the blade only to be buried. The rower should be encouraged to feel the grip of the blade on the water at the catch and ensure that the pressure is held on the blade all the way to the finish of the stroke. Rowing with square blades promotes good effective length under the water.

One progression of rowing with square blades is to move the rower's thumbs on to the top of the handle. Releasing the thumb grip of the inside hand will allow them to feel the optimal release point of the blade at the finish. It will also reinforce the leading role of the outside arm.

Variations and Progressions

Once rowers have mastered the basic square blades exercise, they can move on to further variations and progressions. Working on an individual rower's skill level will help with timing and bringing the handle heights of a crew together, increasing the effectiveness of the blade in the water during the drive and the timing of the blades to the boat.

Practising the variations and progressions can help the rower with transferring the square blades exercise to normal rowing. Delaying the feather until the blade comes out of the water square, rowing with an exaggerated early square or an exaggerated late square can promote relaxation and timing between members of the crew and with the boat. When a crew progresses to a high level, they can try upside-down feathering, where the rower feathers the blade so that the face of the spoon points towards the water during the recovery. This variation promotes shape and a high level of hand skills at the finish, as well as good balance skills, confidence and relaxation.

Double squaring is a further good progression from the square blades exercise and delayed feathering. As they row, the rowers square and feather the blade at the one-quarter-slide position during the recovery before squaring the blade again before the catch. This exercise assists with hand skills, relaxation and crew timing.

Slap Catches

This exercise improves:

- vertical hand movements at the blade entry to the water
- marking a reference blade entry point for the rower
- speed of catch
- handle control

Bladework Exercises: Top Tips

- Rowers and scullers need to pay attention to the correct grip, especially to the wrists being held flat.
- The hand shape and timing at the finish should allow the blade to be extracted out of the water cleanly and squarely.
- The boat needs to be balanced, with the rower's hands deep enough so that the blades do not touch the water during the recovery.
- The blades should be completely square.
- It may help the rower to focus on emphasising a square-shaped catch, rather than being over-attentive to the finish.

Square blades is a simple and extremely effective exercise to improve bladework.

As with the square blades exercise, the path and shape of the rower's hands on the handle are important to make the two turns of the stroke cycle as effective as possible. To work on the shape of the hands at the front turn, the rower can do slap catches. In this exercise, the recovery from the finish is undertaken as normal, but the blade is kept feathered and, at the normal point of blade entry to the water, the rower actively and vertically lifts the handle and slaps the feathered blade down on to the water. This teaches a square handle movement at the placement of the blade. The louder the 'crack' that is created, the better. In a crew boat all the slaps should be timed together so that they sound like one.

Exercise: Top Tips

When practising slap catches:

- Set up with a balanced boat and handle shape at the finish.
- Deep hands on the recovery to enable and emphasise vertical hand movement at the front turn.
- View the recovery and catch as a horizontal movement, followed by an immediate vertical movement – in effect, a 90-degree change of direction. The blade should not be 'sliced' down towards the slap.
- Create a timing point. The slap needs to be at the same catch angle every stroke, marking the blade entry point.
- The louder and sharper the slap, the better.
- Keep a constant forward handle speed and then up and on to the water as you change direction.

The rowers should hear a loud, sharp 'crack' as the blade slaps the water. In a crew boat, any inconsistency in timing will be exposed by the sound.

Recovery Phase: Paused Rowing Exercises

The efficiency of a boat's run between the strokes is a fundamental factor in moving fast and winning races. Sequencing and moving correctly with the boat on the way to the catch will promote the effectiveness of the boat, while doing it incorrectly will impede it. It is the recovery sequence and the timing of the change of direction at the front turn of the stroke cycle that influence the effectiveness and efficiency of the blade's entry to the water – as well as the drive phase sequencing.

One of the first things a beginner is taught in rowing is a recovery sequence of arms, body (trunk), then legs (knees breaking), then a drive phase in reverse: legs, body (trunk), then arms. These sequences need to become part of a rower's DNA. If they have not been ingrained early on, it is very difficult to correct the technique later. One way to think of these recovery sequences is to imagine lifting a chain off the ground. As the first link is lifted, the next ones rises, and so on. From the finish the elbow straightens, then the hips rock over and the knees rise. Naturally, these sequences need to be timed with the hull – it is this aspect that is often interpreted differently by coaches.

The paused rowing exercises improve:

- recovery sequences and front turn preparation;
- balance;
- timing, feel and boat run;
- equal hand heights (and so blade heights) within a crew.

Paused rowing is an excellent exercise, and should be included in any programme for improving sequencing, bladework, moving with the boat and relaxation. Pauses can be at any point in the recovery, depending on which part of the stroke cycle is being targeted:

1. At the finish when the blade is released, to correct a rower's posture and finish timing.
2. Hands away with straight arms: to correct posture, handle height and sequencing the arms to straighten before the rower rocks over through the hips.
3. Hands away and rockover with straight legs: to correct the posture at the finish and the sequence of the arms away from the body, and the initial rockover from the hips. Note; it is not a natural position for the rower to be holding down their knees for so long, so the coach needs to use their judgement to determine an appropriate range.
4. Quarter-slide pause: pausing one-quarter of the way down the slide is one of the most useful exercises a rower can do. The exercise promotes rhythm, timing, sequences, relaxation and balance. The coach and rower can achieve the rhythm and sequences and rockover of the recovery phase of the stroke, arms away from the trunk, the hips rotating and the knees rising. The coach should correct the positioning of each crew member before calling 'go'. For the boat to be balanced, the rowers need to push the boat off the finish with the same handle height at the last moment of the drive phase, tapping the handle down together with the same height and timing throughout the boat. When the boat is balanced the rower should feel in balance with themselves, weight in the feet, hips forward and light on the seat. They also need to feel in balance with the rest of the crew. The pause needs to be long enough so that the rower can become more relaxed and the boat can, as a whole, achieve a 'passive' balance. The more relaxed a rower is, the more they can let the boat run and time their movements with the motion of the boat. Hands, shoulders and hamstrings all need to be relaxed in the recovery. When the rowers release the pause, they should feel as if the footstretcher and stern of the boat are coming towards them (that they are stationary and the boat is moving under them). The boat should feel as if it is skating on top of water. The rower should feel that the stern of the boat is running high towards them and that they are not putting any extra weight on the stern to push the boat deeper into the water. As the boat comes to the rower, they need to time the entry of the spoon to the water as the last movement of the recovery. To achieve this, the hands must be raised early.

This change of direction at the front turn is the most difficult part of the stroke cycle to time correctly and perform effectively. If it is done well, the boat will run high, fast and continuously through the front turn. If it is timed less well, the boat will stop at each catch. Often, the stroke length will be compromised from stopping at the front slide and commencing the drive phase before the blade is in the water. With poor timing, the coach will see and the rower will feel the boat kicking back.

5. Varying length pauses: once the rowers and crew are skilled at pauses at the quarter-slide position, pauses can be done at half-slide, where the rower should have full trunk length, at three-quarter-slide, or even at the front stops. The further the position along the slide length the more difficult it is to control the boat. To increase difficulty, the coach can choose to do two or three slide positions to pause in one stroke, for example, pause at quarter-slide, roll to three-quarter-slide, back to quarter-slide, then roll along the slide and place the blade in the water. These can be done with a pause in each position or just rolling to and back into the position. Relaxation can be improved by introducing blade waves, where the rower pushes their hands down and up to wave the blade at the pause position. Doing this with square blades promotes good balance, handle shape and bladework.

'Feel': Eyes-Closed Rowing Exercise

A rower's 'feel' for timing with the boat and their fellow crew members brings the magic of rhythm, efficiency and the most effective power application. As a complicating factor for coaches, some rowers are blessed with more of a natural feel than others. It is often not related to rowing, but more to their experience and understanding of the pure athletic movement as a whole. Feel is subjective and in many ways cannot be measured, but most coaches would agree that some athletes have more instinct for the sport. They seem to be more gifted, with some undefinable 'X' factor, and this

Pauses allow the crew to focus on sequencing, timing together and feeling for the run of the boat.

Exercise: Top Tips

When practising paused rowing exercises:

- Emphasise sequences, synchronised rockover and rhythm.
- Use the pause to maximise relaxation; come out of the pause more relaxed than before the pause.
- Focus on a smooth, free and relaxed recovery.
- The rowers should move with the speed of the hull.
- With the boat running longer and slower, the rowers feel a greater load at the catch. It is a good opportunity for the rowers to feel the connection and suspension of the placement and catch.
- Be strict when controlling the position of each rower in a crew in a pause. Otherwise, the purpose of the pause is not achieved.

is often amplified by a mental drive and motivation to succeed.

Although not all rowers will have 'feel', they can take some steps towards broadening their understanding of the world around them and improving their own spatial awareness. This will help them to understand the difference between similar movements, or between varying speeds of movements and depth perception. The best rowing coaches in the world have often commented that their best rowers are, first and foremost, good athletes. They can run, jump, swim, spring, cycle – and also row. Coaches can assist their rowers

Coaches and crews can explore their imagination for exercises to develop their feel and confidence for the boat.

by incorporating other skills and sports at different parts of the macro and micro training cycles. For example, in winter, cross country skiing provides a great way to understand the interaction and coordination of the arms and legs, and the benefits of a good breathing cycle. In summer, running, yoga, dance, cycling and swimming can increase body awareness, balance and sensory perception. On top of this, these other sports help rowers remain mentally stimulated, encouraging them to learn and 'feel' new experiences.

The eyes-closed rowing exercise improves:

- feel and timing with the boat and the crew
- balance

Rowing with the eyes closed or rowing (carefully) at night, withdraws one avenue of the rower's sensory feedback and enables or obliges them to 'feel' what is happening with and to the boat. Eyes-closed rowing teaches the rower to feel they are in the right place at the right time with their crew members.

Exercise: Top Tips

When practising the eyes-closed exercise:

- Safety first: the coach needs to steer the boat and keep to the traffic rules.
- Emphasise staying relaxed. It can be a mentally stressful exercise for some rowers.
- Focus first on getting the back turn together.
- Have the rowers listen for the boat and the rhythm while their eyes are closed.
- Keep pressure on the spoon.
- Try some higher rate with eyes closed.

They can also feel whether they are in the right place at the right time – with the boat – during the stroke cycle.

Feedback: Technology, Coaching and Technique

As technology has improved, so has the sophistication of the systems that give feedback to rowers and coaches. Increasingly accessible and affordable, they are now an essential tool in every coach's arsenal. Feedback is essential for development, and technology can also assist a coach in getting their message across more effectively and facilitating change more efficiently. It enables the coach to understand in great technical detail what moves the boat and can help them identify the areas where more speed could be gained. Data can be used to track progress and can be referenced by the coach to support their coaching. The skill of the coach is to interpret the data in order to prioritise the factors that will have the greatest impact on performance.

There are many ways to deliver feedback, so it is important for the coach to recognise that people have different approaches to learning. Effective coaching of the person in front of them demands an appreciation of the risk of information overload. Feedback is crucial to learning and refining a rower's skills. It can come from the feel of a performance, or the outcome of an action, and can be both positive and negative. It can be useful to establish a 'feedback loop': the coach instructs or coaches, the rower and crew listen, hear, understand and implement, then describe what the change felt like back to the coach. In this way, the coach will be able to align the rower's feedback with what they themselves saw.

Types of Feedback

The type of feedback used will depend on the performer and the skill being learnt. Feedback can be in the following forms (MacKenzie, B., 2003):

- **Intrinsic feedback**: information received by the athlete as a direct result of producing a movement through the kinaesthetic senses (feelings from muscles, joints and balance).

Not everything that can be counted counts and not everything that counts can be counted.

(attributed to Albert Einstein)

- **Extrinsic feedback**: information that is not inherent in the movement itself but improves intrinsic feedback. This is also known as augmented feedback. There are two main categories:
  - **Knowledge of performance (KP)**: information about the technique and performance. This can be provided acoustically/verbally from the coach or visually via video. This enables the athlete to establish a kinaesthetic reference for the correct movement.
  - **Knowledge of results (KR)**: information with regards to the result of the athlete's performance, for example, the rower's 2k erg score.
- **Positive feedback**: information for the athlete about what was correct about the movement. Athletes need to know if a movement is correct as this provides a reference point for future execution of the movement. Positive feedback is essential in motivating athletes.
- **Negative feedback**: information for the athlete about what was incorrect about the movement. Negative feedback must include information on the action(s) required by the athlete to achieve the correct movement.
- **Terminal feedback**: information provided to the athlete before or after the performance.
- **Concurrent feedback**: information provided to the athlete during the performance

'Coach's Eye': Communication and Feedback

People learn in different ways, and the coach needs to understand this if they are to effectively coach the person or crew in front of them. They need to prioritise what feedback to give and, with more ways to deliver feedback being developed every day, to be aware of the danger of feedback overload, which might result in their key messages being lost.

The 'coach's eye' has special significance for instructional and training purposes, providing quick feedback through visual observation. However, it can lack precision, as a coach's opinion about what makes an efficient rowing motion and their interpretation of technical faults can vary, and are often subjective. A better approach is to use technology, biomechanical equipment and applied analyses alongside, to act as a more objective 'coach's eye'. As long as the factors are correctly measured and analysed, this will bring a level of precision to the information. It can then be used to give meaningful and applicable feedback to the athlete, to monitor their technique and control the development of their performance. The information gathered (in real time or post-session) needs to be applicable (rowing-specific), coachable (complements the coaching terminology) and trainable (athletes can relate to the information to make technical changes).

Combining the two types of information allows coaches and rowers to examine the different aspects of executing the rowing movement more precisely whilst allowing for individual differences. It can be compared to a 'technical rowing model', which must be clearly defined by certain parameters, including boat speed as a key performance indicator. It also provides a basis for the development of other physical and psychological requirements. Repetitive by nature, rowing makes huge demands on the concentration and attention of rowers. The quality of individual strokes needs to be maintained for a high number of repetitions. Symptoms of fatigue – both physical and of the central nervous type – must be overcome in line with good rowing technique in the daily training environment.

During the execution of the rowing movement, kinaesthetic information (a person's awareness of their position or movement) remains unknown to the rower and reaches their awareness only through connection with information from the outside world (coaching) and through selective attention (feel).

Technique training is understood as a process for optimising movement and performance. It should be the focus of the rower at every session and with every stroke. Coaching and the rower's crewmates allow for the rower to have the transfer of technical information before, during and after the training session. Therefore, there is feedforward and feedback information.

The use of 'feedforward' and 'feedback' in combination with technology, assisting and assessing the rowing stroke at the same time, has been proven to be a highly successful approach (Mattes, 2006). Combining both 'feeding forward' and 'feeding back' turns training into an evidence-based practice for coaches and athletes. Objective information (data) helps the athletes to understand where they are and provides transparency of information. Feedforward is where all the information that is to be given to the rower is gathered together before the activity, for example, an instruction about the ideal technique to be aimed for or about the precise technical points to concentrate on.

Post-training or feedback resulting from completed movements and sessions can be divided into intrinsic and extrinsic feedback.

Intrinsic feedback includes information, which the athlete receives via their sensory receptors – during and as a result of rowing.

Extrinsic feedback means external information that is reported from coaches, crewmates, media, video or equipment measuring systems mounted to the boat. Extrinsic feedback from the coach can be qualitative, for example, correct a rowing stroke that is too long or too short, or quantitative, for example, numeric data from stroke rate, velocity, stroke length and force values. The feedback can also be verbal, nonverbal or visual and varying in frequency.

In conventional training environments subjective external information from the coach plays an important role together with objective biomechanical feedback training measurement and information systems that deliver objective external information in the form of numerical data with higher precision and within a short time frame. Both are necessary for an optimal learning process.

The key for the rower is to compare their subjective perceptions – with that objective information. Then, to reflect on their reflection with their coach and their own internal evaluations.

A good coach understands that people learn in different ways and can flex their coaching to cater for different learning styles.

The Contribution of Rowing Technique to Rowing Performance

The role of technique is common to every sport. The term 'technique' is an abstract concept and has been discussed by many authors (Buchmann et al., 1974; Hochmuth, 1981). For example, Meinel described technique as 'the practice developed and tested method to reach the best possible solution of a sportive movement within the competition rules. It does not characterise something finished, finalised. Its content is characterised by its development' (Buchmann et al., 1974, p.32). Djackov went a step further and described technique as 'the interaction of the internal and external forces of the athletes aiming to apply the forces as effectively and as efficiently as possible in order to reach high sportive performances.' (Djackov, 1973, cited in Buchmann et al., 1974, p.33). Even though there may be a general concept of 'good' technique, it is important to account for individual idiosyncrasies in the performance of technique (Carl & Mechling, 1992). The learning of any motor skill – defining it into 'good' technique - requires information feedback (qualitative and quantitative analysis) in conjunction with practice (training), as it is one of the most important elements of motor learning.

Efficiency of movement can also be considered in terms of how an athlete generates movement solutions to meet the demands of the competitive environment. This is difficult to measure but is no less important for efficient movement. In fact, it is the incredible variability arising in how an elite athlete expresses a competitive skill that sets them apart from the rest.

A coach's language has a direct impact on how an athlete 'focuses' during a movement. It is essential to consider what to say, when to say it, to ensure that the athlete receives the right information at the right time. Importantly, less appreciated yet vital, is 'how' to say it to be in tune with the boat or with immediacy during a time- critical point in the session or in our case, the stroke itself.

There are many different types of feedback possible. Which ones work best during training on and off water scenarios is often also personal choice.

Gorman (2012) proposed the following principles to develop skill acquisition in rowing:

- Identify the problem: What is the main issue that is applying the handbrake to performance? e.g., Poor angle at the catch.
- Identify the *core* problem: Which particular issue is the primary cause of the main problem? i.e., poor timing of leg drive & handle/upper body movement during the last 1/3 of recovery towards catch (catch preparation).
- Design drills/activities to address the issue.
- Catch preparation drills.
- Promote transfer and encourage adaptation.
- Partly/fully executed rowing sequence both on the water and the ergometer.
- Objective coach's eye – Evidenced-based Coaching with Technology.
- As technology has improved, so has the sophistication of feedback systems for rowers and coaches. Feedback to rowers is essential for their development, and technology can assist a coach as an effective objective 'messaging tool' to

enable a change more efficiently and more effectively.

Technology also enables the coach to understand in greater detail what forces and factors are affecting their boat. What factors make it fast, and what factors are slowing it down. Technology assists us in identifying the specific areas, where an athlete/the crew can gain more boat speed and reduce limiting factors. Data is an excellent way to track progress. A coach needs to have the ability to use objective information to support their coaching and training plan, as well as underpin the ability to prioritise, which parameters and areas will have the greatest impact on improving performance. Technology has been rapidly improving, and so has the sophistication and access to feedback systems, instrumented sport-specific equipment and software applications for rowers and coaches. With increased data availability, affordability, accessibility and usability, objective feedback has become an essential tool in a coaches' tool box and the athlete's backpack. There is no question anymore if or whether technology assists coaching feedback. The importance lays in its applicability. There are three components to this:

1. Applicability to the sport-specific characteristics of the rowing movement and racing in different environments (ergometer (stationary/dynamic) or on-water (flat/open water).
2. Coachability, that the data provided assists coaches in their training plan, technical coaching and competition preparation and review.
3. Trainability, that the athlete can relate to the objective feedback to influence actively their technical and performance execution.

In general, sports are investing more and more in simple tracking data and 'wearables' systems alongside the more comprehensive and detailed biomechanical instrumentation systems – so they can more easily quantify technique, performance, training and competition characteristics. Information can support evidence-based practices, objective decision-making for the training planning and load, as well as managing the risk of injury.

The selection of 'parameters' requires a critical process to be able to describe, plan, monitor and evaluate training and competition characteristics and importantly assess and utilise the real-time information for crucial technical skill development and performance assessment. In order to provide complete athlete monitoring and technical and performance development, coaches and support staff often need to combine the tracking data from multiple systems. Understanding the differences between systems is important for practitioners, in order to track meaningful changes in individual and crew related technical and performance-related profiles.

The cycle of planning and monitoring is an ongoing, interactive process in which the quantification and evaluation of planned and implemented load alongside training responses and outcomes can be beneficial to practitioners towards the coaches and athletes they strive to support.

Coaches and athletes love the thought of the multitude of collected data from all

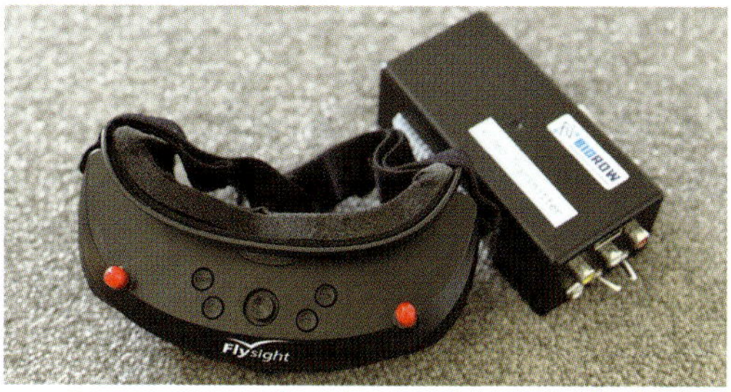

Live video feedback system to the rower.

the various tracking systems. However, at the same time they can be overwhelmed by the amount of information presented. The key is in selecting and categorising the most pertinent information. In other words, there is a need to distil the myriad of metrics into concise, meaningful and easily absorbed and acted upon information.

In the applied sport environment, decision makers (such as coaches and support staff) require simple, accurate and coherent feedback, including succinct conclusions from data, in a timely manner. Also it is advisable to include all relevant stake-holders in the metric selection process, to ensure that the data is SMART (Specific, Measurable, Applicable, Results based and Timely).

Purposeful interaction with technology is the key here, though. Technology-supported (not technology-led) coaching allows us to understand how athletes perform and what we can do to positively affect this performance.

Even with all the technology that is now available the most basic is often the most effective in providing feedback and eliciting and maintaining a technical change in rowers. The video camera and the use of still photos still allows coaches to better appreciate and identify effective rowing mechanics.

Feedback, Sensors, Systems and Trackers

There are a number of established sensors, systems and trackers currently available.

Drone technology has transformed the way video feedback can be made. It has not only opened up the possibility to use for overhead footage enabling the coach to better assess angles, rhythm, bladework and timing. It also has the capacity to use their pilot goggles for live video feedback to the rower from the coach boat.

To get detailed insight into a crew or sculler's technique and performance there are biomechanical systems commercially available. Chapter 2 delves deep into biomechanics and analysis from the Peach system. Biomechanic systems explore in depth the rower and crew's mechanical properties and boat-moving capacity. They provide excellent feedback to analyse, assess and improve performance.

Inertial Measurement Units (IMU), for example 'GPS MiniMaxX' units, have now been widely used for several years. With this development there is now an even greater need for a pragmatic and systematic approach to data collection, analysis and interpretation.

It is not enough to develop a reliable and valid testing battery, collect data, and determine whether the changes are worthwhile or not. If the information is not presented to the coach or athletes in a meaningful and truly accurate way, then the ability of that information to make a difference to the performance of the athlete and/or the crew are reduced. To assist with interpretation of the results, we first need to make an assessment about the magnitude of the change, considering the reliability of the test. It is important to present the results in a way the coach and athletes can understand. This can be done in different ways and by using a combination of methods.

Best practice is to research how individuals prefer to receive information. This may be verbally; numerically within tables; or displayed visually, such as in graphs. Although time and/or data management limitations may not enable each and every preference to be served, this is an approach practitioners are encouraged to strive to achieve. This also highlights the requirements of practitioners to have variation and flexibility in their approach to data presentation and communication.

Another key part of the reporting process is the time taken to give these results to coaches and athletes. This needs to be done as quickly as possible so that coaches have time to implement changes in training programmes to correct any identified weaknesses. Just as the poor presentation of testing data can limit the impact for improving athletes' training results, taking excessive time to deliver the information to the key stakeholders can also have a negative impact.

Likewise, the data gathered must be accurate and accurately gathered, or the implications drawn from results can be misinterpreted or even incorrect. For example, many simple biomechanical systems 'filter' or average results. This data can be misleading and can miss key items affecting boat speed.

Modern sports programmes have created systems to monitor an individual athlete over time. It is now common to use athlete data management systems for the storage and organisation of data in the applied environment. Similarly, practitioners with certain skill sets or who are collaborating with others within the organisation, may be capable of building such solutions internally or integrating data sources with specialist data visualisation tools. Dashboards can be an effective method for communicating data in a meaningful and engaging way. They may also enable interactive solutions that allow the user to explore the information by dynamically changing the athlete, test, metric or time frame being displayed. Practitioners have been encouraged to employ such interactive dashboards, along with filtering and highlighting tools, to tell an engaging story to coaching staff (Mackenzie 2003).

Despite the importance of data visualisation as well as the increased application of dashboards in the applied environment, the importance of communication and interpersonal skills in relation to the delivery of data should not be downplayed.

Given that performance is often poorer when athletes are trying to acquire new knowledge and skills, avoid assessing their level of performance whilst they are engaging in the learning process.

These systems can measure gate force, oar force, feet force, slide timing, boat acceleration and velocity, and produce a report for analysis.

In a biomechanical sense, modern rowing technique is based on the laws of physics (mechanics kinetics) and these biomechanical principles are considered together with the hydrodynamics effects of boats moving in the water.

Practitioners should aim to provide testing reports that are meaningful, timely and inclusive of specific recommendations for the coach and athletes.

Description, Planning and Monitoring

Data has always been integral to training routine, but now we have the ability to deep dive and truly understand performance:

- Interdisciplinary – Objective insights can be used to analyse performance data, optimise practice sessions, monitor injury rehab and post-training/race recovery, track sleep patterns and blood oxygen levels, and much more. Teams and athletes are uncovering a new competitive advantage.
- Software is helping teams work efficiently, and we're still in the early days of sport's digital transformation. *See* Chapter 7.
- Manufacturers have some version of this technology live available for competition use and feedback to the coaches/ spectators.

These objectives can be condensed into the following over-arching and overlapping purposes: Describing, Planning and Monitoring.

Training plan development involves combining both an objective (for example external load) and subjective (such as coach experience) understanding of the sport's characteristics. In rowing, performance is complex (individual-crew-team/on-water vs ergometer) and the training process involves more consideration than physical inputs alone. Planning is an essential part of the training process, whereby tracking system data can play a vital role.

Top Tips

- It is vitally important to use laboratory or performance tests that satisfy the most important criteria. Changes in test results need to be directly related to changes in competitive performance. In simple terms, know what you want to measure, and determine the simplest and most accurate way to measure and record that data.
- Once the precision and accuracy of a tracking system are quantified, attention can turn to the analysis process. Tracking data can be used to identify key competition characteristics, including the most demanding situations, in order to objectively manage physical preparation, readiness, and return-to-play.

4 Considerations for Rowing Technique Training and Performance

This chapter aims to explore the connection between a rower's physical conditioning and strength and the quality of their technique. It will look at the type of training required, delve into some research and consider the implications of injury and illness. Dr Nico Furlan, strength and conditioning coach to World Championship and Olympic rowers, rowing researcher Dr Caryn Urbanczyk and national team doctor Dr Andrew Griffin have all contributed their considerable knowledge and expertise.

Key Principles in Designing a Training Programme

The physical, mental and technical demands of a 2000m rowing race are immense. By virtue of facing backwards the race is started with a sprint where the rowers build lactate in their muscles and go into oxygen debt. This debt is not paid back until the race is over. The rowers need to be not only powerful but also rhythmical and efficient to maintain optimal boat speed in the middle of the race. They need to have enough energy to increase their stroke rate and power to sprint into the finish line, either to challenge the leader or defend their position. Rowers need not only to produce the gold medal speed but also to go the gold medal distance. There are multiple challenges from other boats and race margins can be as fine as a couple of hundredths of a second. Training, and the daily training environment, prepare rowers for this challenging competitive experience. The level at which a crew trains determines the level at which they will race. The more strokes of gold-medal quality a crew completes in training, the greater the chance of them challenging for a gold medal.

Generating a large amount of force over a relatively short amount of time and effectively transferring that on to the water to power the boat is the singular over-arching goal in rowing. However, the way in which an individual achieves this goal depends significantly upon their own individual attributes, including but certainly not limited to their height, weight, gender, age, years of experience, injuries, and the good and bad habits they have developed. To maximise the performance and technical development of the rower, a series of variables needs to be considered. Stroke length, distance per stroke, individual and crew biomechanical efficiency, as well as compatibility and rhythm are influenced by the rowers' anthropometric make-up (height and limb length), flexibility and mobility, ability to generate force and time it together with other rowers, and maintain appropriate form under duress, as well as relax and move with the boat and the crew.

There are a number of key principles that a coach should consider when planning a rower's physical development and training programme, and their relationship to a technical model and technical development process. This will enable the rower to optimise the opportunity to achieve the required technical components by focusing on developing the physicality that underpins technical development. In designing a programme of physical conditioning to improve technique, the coach should look to build a periodised model, moving from flexibility to conditioning to strength to endurance. Depending on the rower's stage of physical development and the point in their career, in practice these attributes will be worked on concurrently.

Resistance and weight training have many benefits, developing a robust and resilient rower, and increasing muscle mass, power and force generation. Other aspects of physical training that are often overlooked revolve around posture and quality of movement. If trained appropriately, these can enhance rowing performance, support the rower's technical development and reduce the chance of injury. Chapters 3 and 6 look at training methods to develop physicality and sustain technical proficiency throughout a race, including exercises and drills that promote technique development and stroke correction.

Training the Rowing Stroke

The rowing stroke movement is composed of two main phases: the drive and the recovery. In the drive phase, the rower performs a powerful sequential extension of the ankles, knees and hip joints from a position of deep triple flexion (the catch). The rower's trunk and shoulders hold isometrically to ensure the muscular forces applied to each body segment are transferred to the oars and boat as much as possible, and finally contribute by rapidly extending towards the finish. During the recovery phase, the rower performs a controlled and effortless flexion of hips, knees and ankles from an extended position (the finish), initiating the movement by sitting the pelvis up, letting the boat flow underneath them and actively preparing for the following drive phase. This combination of powerful and relaxed movements is to be repeated with high precision approximately 240 times during a 2000m race, in an unstable object (the boat) and in unison with the other members of the crew, all while performing at the upper end of extreme physical exertion.

When asked to describe the ideal rowing stroke, coaches will commonly use words such as 'long', 'strong', 'efficient' and 'consistent'. These simple adjectives perfectly exemplify the factors that need to be trained to improve a rower's ability. Looking at the single stroke as the minimum trainable component of a 2000m race allows the coach to establish an effective and well-organised programme that focuses on the relevant outcomes to be achieved. In designing a physical performance framework, the coach will be seeking solutions to the following questions:

- Is the rower flexible enough to achieve the desired positions?
- Is the rower strong enough to hold positions and produce a powerful acceleration?
- Is the rower conditioned enough to keep posture and manage fatigue?
- Is the rower efficient enough to move well?

Once the rowing stroke determinants and their underpinning qualities have been identified, the training strategies – content, priorities, distribution and modalities – can be laid down, based on the individual's needs and the constraints. There is a range of methods that can be used as part of a training plan. Fundamentally, achieving and maintaining a fast boat speed over 2000m is the most important training outcome.

Training for Flexibility and Mobility

Boat speed is influenced by distance per stroke – roughly, the product of forces applied and the length of each stroke. Flexibility and mobility underpin the rower's ability to optimise stroke length. Moreover, removing any restrictions that impair the rower's desired positions on the boat can improve consistency and control around the catch and the finish. An ability to lengthen muscles passively and to move actively through a range of motion plays an important role within a comprehensive physical development plan. Due to the cyclical nature of the sport and the high number of close skill movements performed in training, rowers are generally tight in the hip flexors, hamstrings, thoracic spine and shoulder girdle. This can be addressed by establishing a basic flexibility programme to promote lengthening in these areas. However, the coach should always consider each rower's individual needs, based on their capabilities in relation to the positions that are to be achieved on the boat.

Movement restrictions at the ankle and hips are likely to disrupt the rower's ability to reach the desired position at the catch, which is when these joints are close to their full flexion potential. Indeed, these two factors alone explain 50% of the variance at maximum handle force. Hip mobility is also largely associated with reductions in lumbosacral angle at the catch, which is a potential risk factor for the development of low back pain in rowers. Furthermore, the ability to perform an unrestricted lumbopelvic rockover in the first part of the recovery means that the rower will be well prepared to time the entry of the spoon at the front turn and catch the boat, using the big leg muscle groups effectively to accelerate the boat (as detailed in Chapter 2).

Descriptor	Determinant	Underpinning Qualities
Long	Stroke length	Anthropometrics, mobility, flexibility
Strong	Neuromuscular capabilities	Maximal force, power, posture
Sustainable	Conditioning	Work capacity, physiological profile
Efficient	Motor control	Rhythm, timing, balance

During the recovery a tight thoracic spine in extension or rotation can impair stroke length and timing through the front turn. Rowers at all athletic levels need to have good length through the upper back (latissimus dorsi, teres major, serratus anterior, middle and lower trapezius) to attain a stable rockover sequence during the recovery with a spine that is neutral (in alignment and with the least amount of stress through it).

Mobility and flexibility interventions can be included as part of the rower's daily preparation routine, in warm-ups, after training or as short and targeted sessions. It is important to create a structure that facilitates adherence and practicality as daily exposure and intentionality are necessary to ensure change is achieved and maintained. Muscle flexibility can be achieved by passive or assisted lengthening work (*see* examples below), applying a constant tension for several 15- to 30-second repetitions. Anecdotally, administering a total daily dose of three minutes of tension per muscle is sufficient to produce results – as long as consistency is achieved. Flexibility can also be supported by eccentric exercises that aim to increase muscle fascicle length. One example of these is the Nordic curl exercise.

Ankle dorsiflexion stretching. Keep the leading foot flat on the ground for the most effective stretch. Your knee position is important; a flexed knee will stretch the soleus muscle (the deeper calf muscle), which is important for ankle dorsi flexion. You should feel a pulling stretch in your calf muscle and Achilles tendon.

Hip flexor stretching. Set your pelvis by drawing in your tummy muscles and tilting your pelvis. Squeeze the glute of your back leg. Done correctly, you should feel a deep stretch at the front of your groin.

Gluteal stretching. Keeping your spine in a neutral position, find the position where you can feel the stretch in the gluteal muscles, not your back. The stretch needs to come from your hip motion; you will feel a deep dull stretch in your gluteal muscles.

Piriformis stretching. Set your hips and draw in your lower abdominal muscles and avoid twisting. The piriformis is a deep and small muscle, so pulse to stretch. You should feel a deep stretch in your buttocks.

Hip internal rotation stretching. Set and stabilise your hips; a better stretch comes from controlled pulses rather than forcing positions. You will feel a stretch deep in your hips.

improves this quality by demanding force applications that exceed peak rowing forces by several times, resulting in a strong training stimulus. Additionally, having a great strength reserve allows for greater economy when the rowers are at mid-race pace. The ability to reach peak forces quickly, otherwise referred as 'rate of force development' (RFD), is also greatly valued as it means a rower can produce more work per stroke, discounting all other variables, resulting in an increase in distance per stroke. Additionally, rapid knee extension during the drive is beneficial to maximise the horizontal component of force applied to the footstretcher (Buckeridge, 2014, 'Biomechanical determinants of elite rowing technique and performance').

These two qualities are often referred as 'power' and seen as one of the key outcomes of land-based training, whether in the gym or on the ergometer. Although 'powerful' athletes are often referred to simply as 'strong', it is important to establish and use terminology that is more meaningful. This can then be understood and shared between the athletes, coaches and support staff to ensure there is mutual understanding among all stakeholders. According to Wolf in *Strength and Conditioning for Rowing* (Crowood Press, 2020), the terms 'strength' and 'strength training' are too generic and do not provide the right context for the desired training outcome. Instead, the more specific concepts of 'maximal force' and 'rate of force development' may be used within the training framework. Maximal force training requires heavy loads above 80% of one repetition maximum to be targeted appropriately. Rate of force development can be trained by using loads ranging from very light to moderately heavy and can be performed using very fast and explosive training modalities such as jumps, throws and weightlifting variations.

The legs, trunk and arms account for 46%, 32% and 22% of the force generation in the drive phase, and express 95%, 55% and 75% of their work capacity, respectively. As the technical model promotes a leg-initiated and leg-driven stroke, lower-body force production is one of the protagonists of land-based training. With knee and hip extension sharing similar proportions of joint work done during the drive phase (Buckeridge, 2013 PhD thesis, 'Biomechanical asymmetries and joint loading in elite rowers'), exercises targeting these patterns concurrently are great options:

- leg press
- back squat
- front squat
- single-leg squats and variations
- lunges and split squat variations

With hip kinematics being the most important variable for generating large resultant foot forces (Buckeridge, 2014), a training programme should consider additional movements targeting hip extension from a deep flexion position. These might include hip thrust (with the back placed on a box), snatch grip deadlift, and clean pulling derivatives with deficit.

A strong trunk is also required to ensure the force produced by the legs is transferred effectively to the hanging arms and to the oar. Accessory exercises requiring the trunk to produce high forces include the

Australian rower Fraser Miscamble straining under the weight of the leg press. Leg strength is crucial in rowing and the leg press is an ideal exercise to achieve it. (Photo Jan Legg)

Romanian deadlift, 'Good Mornings' and back extensions (performed on a bench, GHD or Roman chair).

It is important to remember that the intended outcome, which is to develop high and/or rapid forces at knee and hip joints, must guide exercise selection. When targeting maximal force generation in the squat, the load the rower can lift is most often limited by their trunk strength, not their legs. Isolating the legs and utilising the leg press exercise means that the legs can express more of their potential, and the programme will effectively develop force capabilities of the targeted musculature.

Research has shown that hip kinematics is the most important variable for generating large resultant foot forces.

The rower's technical proficiency and ability to move through an adequate range of motion will also play an important role in exercise selection. For example, if a rower performs a barbell snatch from the floor with poor execution due to lack of mobility or competence, it is unlikely that the targeted musculature will receive an adequate and safe training stimulus. In this case, other options should be considered, taking into account the rower's capabilities and the desired end result.

Strength development in the lower body and trunk is essential but so is the ability for the rower's kinetic chain not to 'leak' any Watts through the drive phase. To do that, the trunk needs to possess the ability to create forces of equal magnitude and rate offering directional resistance to the high forces exerted by the limbs. When training for maximal force, the exercises mentioned above will provide a strong stabilisation stimulus to the spine if the trunk is involved. However, with rowing force production being predominantly extension-based, the anterior quadrant should receive special attention when training the trunk. A well-prepared abdominal wall ensures a proper rockover can be performed to start the recovery and improve force transfer when the blades are put in the water. This avoids over-reliance on hip flexors during the recovery phase and decreases lumbosacral stress during the propulsive phase.

General exercises that can develop the anterior trunk include:

- sit-ups and variations
- abdominal curls and variations
- Swiss Ball wrestling
- suitcase and farmer's carries
- jacknife (on Swiss Ball or on the ergometer seat)

A large portion of trunk training is also allocated to the development of work capacity (*see* below).

The rowing ergometer is also good at helping with the generation of force by the legs and with trunk stiffness. Several modalities can be introduced to provide a bridge from the weight room to the boat:

- 'Legs only' drills at full strokes. This drill aims to focus on early leg drive and holding the trunk so that the hip can produce a large force moment later in the drive.
- Drag factor and stroke rate can be manipulated as a constraint for rate of force generation. This is also a great learning tool to understand how power can be generated with different combinations of force and rate.
- Short sprints of less than 150m or power strokes can be incorporated during gym sessions as a tool to develop rate of force development, challenging the athlete to produce peak power values.

The rowing ergometer is an excellent tool to help generate leg force and trunk stiffness.

- With the handle securely tightened (for example, with a boat strap), rowers can perform a maximal isometric push in peak handle force position (~110 degrees at the knee, trunk relatively upright, arms very slightly bent). Rowers should aim to maintain a strong and neutral back whilst gradually exerting as much force as possible through the footstretcher and the handle over five seconds, three to five times per set. Due to the high force demands placed by this exercise, it is vital to ensure that the set-up is safely arranged.

Despite its smaller contribution to total forces, the upper body has a crucial role in developing a powerful stroke. Concentric contraction of muscles (where muscles shorten while generating force) around the hip and knee joints generates force, while isometric contraction (a stabilising muscle contraction without motion) of the trunk and upper extremity muscles (pectoralis major, trapezius, latissimus dorsi, teres major, serratus anterior) transfers kinetic chain to the handle. Through the late drive phase and into the finish position, the upper body continues the momentum from the back and legs through concentric contraction of the arm extensors and internal rotators. The rhomboids retract the scapula, biceps brachii flex the elbow, and triceps brachii draws the arms into the body and the finish position. The change of direction at the finish position is supported by the contraction of the biceps brachii long head and subscapularis. If the trunk and arm muscles are unable to sustain the force generated by the legs, suspension and load transfer through the drive will be lost, and the athlete will be more vulnerable to injury (Thompson & Wolf, 2016). Overloading the lats, shoulders and upper back develops a strong finish and good stability during the drive.

Exercises supporting the development of relevant muscle groups include bench pull, bench press, seated row, bent-over row, supine row and pull-ups. Bench pressing plays an important role in targeting muscle groups that are typically underdeveloped in rowers whilst developing resilience in the rib-cage area, a typical site of injury within the rowing population. Moreover, a properly executed bench press targets thoracic extensors, which could be beneficial for overall posture. Looking to improve a rower's upper body strength through bench pulls can come to a ceiling and the breakthrough will happen from focusing on bench press.

Training for Conditioning

To ensure that boat speed is maintained, or increased if required, a rower's body needs to be able to maintain consistent force outputs throughout all 240 strokes of a race. On the water, as a rower fatigues either during pieces or over the course of the training session, the coach needs to reinforce the quality of technique and fundamentals that underpin boat speed. Rowers need to be constantly challenged on this component in all training – on the water, on the ergo and in the gym – until it becomes part of their DNA. Fatigue is a complex phenomenon in which interactions between perceptual and performance variables lead to impaired physical and cognitive function. It is beyond the scope of this book to discuss the intricacies of fatigue development from a physiological and cognitive perspective, but it is useful to focus on aspects related to the ability to hold appropriate posture whilst maintaining relaxation and rhythm.

Work capacity can be defined as 'the ability to produce or tolerate variable intensities and durations of work and contributes to the ability of an athlete to perform efficiently in a given sport' (Spencer, 2016, 'Spinal-Exercise Prescription in Sport: Classifying Physical Training and Rehabilitation by Intention and Outcome'). Muscular work capacity is generally targeted by rowers using high repetitions (20 to 30) circuits of eight to ten whole-body exercises performed at moderate to light loads. These circuits, usually referred to by the generic term 'strength endurance', can generate anatomical adaptations at the muscle and tendon level, promoting hypertrophy and increasing loading capacity. It should be reminded that, for trained rowers, these metabolically demanding circuits will only increase force capabilities if they result in substantial increase in muscle cross-sectional area. This is because the moderate intensities used in this training modality are too low to target maximal force capabilities (*see* above).

Traditional rowing training promotes strong global strength and loading ability, particularly for the muscles driving the stroke, such as the quads, the back extensors and the lats. Smaller muscles and antagonists are often left out, and this can impede good posture and sequencing, as well as having a negative impact on training. Understanding the role played by these muscles and their conditioning in supporting the rower's training and performance is vital. For example, a lack of sufficient work capacity in the abdominal wall will lead rowers to rely on hip flexors to initiate the recovery. This is likely to result in poor posture and a compromised stroke. Additionally, the already overworked hip flexors could further hinder training that is supposed to mitigate their over-activity. One example of this is when a rower does abdominal work such as sit-ups. Strong hip flexors can take over and there is no benefit to the abdominal muscles, which are the ones that need to be strengthened. In this case, exercises putting the hip flexors at a mechanical disadvantage and isolating rectus abdominis can offer a solution until enough work capacity is achieved.

The Shoulder Joint

The shoulder joint has a relevant role in achieving correct rowing posture. Due to its anatomy, it requires a sophisticated system of muscles to provide stability. These stabilising muscles need to possess sufficient work capacity to endure the demands of training and racing.

Rowing training often promotes global strength and ignores smaller muscles and antagonists, which can compromise a rower's development.

Serratus Anterior and Rib Stress Fractures

Handle force output is strongly related to muscle force magnitude and the timing of the latissimus dorsi, teres major and pectoralis major during the early- to mid-drive phase. The trunk and arm muscles spend much of this time in eccentric or isometric contraction. Eccentric contractions are where the muscle is active while lengthening under load; isometric muscle contractions are contractions without movement. Applied strain and strain rate while a muscle is lengthening have been identified as factors in muscle damage (Lieber & Fridén, 1993; Proske & Morgan, 2001). The trapezius and rhomboid major contract concentrically during drive-phase scapular retraction, producing large eccentric loading in serratus anterior. Serratus anterior actively keeps the medial border close to the thoracic wall (Prinold, 2012) and stabilises the rib cage during forced respiration (Warden et al., 2002). Results from rowing biomechanics literature have previously implicated serratus anterior in the occurrence of rib stress fractures among rowers (Abbot & Hannafin, 2001). Variation in force output and peak force timing among serratus anterior, trapezius and rhomboid major (Urbanczyk et al., 2022) suggest that forceful antagonistic co-contraction, over thousands of strokes, potentially leads to rib stress fractures (Vinther et al., 2006; Rumball et al., 2005; Karlson, 2000) and may be a factor in scapular dyskinesia (Noguchi et al., 2013).

The Rotator Cuff

The rotator cuff muscle group lends stability to the shoulder joint. Variation in peak force timing suggests different roles for each of the rotator cuff muscles. Subscapularis (shoulder blade) contraction during the late-drive phase protects the shoulder joint by supporting arm deceleration into the finish position, the sharp change in direction, and then arm out into the recovery phase. In contrast, peak force timing of infraspinatus late in the recovery phase suggests that its main role is to restrain the humeral head from sliding forwards when the arms are fully extended (straightened). Infraspinatus works in tandem with the anterior deltoid as the handle is elevated into the catch position to help set the rower up for a relaxed but sharp catch with a stable scapular position. High humeral elevation, internal rotation and reduced scapular posterior tilt contribute to impingement injuries (Persad, 2016; Prinold, 2012). Contraction of subscapularis during the late drive, and relative quiescence of middle deltoid function to depress and retract the scapula, and centralise the humeral head, protect the tendon from impingement and damage.

Biceps Brachii and Epicondylitis

Epicondylitis (inflammation of the tendons) can arise in rowers due to incorrect initiation of the drive phase by flexing the elbows with pronated forearms, (Bompa, Hebbelinck & Van Gheluwe, 1985). Full extension of the upper limb should be maintained through the early drive, giving triceps brachii an advantageous line of action. If, at the catch, the elbow is slightly bent in flexion, biceps brachii can potentially overpower the triceps, decreasing load transfer efficiency (Cookson & Nolte, 2017). Strengthening triceps brachii to stabilise the elbow during the drive phase and de-emphasising early contraction of the elbow flexors can mitigate against elbow injuries.

Developing an Individualised Programme

An integrated assessment of the rower's technical flaws, musculoskeletal testing and injury history can all be used to inform the development of an individualised plan to incorporate isolated muscle work capacity, prioritising two or three major points. Short and targeted sessions, involving three to five exercises with low load and high repetitions, can be included in warm-ups, at the end of strength sessions or around water training. Anecdotally, a minimum of 100 repetitions per muscle (for example, four sets of 25 repetitions) performed at least five days a week can produce results within a six-week period. This volume, which can also be achieved with multiple exercises targeting the same musculature, should be progressively introduced to avoid delayed onset of muscle soreness due to the rower initially lacking tissue tolerance.

See below for two examples of how this type of work can be designed and incorporated into a rower's training schedule.

Athlete 1	**Sculler**	**Week 4**
Technical flaws	MSK/Physio screening	S&C movement flaws
Does not rock over properly	History of low back pain	Deadlifts with slight spinal flexion
Dives into the catch with thoracic flex	Tight hip flexors and hamstrings	
Work capacity plan (extras – 5× per week)		
Cat camel (lumbar, thoracic, integrated) McGill Birddog Aleknas Deadbug Hip hinge 10kg plate on chest (2s hold) Prone thoracic extension (2s hold) Push the ceiling in catch position		4×10 each 5×10 each side 5×20 4×15 4×20 5×20
Work capacity plan – at the end of each session		
L-sit stretch against the wall Couch stretch (hip flexors)		5 minutes 3 minutes each side

Notes: Athlete 1 presents a blend of postural flaws related to a lack of mobility, work capacity and motor control. The prescription aims to improve on these areas by increasing capacity across key musculature whilst removing movement restrictions and allowing the athlete to build competence on targeted postures and movements.

Athlete 2	**Sweep rower**	**Week 1**
Technical flaws	MSK/Physio screening	S&C movement flaws
Sits a little low at the finish	Sore R hamstring after 18km+ sessions	Hamstrings cramp during hip thrusts
Work capacity plan – at the end of every warm-up (pick two exercises)		
Glute bridge walk-out Single-leg (R) Romanian deadlift Single-leg (R) glute bridge Banded (R) leg curl prone		
Work capacity plan – at the end of strength training sessions		
Hip thrust (3s pause at the top) 55kg Bench reverse hyper Banded assisted Nordic curl		

Notes: Athlete 2 often reported specific muscle soreness in the hamstring following long water and ergometer sessions. Additional work was distributed over each warm-up three times a day, and at the end of the four weekly strength sessions. In this case, exercise prescription could be extremely targeted towards building resilience in the hamstrings and spread over the daily activities of the rower. The work progressed in volume throughout the weeks to reach four sets of 25 repetitions by Week 3 for the additional exercises performed at the end of the strength sessions.

Using Holds for Conditioning

Work capacity in the trunk can be developed using several exercises. Initially, exercises targeting non-specific positions should be used to develop the ability of the spine to hold neutral position against deformation forces through one plane of movement. Exercises should target all trunk quadrants – in other words, anterior, posterior and lateral (left and right). Consideration of the training objective is once again the priority, and the exercise prescription should follow suit. Planks are often selected due to their practicality, although the shoulder girdle is often the limiting factor impeding progress. Removing the shoulder from the equation allows an exercise to target the trunk directly. For example, horizontal bench holds have the potential to strengthen and improve conditioning in all four quadrants of the trunk.

Bench holds can be performed as a pair, with one rower lying on a bench or box with hips on the edge so that the trunk is unsupported and holding against gravity. The partner athlete sits below the knees to provide support. It is imperative to maintain appropriate alignment and hold the position with the rower's hip fully extended and with a neutral spine. Training can be arranged in a circuit format, with the rowers swapping between positions every 30 seconds with no rest, for a total of around 10 minutes of continuous work. Progression can be introduced by adding weight and/or dynamic movements to increase the difficulty of the exercise. Including rapid perturbations to the rower performing a bench hold is a great way to challenge the ability to create rapid trunk stiffness.

Developing work capacity in key positions of the stroke is another strategy that creates cohesion between physical preparation in the gym and the boat. In this context, isometric holds can be used at key positions of the drive such as the catch, mid drive and the finish. In similar fashion to the maximal isometric push described above, a nylon boat tie can be used to secure the handle so that the rower can practise safely. These isometric holds are used to practise suspension, which is a key skill in rowing that allows for effective horizontal transfer of force. Rowers should be using their glutes and abdominals to slightly remove weight from the seat whilst hanging from their lats with shoulders relaxed.

Once positions are mastered, work capacity can be developed by accumulating multiple short holds (for example, starting at 10 seconds) and increased with longer durations, up to 60 seconds, or a higher number of sets. Coaches are instrumental in checking for and reinforcing correct posture, which is essential for progression.

Holds can also be performed on the static Concept2 ergometer. With the rower's permission, the coach will have

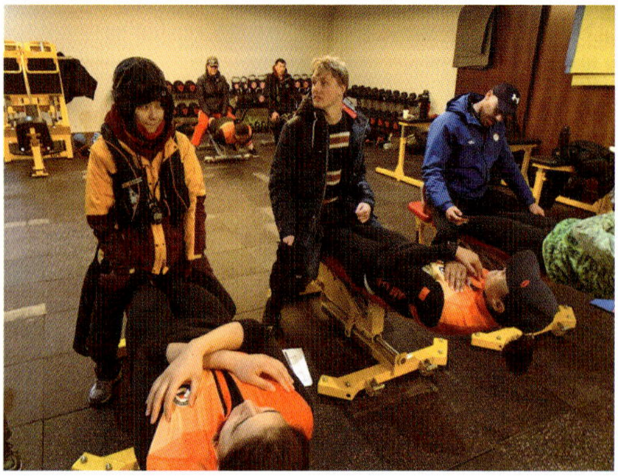

The Chinese rowing team training with bench holds.

the opportunity to manipulate their body into the positions they need and to emphasise the local muscle activation and relaxation. The rower will hang during the drive phase and should be feeling that they are working only the muscles that are moving the boat. In the boat the rowers will also feel the run of the boat, the timing and the work of their crew mates. During the recovery, the rowers need to switch off and relax. These two components of the stroke combine to produce the boat's rhythm. Connecting dynamic ergometers together with bars or rope enables the rowers to feel each other's timing and rhythm. The dynamic Rowperfect also enables the rowers to better feel the timing of the leg drive and the knees dropping. It can be connected to other rowers at the footstretcher and handle.

Making Technical Changes

During ergometer training the components of the stroke need to be constantly emphasised. Unless the coach has access to a rowing tank, the ergometer is an excellent tool to develop and reinforce gross technique and introduce new concepts to the rower. Although competence is measured on the water, land training provides a good opportunity to explain and develop what underpins technique, to help the rower understand what they need to do on the water, and provides more exposure to developing good technique. Technique training is not a light recovery session. There should be a skill and rhythmical component in all training sessions. With the ultimate technical test of a crew being under race pressure, technical training needs to have a mental component as well, with rowers being required to hold their technical form under physical duress and racing conditions. Producing changes in a rower's technique requires time and a good amount of deliberate practice. If mobility and work capacity limitations have been addressed, exercises emphasising motor control of the movement can be used as a training tool.

A classic example of this is training drills targeting the rockover:

- At a very basic level, the coach can ask the rowers to place their hands between the seat and their sitting bones, rocking back and forth.
- Postural feedback can be provided with elastic bands to ensure the trunk is in the right position. If the rower finishes the drive with a flexed upper back, the band should pull backwards on their trunk to generate a reaction in the desired direction.
- The rower holds a wooden stick at the finish and hangs off it whilst the coach attempts to pull it away. This action generally results in a good abdominal and gluteal activation, which is required for a smooth finish and a rapid turn point and release.
- To build correct rockover timing, a light medicine ball can be used in different ways to emphasise a quick hand release with hips following through, or control of the hips and trunk while receiving and returning the ball in a dynamic fashion. Medicine ball placement can also be changed to cue for a neutral thoracic spine.

- For the development of an active rockover after the finish, rowers can perform 'rebounding' drills at the finish position in pairs. The task in this case is to perform an active rockover, with the challenge being to maintain posture and rhythm at increasingly higher movement rates.

Medicine ball throws being used to challenge a rower's postural control and timing on the ergometer.

Once there is clarity around the technical changes that are to be made, these 'functional training' drills can be prescribed as individual sessions or before water training. When administering these drills, a coach should ensure a quiet environment that will foster concentration and attention, explain with clarity and aim for simple cues. The rowers should be encouraged to provide feedback and to take an active part in the planning of these drills. Long-term buy-in is required to ensure learning and transfer occur.

Rower learning how their sit bones relate to the rockover. The ergometer provides the ideal opportunity for coaches to help rowers with understanding how they move.

Biomechanical Considerations in Rowing

Using Musculoskeletal Modelling

The Biodynamics Group at Imperial College, London, led by Professor Alison McGregor, has undertaken rowing research for over 20 years. This body of work has investigated the rowing technique of some of the best rowers in the world and underpins British Rowing's technical model. It has been the catalyst to identify technique and training to both maximise performance and mitigate against injuries.

Dr Caryn Urbanczyk's research, utilising computational modelling, investigated how muscle forces drive the variation seen in movement patterns, which impact joint forces, and thus injury. Repetitive loading with poor mechanics or movement control was found to lead to an increased risk of shoulder injuries during ergometer rowing. Her interesting and compelling research also identified differences in male and female rowing technique that could not be attributed to anthropometrics (body shape and size) alone. The work demonstrates that computational modelling can enhance a coach's interpretation of rowing performance data, and provides many practical tips to coaches and rowers.

Assessing the quality of an athlete's performance and facilitating improvement are fundamental coaching paradigms, but there is much more to prescribing training plans than a simple technical understanding of movement. Rowing is a highly coordinated, whole-body activity that utilises 95% of lower extremity muscular capacity, 55% of trunk muscle capacity, and 75% of upper extremity muscle capacity with every stroke (Thompson & Wolf, 2016; Soper & Hume, 2004; Kleshnev, 2006). A rower must produce maximal and repeatable force, smoothly and consistently, over hundreds of strokes.

Generating a large amount of force over a relatively short amount of time and effectively transferring that into the water to power the boat is a singular over-arching goal in rowing. However, the way in which an individual achieves this goal depends significantly upon their own individual attributes, including but certainly not limited to their height, weight, gender, age, years of experience, injuries, and the good and bad habits they have developed. Rowers at all athletic levels need to have good length through the upper back (latissimus dorsi, teres major, serratus anterior, middle and lower trapezius) to attain a stable rockover sequence during the recovery with a neutral spine (where the spine is in alignment and there is least amount of stress through it).

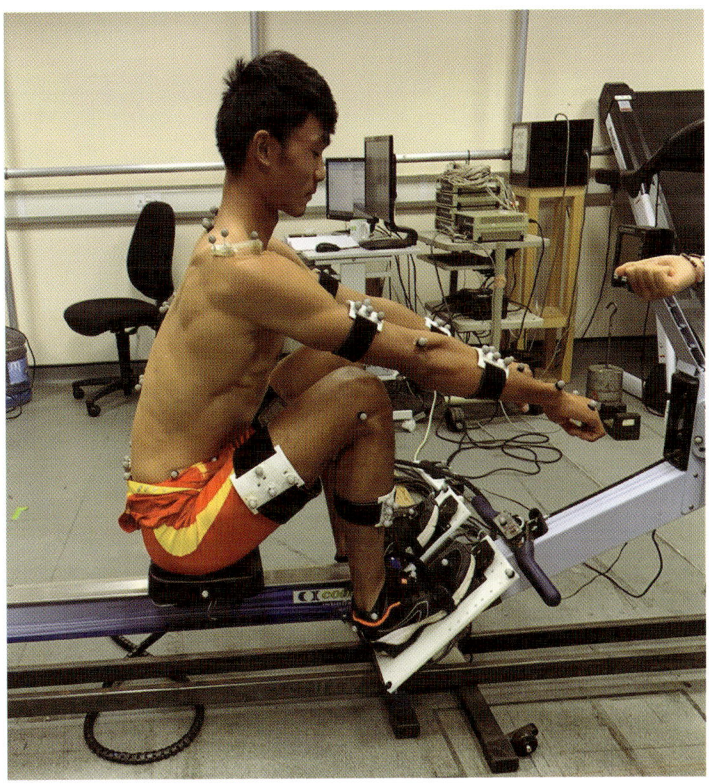

An international rower undertaking testing at the biodynamic laboratory at Imperial College, London.

Engraining musculoskeletal control of the finish and catch positions will increase stroke efficiency and consistency for the same physiological workload (McGregor et al., 2016). Over-use of rhomboid major, upper trapezius, levator scapulae and serratus anterior contribute to a rounding of the upper back and compromised scapula (shoulder blade) positioning (Kibler et al., 2002; Page, Frank & Lardner, 2010). Excessive flexion at the shoulder may yield rotator cuff tendinopathy, anterior instability, or impingement (Thornton et al., 2017).

Poor scapular mechanics are commonly implicated as a cause of over-reaching or 'lunging' at the catch (Nugent et al., 2020). Scapular positions commonly exaggerated in the outside arm of sweep rowers include large scapular protraction and anterior tilt (Ludewig & Reynolds, 2009). Large scapular protraction and anterior tilt (lunge) leading into the catch decreases the latissimus dorsi connection and increases load through the upper trapezius and is usually associated with a stooped posture in the upper back. A key deliverable for any training programme is to maximise load adaptation of the musculoskeletal system, by monitoring training to achieve consistency in compliance and progression.

Gender Differences in Muscle Mechanics

It is well documented that men have faster race times than women across weight classes (Keenan, Senefeld & Hunter, 2018). This is attributed to the greater height and mass of male rowers; however, sex differences seen in rowing performance are not fully explained by anthropometry alone.

Examination of average muscle force time profiles, independent of stroke rate, shows that males appear to generate force primarily through activation of the prime shoulder movers and select scapula stabilisers. There is preferential recruitment of large superficial back muscles during the drive phase, including the latissimus dorsi and teres major. Males generate higher peak muscle force than females in teres major, latissimus dorsi, serratus anterior, subscapularis and supraspinatus. However, females share cumulative force across a wider distribution of back and shoulder muscles. For example, females display higher peak muscle force than males in pectoralis major and trapezius, which suggests a more global approach to isometric stabilisation of the upper extremity during the drive phase. These differences in muscle force distribution contribute to subtle differences in external movement patterns at the shoulder and lumbar spine (McGregor, Patankar & Bull, 2008). This appears to be a beneficial tactic. As Mason (1988) noted, female rowers showed higher effective work output, attributed to better muscle sequencing.

Age Differences in Muscle Mechanics

Age is a powerful predictor of performance variance across competition levels (Seiler, Waneen & Martin, 1997). This performance variation is influenced by aerobic capacity (Ingham et al., 2002) and rowing expertise. In turn rowing expertise is correlated with variation in muscle synergies, which adjust mechanical output (Turpin et al., 2011).

Novice athletes show poorer muscular coordination, higher rates of fatigue onset, and lower stroke efficiency than more experienced rowers (Green & Wilson, 2000). Coordination of forced respiration with contraction of serratus anterior during the stroke cycle is implicated as a precipitating mechanism of rib stress fractures in rowers (Abbot & Hannafin, 2001). High serratus anterior force among club athletes supports the idea that co-contraction of the scapular muscles creates a compression force on the rib cage. This highlights the importance of trunk muscle strength and conditioning for young, highly competitive athletes.

Masters rowing has a large and growing membership throughout the United States, Europe and Australasia. Rowing continued with advancing age is attributed to attenuating an age-related reduction in aerobic fitness and skeletal muscle mass (Arumugam et al., 2020; Boland & Hosea, 1994). However, this is not the case for muscle power (Volianitis, Yoshiga & Secher, 2020). Between the ages of 20 and 50 years, ergometer performance declines by 3% per decade, and 7% per decade from age 50 to 70 (Seiler, Waneen & Martin, 1997). Masters rowers have the lowest peak force output among the prime movers and scapula stabilisers but show higher peak muscle forces in arm accessory muscles. Recruitment of smaller muscles suggests that masters rowers have a more pronounced use of the upper limbs during rowing. This may be the result of better muscle load sharing developed through greater experience, or represent a reflection of compensation for reduced global strength.

Injury Mitigation

To decrease risk of injury (and simultaneously improve performance), an important emphasis should be placed on implementing strength and conditioning programmes that focus on scapula-thoracic muscular strength and endurance, to avoid development of muscular imbalances, minimise fatigue effects, and engrain positive postural coordination. Alternate pushing and pulling exercises, performed over a full range of motion, build shoulder stability and anterior/posterior muscular balance (Urbanczyk et al., 2020). Additional focus on muscles involved in shoulder rotation are particularly beneficial to female athletes (Attenborough, Smith & Sinclair, 2012). Regular strength and conditioning of serratus, latissimus and rotator cuff muscles will benefit masters athletes, to reduce decline in muscle strength, ensuring glenohumeral stability thereby reducing symptomatic and asymptomatic rotator cuff damage with age (Teunis et al., 2014).

Medical Considerations in High-Performance Rowing

Dr Andrew Griffin has over a decade of extensive rowing experience, having been a Great Britain Rowing physiotherapist,

Australian Olympic team doctor as well as an Australian Rowing team doctor. Here, he outlines common rowing injuries and illnesses and how they can be avoided.

When coaches are considering athlete training loads and technical coaching interventions, the potential for injury needs to be considered. Rowing presents extremes challenges to the athlete in relation to cardiovascular fitness, strength and power output. It is a sport that demands high-volume training and repetitive biomechanical movement. The volume of training and the repetitive nature of the movement patterns are associated with certain injury and illness presentations. The most common injuries involve the chest wall, low back or forearm. They often, but not always, present following a change in training or athlete load.

Chest Wall Injury

Issues with the chest wall are very frequent, accounting for up to half of athlete time lost to injury. The most common specific injuries identified include:

- rib stress injury and rib stress fracture;
- acute muscle tear, particularly in the intercostal muscles (the muscles that run diagonally between the ribs);
- inflammation or irritation of the costo-chondral joint (the joint between the rib and the rib cartilage).

Rib stress injury can present with a myriad of symptoms in either a sculling or sweep rower. Diagnosis is made via MRI scan, CT scan or bone scan, with MRI being the preferred imaging modality. Bone stress injuries can occur anywhere throughout the ribs and may present with pain away from the site of the injury, most likely due to the complex neural pathways and referral of pain. They may occur on either side of the body and anterior to posterior.

It is important for an injury to be assessed and diagnosed by a qualified medical practitioner or physiotherapist, ideally, someone who is knowledgeable about rowing injuries. A range of diagnostic objective and subjective tests is used for assessing risk of rib stress. These tend to be more accurate for anterior and antero-lateral rib injuries. It is important to still consider a posterior rib stress injury with persistent posterior discomfort, often associated with muscle spasm and tightness.

Scanning immediately at the time of the onset of symptoms may not identify a developing rib stress injury. In the elite team environment, it is most common to seek a diagnostic scan around five days

Muscle Mechanics: Top Tips

- Muscle forces drive the variation seen in movement patterns, which impact joint forces and affect injury risk.
- Use strength and conditioning wisely to focus on areas of weakness and improve muscular balance.
- Coaches and trainers need to consider their individual group of athletes to tailor training programmes for technique optimisation and strength and conditioning.

after the onset of symptoms, and with continuation of these symptoms, to best identify the pathology.

Ignoring chest wall symptoms and continuing training will most commonly lead to a development of the stress injury, and it may even cause a rib stress injury to progress to a rib stress fracture. Failing to adequately rest and rehabilitate from a rib stress fracture risks a non-union of the fracture and this lack of healing may have long-term negative health effects for an athlete. For this reason, it is strongly recommended that any athlete with chest wall symptoms be removed immediately from on-water and ergometer training for a minimum of four days. In a substantial number of athletes, this time will allow the pain and discomfort to settle, and they will be able to return to training.

If an injury is identified following a medical review, recovery time will vary depending on the nature of the pathology. A rib stress injury involves bruising within the bone, without a break to its outer cortex. In the elite setting, with daily monitoring and assessment, the athlete can return to full training load in an average of 38 to 57 days.

A rib stress fracture involves a break or separation of the outer layer of the bone. This may be partial or complete. A return to full training takes on average 57 to 69 days, although for some the time lost may be significantly longer. It is important to note that these time frames relate to an elite setting, where there is daily monitoring and the athlete's rehabilitation programme is being constantly adapted. A more prolonged period of recovery is recommended for community and club-based athletes.

When a rib stress injury occurs, it is important to consider the broader factors that may have contributed to it. Issues with the chest wall often present following a change in training. This may be an increase in duration or intensity, or both, or a return to training after a break period or other injury or illness. Regular loading of the chest wall, such as in gym work or in bodyweight-based exercise, particularly during times of disrupted training, will help load the structures of the chest wall and minimise change in load with the athlete's return to training.

Further investigation and consideration of bone health may also be indicated, such as assessing for adequate energy intake, menstrual cycle irregularities and the presence of nutrients such as calcium, iron and vitamin D.

Low Back Injury

The prevalence of low back pain in the rowing population is high and causes a significant loss of training time. Of particular note is evidence that junior rowers aged 14 to 18 years report much higher rates of low back pain than the general population for their age.

A presentation of low back pain may relate to a wide range of pathologies. It is imperative that red flags and neurologic symptom evaluation are considered on initial presentation, and if concerns are present that immediate further investigation and medical care occur.

While a great proportion of low back pain may resolve within weeks, it has the potential to cause ongoing pain and concern in athletes. Initial management of low back should involve the following:

- A medical review as soon as possible, with presentation to a physiotherapist or doctor. Early presentation can enable early consideration of medication management and perhaps physically offloading the athlete, if appropriate. Early management has been shown to minimise training time lost.
- Early control of pain is a priority. The presence of pain can cause muscle inhibition, which can then lead to altered biomechanics and loading. This can be deleterious to performance and cause further and ongoing issues.

Chest Wall Injury: Top Tips

- Early recognition of chest wall symptoms can significantly minimise lost training time.
- Injuries following changes in training load and intensity, or following periods of broken training, must be treated with extra care.
- Diagnosis using MRI or other available scan will help guide recovery time.
- Four days out of rowing training with chest wall symptoms can significantly improve an athlete's outcome.
- Further assessment and diagnosis are essential for athlete management.

- Following an assessment of the nature and presentation of low back pain, an individualised management plan will help return an athlete to full training.
- Imaging may be indicated for some athletes. In rare cases, if pathology is correlated with ongoing severe symptoms, an athlete may require referral to a medical specialist such as a radiologist or surgeon.

The majority of low back pain in rowing athletes is associated with flexion stress of the lumbar spine, with a smaller group related to extension loading. Presentation of pain is commonly associated with on-water or ergometer training, but may also be related to gym activities. The injury is likely to be related to highly repetitive loading of the lumbar spine, in conjunction with other factors including biomechanics, kinematics, training volume and modality, posture in and out of the boat, genetic predisposition and other daily activities. Adequate range of motion in the hip, hamstring length, abdominal strength and endurance are all important to help maintain a good lumbar spine position throughout the rowing stroke.

The strongest predictor of low back pain is a previous history of the issue, but other causative factors include the following:

- A large volume of training on rowing ergometers. To avoid this, ergometer sessions should be broken up into blocks of 30 minutes or less, with the athlete getting up and moving around between blocks. The athlete should be monitored for postural fatigue during ergometer training sessions to avoid increasing lumbar spine flexion.

- Significant and rapid changes in training. This can relate to volume, frequency or intensity, or a combination of these. It is important to consider carefully any reasons for changes that are due to factors other than the training schedule – for example, time away from training due to personal obligations, illness or other injury.
- Reduced range of movement in the hip and an incorrect pelvic position. Achieving a vertical or anterior pelvic tilt at the catch of the rowing stroke will decrease lumbar flexion and is believed to reduce stress on the lumbar spine. Achieving a vertical position at the catch – aiming for greater than 130 degrees of hip flexion prior to pelvic movement – requires a good range of movement in the hip. Thoracic spine (upper back) flexion on top of a vertical pelvis will ensure that load is spread throughout the spinal segments.
- Changing lumbar flexion through the stroke. While starting with an initial flat low back position at the catch, it is important not to drop into excessive lumbar flexion through the drive phase and the end of the stroke. A flexed lumbar position may be driven by a posterior pelvic tilt at the end of the stroke. This pelvic position in turn also requires adequate hamstring length. If the hamstring muscles are tight, they will pull the pelvic to a posterior tilt position, which in turn will increase lumbar flexion. Further, adequate lower abdominal strength will support the lumbar position throughout the stroke, but especially in the back half of it.
- Lack of trunk strength and endurance. Poor abdominal and back muscle strength and endurance are associated with a higher risk of developing low back pain.
- Technical changes have the potential to load different tissues in a different way. If technical changes are being made, it may be worth decreasing training volume while the athlete adapts to the change.
- Equipment set-up and biomechanical position. The height of the feet, seat and gate will all have a big impact on how an athlete is positioned in the boat and the posture they assume. Every athlete has a different body shape and may require a different set-up from others. A new rowing combination in a different boat may be unstable and lead to increase lateral instability, which can put a higher lateral load on the low back.
- The most common environmental factors relating to low back pain are rough water and windy conditions. These are particularly relevant for athletes with a history of low back pain. Rough water decreases the stability of the boat, requiring greater trunk muscle and lateral control of the boat, which can increase load on the low back. This can be mitigated by teaching athletes the skills to maximise boat stability.

Forearm Intersection Syndrome

Intersection syndrome occurs when tendons and their connective tissue from the thumb rub over the top of tendons from the back of the wrist causing inflammation of the tendon coverings. This may result in a localised pain, swelling and crepitus (squeaking feeling with thumb and wrist movement) approximately 5cm above the wrist on the thumb side, where the tendons and connective tissue cross. Pain and swelling will limit grip strength and the range of movement in the wrist, making it difficult to hold and control an oar. While it is not as common as other injuries, rehabilitation from intersection syndrome can be time-consuming and difficult.

The risk factors are familiar: rapid changes in training load, volume and intensity, along with technical changes. Increases in repetitive movement, particularly feathering, and increase in grip strength all contribute to load through the forearm tendons and forces between tendon groups.

Equipment is an important factor influencing the grip. The size of the handle and its covering will dictate the level of grip strength required, the wrist position and the forearm muscle contraction. If the oar handle is slippery, this can have an impact on the grip strength required, as can windy or rough water conditions. It is important to assess where and how an athlete takes up load from the oar during the rowing stroke. Assessing shoulder girdle and arm strength and movement control may help inform why an athlete is over-gripping the handle.

Intersection syndrome can present and progress very quickly. It is important to offload the forearm quickly, avoiding gripping and load or stretch through the forearm. A wrist brace that does not compress the inflamed area can help rest it. Regular icing and a review with a medical team doctor or physiotherapist are recommended to come up with a plan for a graded return to rowing. In the event that conservative management fails, intervention including injections and/or surgery may be the next option.

Infectious Diseases: Respiratory and Gastrointestinal

The COVID-19 pandemic brought into light a focus on medical well-being within the whole population as well as within athlete groups, with great efforts being made to minimise the risk of the illness spreading. The outcomes were significant, with an impact on the spread of all infectious diseases, not just COVID-19. As an interesting example, at the 2021 Tokyo Olympics, which took place in crowd-less stadiums under strict mask and distancing rules, recorded cases of respiratory and gastrointestinal infectious illness were at a fraction of previous Olympic Games.

The challenge now is to amalgamate the learnings from the pandemic with the practicalities and comfort of the daily training environment, travel and competition. The single most effective key in reducing the number of days lost to training is the minimising of the spread of respiratory illness within the team environment. This requires athletes and staff to recognise and acknowledge respiratory illness, and to take appropriate action.

These measures are also effective in decreasing the risk of gastrointestinal illness spreading within the group. In addition to providing multiple easy opportunities for good hand hygiene, food preparation areas must be clean, and everyone needs to be mindful of environmental exposure. In a team environment, open food buffets and

Reducing the Risk of Injury: Top Tips

- The greatest risk comes with sudden changes – to overall load, duration, intensity and technique – in training.
- Significant changes to technique will load the body in different ways. Decreasing overall training load at these times will allow adaptation to new physical challenges.
- Appropriate recovery, rehabilitation and self-management of strength and flexibility will help minimise the risk of common injuries.

the sharing of serving devices can easily spread pathogens. Where possible, meals should be taken outdoors or in areas with good space and ventilation.

Water bottles must be kept clean. If left unwashed for a period of time, they can harbour mould and other pathogens, especially when used for sports drinks as well as water. Water bottles should regularly be thoroughly cleaned and put through a hot dishwasher if available. In rowing, there is a particular risk of illness from a water bottle sitting in the bottom of a boat, which may be contaminated by a simple splash of lake water. It is important to be aware of water quality and the risks of exposure to pathogens such as parasites and bacterial infection.

Skin Issues

Skin infection and damage are key considerations for athletes that are sometimes overlooked. The risks can be both short-term and long-term. Training in an outdoor environment puts athletes at risk of sunburn, which in turn increases the risk of skin cancer. Annual skin checks are recommended, especially for athletes who have spent time training in environments with significant sun exposure.

Skin infections are not uncommon in rowing. They may relate to a range of causes, but there are ways to help minimise the risk:

- Wear clean clothing for every training session.
- Change out of training gear following a session. Do not stay in training gear for prolonged periods.
- Shower after a training session using soap and a clean, dry towel. A damp towel can harbour bacteria that can cause skin irritation and infection.
- Monitor, clean, treat and cover skin breaks. This includes so-called ‘slide bites’ (skin cuts on the lower leg from the seat runners), insect bites, skin breaks or sores on the buttocks, and open blisters. Seek early medical assessment and treatment if any of these areas develop signs of infection.

Blisters are extremely common in rowing and have the potential to cause significant illness. A blister is typically a separation of the layers of the skin, which fill with fluid as a result of repeated friction, rubbing or pressure. As with many injuries in rowing, the development of blisters can be related to changes in load, technique, environment or equipment, or any combination of these. It is important to

Stopping the Spread of Respiratory Infection: Top Tips

- Develop a team culture around illness that supports athletes and staff to recognise and acknowledge illness early. They should resist simply 'pushing on through' for the team. Training may continue, depending on the individual case, but a strategy should be put in place to minimise the risk of spreading it to others within the group.
- Prolonged time in an enclosed environment is a key risk in the transmission of infectious respiratory disease. Indoor social spaces and restaurants, kitchens, cars, airports, aircraft and buses are all high-risk areas. Mask wearing may be appropriate in some situations.
- Ensure effective air flow in an enclosed gym environment, particularly during a prolonged ergometer training session. All windows and doors should be opened (ideally behind and in front of exercising athletes) to allow this. Any fans should be set up behind the athletes, all facing forwards in the same direction to direct air flow away from other athletes. Athletes can also be aligned side by side, all facing the same direction.
- Encourage hand hygiene – washing under warm running water with soap for at least 20 seconds. Alcohol gels are also effective, but may not kill all pathogens, particularly some viruses.
- Where possible, meetings with athletes or teams should be held outdoors or in a well-ventilated open environment.

manage blisters to minimise the risk of infection:

- Early blister development can involve collections of fluid under the skin. If these become problematic, they can be drained via a small opening, which must then be kept clean.
- Open blisters or areas where the external skin has been worn away should be thoroughly washed with warm soapy water to minimise the risk of infection.
- Keep the oar and ergometer handles clean by washing and wiping down after every use. They can be dipped in a bucket of soapy water or disinfectant to assist in further cleaning.
- If a callus or area of skin becomes thickened and raised, it may be trimmed or worn down using an appropriate skin file.
- Trim off loose or torn bits of skin if they are not providing effective protection.
- Antiseptic creams are useful for open and cracked areas of skin.
- If there are any concerns about infection, medical assessment and management must be sought quickly. Ignoring or putting up with it can lead to severe injury and illness in a relatively short period of time.

5 Equipment, Technology, Rigging, Gearing and the Rower

This chapter aims to explore rowing equipment and how it can be manipulated, rigged and geared to enable the rower to be at their best in any wind or water conditions. It will look at how to select and maintain rowing equipment and consider what the future may hold.

Rowing equipment, rigging and gearing play an essential role in performance preparation for any competitive rower. The right rigging optimises performance by enabling the most effective stroke length and timing to be achieved, both individually and with the rest of the crew. Individualisation of the set-up facilitates optimal power application and synchronisation. Rigging adjustments can achieve rower comfort and biomechanical alignment, along with better load distribution through the rower, which assist with injury prevention. Gearing of the boat, as in cycling, enables the rower to achieve an optimal stroke rate and power output to achieve efficiency over the race distance.

A boat must be set up precisely, and rigged as individually as possible in order to achieve the following:

- to generate boat propulsion effectively and economically;
- to fully exploit the individual's performance capabilities;
- to achieve crew unity (synchronisation) and the ability to row fast;
- to help the rower to learn and practise sustainable technique;
- to prevent health problems and injury.

Rigging and Gearing

Rowing is a mechanical sport based on levers and equipment. The set-up of the boat – the rigging and, consequently, the 'gearing' – can be adjusted and adapted by the coach to get the most out of the individual's anthropometric and physiological qualities. Making every rower comfortable and matching up individuals within the crew will enable the crew to row and race more effectively and efficiently.

The first step in understanding the most effective rigging for both an individual and a crew is to accurately measure and capture the rower's standing height, sitting height, upper and lower leg length and arm span. When considering the appropriate gearing for a crew, it is vital to take into account their anthropometry and physiology. Taller rowers with long strokes and less power than shorter rowers with shorter more powerful stroke rates will need different race style and gearing.

Tristan Shipsides is a rowing expert and has been a senior physiotherapist with the Australian rowing team for many years. His guidance on the anthropometric and biomechanical considerations for optimising rowing performance is written from a physiotherapist's perspective:

> *The anthropometric considerations in rowing are well researched. Rowers tend to be taller, have longer limbs and torso height as well as high arm span to height ratio. These longer levers provide a mechanical advantage, improving stroke length and greater power application. Achieving an Optimal rowing position requires 3 further critical components. 1) Essential range of movement across multiple joints in the body to achieve an effective catch. 2) Strength and endurance, particularly in the lower limb to generate power and in the trunk to transfer force from the spoon and the handle to the foot plate, and endurance to maintain optimal trunk positions throughout a training session or race. 3) The ability to coordinate and sequence the movements of the joint to prepare and put the rower into effective positions. A rowing Physiotherapist must strive to optimise the athlete's position whilst minimising their injury risk. Their expertise lends itself heavily to the first two components, but they may also influence the 3rd component in conjunction with the coach. These areas should be addressed prior to considering changes to the rigging.*

Pelvis

The pelvis must be able to achieve at least a vertical position during the rockover to ensure that the lumbar spine is maintained in a neutral position. This not only ensures optimal trunk activation and thus power transfer from handle to foot plate, but also preserves tissue health of anatomical structures in the spine, such as the intervertebral discs and posterior longitudinal ligament.

By not putting forces in excess of their capacity for prolonged periods of time, a key biomechanical risk factor for LBP is reduced.

This angle of rockover can be measured easily using an inclinometer. With the athlete in a

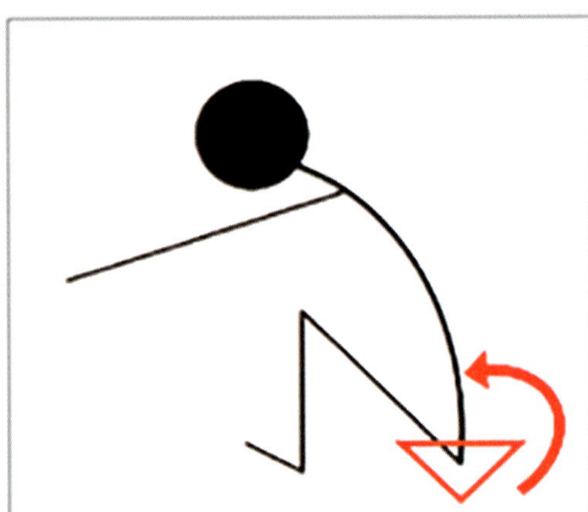

The rower's pelvic rockover.

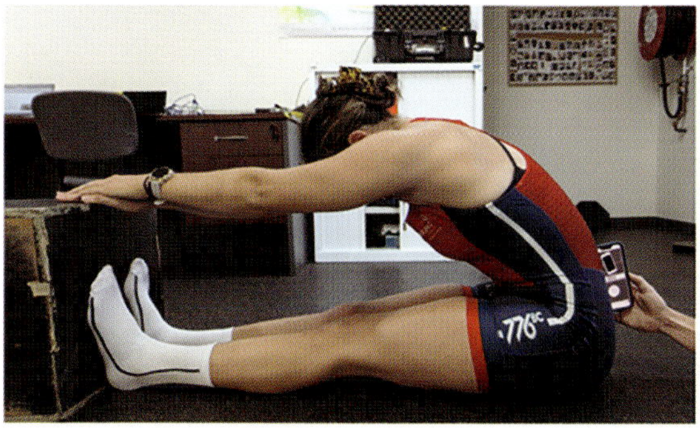

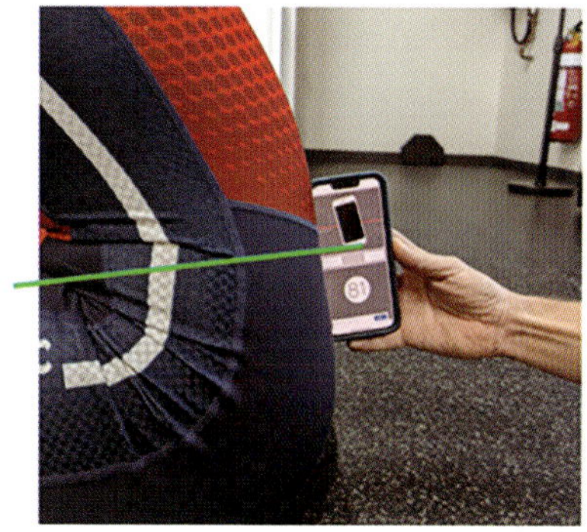

Measuring and tracking the pelvic rockover.

sit and reach position and an inclinometer on the flattest part of the lower lumbar spine and measuring how far over the pelvis, can tilt, medical staff and coaches can regularly and easily check this angle. An angle of at least 0 degrees is desirable.

Hip

The hip requires a minimum of 130 degrees of flexion to achieve an optimal position at the catch. This again allows for the pelvis to remain at least vertical and reduce excessive load on tissues of the lumbar spine.

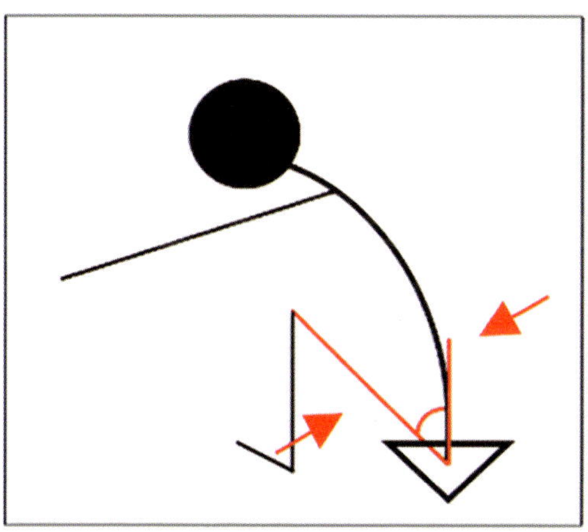

The hip requires a minimum of 130 degrees of flexion to achieve an optimal position at the catch.

Hip angle can be measured with a goniometer. The athlete lies on their back and takes one knee towards their chest. The athlete must not use their arms to help and must leave the other leg flat on the ground to ensure the pelvis doesn't rotate and over inflate the athletes available hip range. An arm of the goniometer follows a line parallel with the athlete and the other arm follows a line though the middle of the femur. The angle between the arms is then measured

Ankle

The ankle requires enough flexibility to achieve a vertical shin at the catch. A large part of this comes down to the flexibility of the calf complex.

Calf flexibility is best measured using the 'Knee to Wall' test. A value of 12cm is desirable, with a reduction in dorsiflexion range being a risk factor for lower limb injuries. Ensure the athlete keeps their knee directly over their toes and their heel on the ground when undertaking the test. The value recorded is the distance from the wall the tip of the big toe achieves whilst still being able to touch the wall with their knee.

Trunk endurance

The ability of the trunk musculature to maintain optimal rowing posture and transfer power from the handle to the footplate is key. During the drive, this is dominated by the back extensors with the abdominals being relatively quiet. These trunk flexors then take over working to eccentrically control the end of the drive and assist with rockover. There is no definitive way of strengthening these muscles, but focus should be on dynamic and functional exercises rather than static ones involving excessive muscular co-contraction. Both the endurance and the strength and power aspects of the sport must be considered when designing a programme to optimise trunk function.

Many rowing federations look at iterations of trunk isometric holds to test an athlete's capacity. The Bering Sorensen test is commonly used to test back extensor endurance for example. Again, there is no minimum time requirements in the literature, but in a study of school-level rowers, less than a 90 second hold was a risk factor for developing low back pain. In the elite rowing population, anecdotally the author considers a minimum of 150 seconds as a base line.

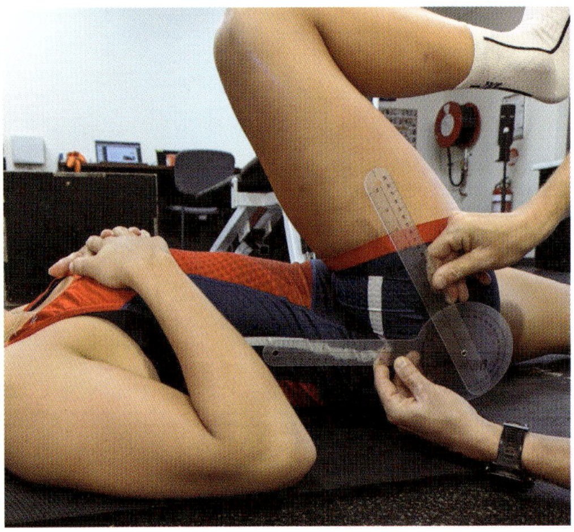

Measuring a rower's hip angle with a goniometer.

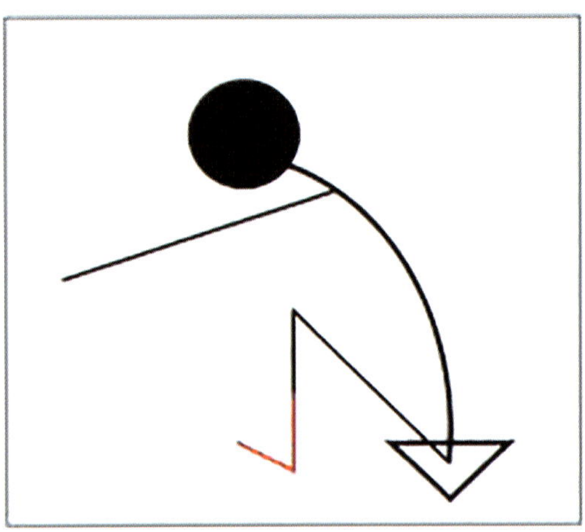

Measuring calf and ankle flexibility.

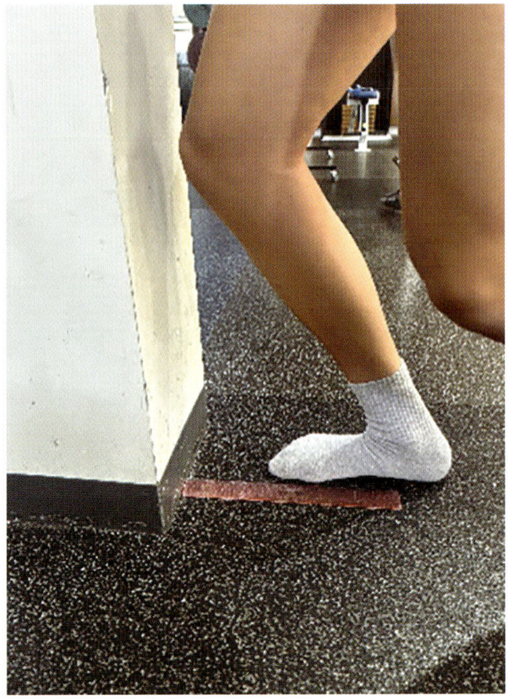

Demonstrating how to measure calf and ankle flexibility.

Tilting the seat can assist with achieving an optimal spinal position.

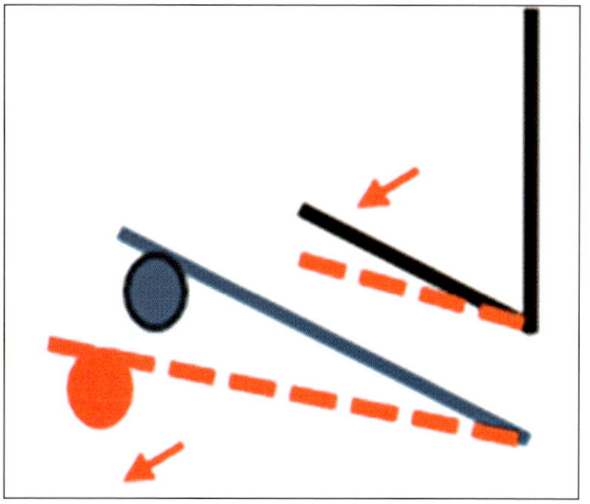

Footstretcher angle.

Rigging considerations

If an athlete is unable to achieve an optimal position themselves, considering the requirements above, altering the rigging may be helpful.

Seat tilting

Tilting the rear of the seat may assist those with borderline pelvic rockover achieve an optimal spinal position. Adding tilt will increases the pressure on the anterior aspect of the athletes sit bones and proximal hamstring tendons. This can increase the risk of tendinopathy or bursitis. Generally, a 5mm raise will suffice.

Foot plate

It is possible to alter the angle of the footplate, the rake, to a shallower angle if ankle flexibility is reduced. In reality, the athlete will just lift their heels off the footplate earlier if their range is limited. However, you still may want to consider reducing the angle to allow for quicker contact of the heels onto the footplate and thus optimal posterior chain activation during the drive.

The other consideration with the footplate is height. If an athlete has a reduction in hip range, having the feet too high with reduce the ability of the pelvis to rock over. Lowering this height will increase the athlete's available range to get into an effective position and improve their catch angle.

Seat pads come in a variety of forms.

Seat pads

Seat type is heavily based on athlete preference. Flat, holed, wooden, carbon, there are multiple options. Pads can add comfort and reduce compressive forces around the sit bones.

Pads can be as simple as taping a piece of foam matting to an existing seat to having custom-made foam seats with silicon inserts made. Measurement of sit bone width is required for these custom seats.

Terms and Definitions

Coaches and rowers need to understand a series of basic terms and definitions of the boats and oars, as well as consistent measuring points on the boat. These terms vary slightly between sculling and sweep boats (see below).

In sweep rowing the distance between the centreline of the boat (keel) to the centre of the rigger pin is referred to as the 'spread'. In sculling, the term is 'span', as it represents the span across the two riggers, from the centre of the rigger pin on the port side to the centre of the rigger pin on the starboard side. The overall length of the oar or scull is the distance measured down the loom (shaft) of the oar from the tip of the blade to the end of the handle. The distance between the end of the handle to the outboard side of the oar or scull's collar is called the 'inboard'. The measurement from the outboard side of the collar to the tip of the blade measured along the middle of the oar or scull's loom is the 'outboard'.

Top Tips

- Encourage your athlete to undertake a musculoskeletal screening with a rowing-specific physiotherapist to understand areas to optimise mobility, strength and endurance.
- Attempt to optimise the athlete before modifying the rigging.
- Any changes to rigging must be done gradually over a period of time to ensure the athlete's tissues can adapt to the changes in the demands placed upon them. This graded approach will reduce the likelihood of injury.

When measuring and rigging a boat, consistency is essential, measuring in the same place every time. Every coach will measure slightly differently so if there is more than one person rigging a boat always keep each individual to the same task. Coaches also need to keep detailed records to track rigging changes across the season.

Commonly used sculling terms.

Basic rowing terms.

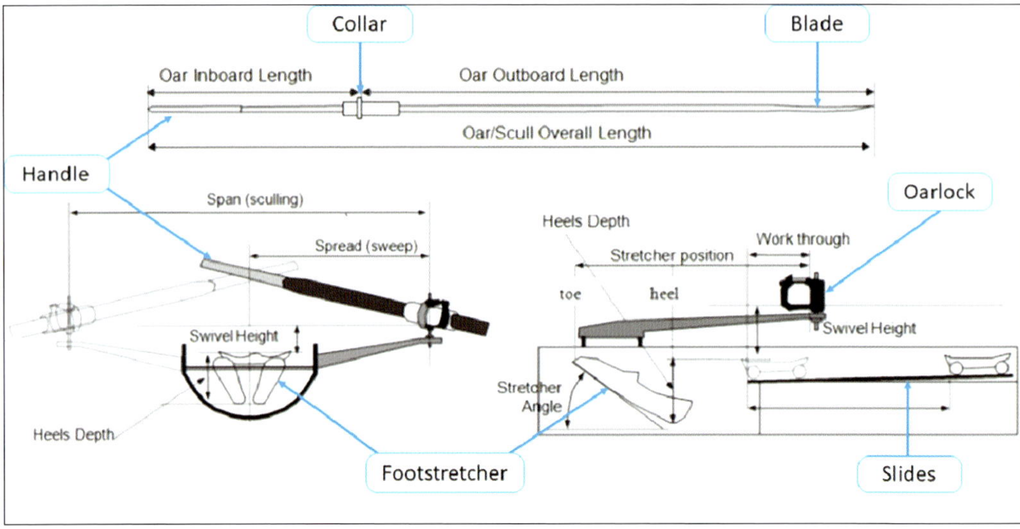

Boat and oar set-up with adjustable rigging parameters (Voordouw, J., 2018; figure adjusted from Gianchandani).

Gearing

The mechanics of the rowing stroke and the principles behind it (*see* Chapter 2) – stroke length, rate of force application, effective work and distance per stroke – are all influenced by rigging and gearing. Reducing the span (in sculling) or spread (in sweep) with long oars will increase the mechanical load on the rower and crew. This adaption of the load is referred to as 'gearing'. A wider span and spread with shorter oars reduces the load on the rowers and in this context the gearing is being eased. Harder gearing will place a greater load on the rower. Their rate may be too low, and they may not be able to hold their pace for the whole of the race. If the gearing is too light, the stroke rate will be too high and the work per stroke and distance per stroke will be too low. The result of this will be that the crew's rhythm will not have enough ratio and, due to the physiological cost of the extra strokes they are taking and the lack of power per stroke, they may not be able to increase their speed when challenged in the second 1000m of the race.

The measurement of the span or spread affects the gearing of the boat. Increasing the span or spread causes the arc of the blade in the water to be smaller, making the gearing lighter. Reducing the span or spread will increase the size of the arc of the blade in the water, making the gearing heavier.

Effects of Gearing

A coach needs to understand how to select the right gearing for each boat type and for the attributes of the rower(s). This is key to determining the crew's rhythm – the relationship in time of the drive phase and recovery phase. Eights, fours and quads tend to have heavier gearing than singles, doubles and pairs. This is for a variety of reasons:

- Bigger boats move faster so the rowers need to catch and apply their force

Rigging the boat properly will not necessarily win a race. However, a poorly rigged boat will impede the performance of the rower(s) and can 'cause technique problems that are difficult to correct or may contribute to injury'. (Rowing Australia, 1997, p.1.)

quicker, to get a better purchase on the water and to make the force effective.

- Bigger boats have a greater mass and momentum, so they require a higher gearing if the rowers are to effectively apply their force and accelerate throughout the drive phase.
- The collective power output is higher in the bigger boats, allowing a harder gearing to be tolerated.

A boat that is rigged too hard for the rower will increase the load on their body and may lead to additional load and stress on the lower back and rib cage, potentially contributing to injury. The repetitive, cyclic nature of rowing and the volume of training required means that even small changes in rigging can have a significant effect on the way a rower moves, and the potential for injury. It is good practice always to make small and incremental steps. Rowers will often have imbalances in leg length, which can be real or apparent, or they may have issues around ankle or hip flexibility. These can all be mitigated by the correct rigging, which will enable a longer, more symmetrical and effective stroke.

Rigging and gearing can influence technique both positively and negatively. If the gate height is too high, the rower will have difficulty keeping the oar buried at the end of the stroke. If it is too low, the rower will tend to lift the handle up making the oar go too deep in the water. There are similar implications with the gate and oar pitch. If the angle between the gate and the shaft of the oar is too high, the blades will skim rather than stay gripped to the water. If the pitch angle is too low, the rower will feel as though they are struggling to get the oar out of the water. A well-rigged boat should enable the rower to hang their bodyweight and apply their force in the most effective manner and also time the stroke with their crewmates and move comfortably, with each other and most importantly, the boat.

Biomechanists Valery Kleshnev and Volke Nolte researched the various effects of changing oar lengths in the September 2011 edition of *Rowing Biomechanics Newsletter*, **www.biorow.com**). Their research found that the main differences between heavily and lightly geared boats was in blade efficiency with the lighter-geared rigs. This was due to the rowers having to spend more energy moving water at the blade. This makes for a faster drive phase with lighter gearing than with harder gearing. The rower's forces, power and boat speed are not significantly altered. It is more convenient to adjust the oars and sculls than the spread and span, so the researchers' recommendation is to experiment with big changes in a rower's outboard oar length when looking to reduce or increase load.

Calculating Gearing Ratios

To understand and compare gearing changes, coaches can use a simple gearing ratio calculation. This can measure the changes they are making and record the ratios that work most effectively in various conditions and situations and with various crews.

There is an assumption in the equation that the centre of blade pressure is 12cm from the tip of the blade. As there are a host of blade shapes being developed, for consistency, this hypothetical centre of pressure is used for both sculling and sweep equations.

Sculling

$$\frac{\text{Scull length} - \text{inboard} - 12}{\tfrac{1}{2}\text{ scull's span}}$$

For a sculling boat with a span of 159cm, overall scull length of 289cm and an inboard of 88cm the equation will be:

$$\frac{289-88-12}{79.5} = \frac{189}{79.5} = \text{a gearing ratio of } 2.377$$

On a sculling boat with a span of 160cm, overall scull length of 288cm and an inboard of 88cm, where the gearing ratio is 2.350, the ratio is less, and therefore the gearing is lighter than in the heavier rig with a 2.377 ratio.

Sweep

$$\frac{\text{Oar length} - \text{inboard} - 12}{\text{Spread}}$$

If a sweep boat has a spread of 87cm, oar length of 377cm and an inboard of 117cm the gearing ratio equation is:

$$\frac{377-117-12}{87} = \frac{248}{87} = \text{a gearing ratio of } 2.850$$

In comparison, on a sweep boat with a shorter spread and inboard (86cm and 116cm) and oar length of 377cm, where the gearing ratio is 2.895, the rig is harder than the boat with a 2.850 ratio.

Rigging for Training and Racing

Rowing performance is about optimising the physical, mental and technical attributes of the rower and crew. Races are not won only by the strongest, the most technically proficient or those who have done the most training. The crew who can combine effectively all those parameters will put themselves in the best winning position. Technical proficiency plays a significant role in ensuring strength, endurance and other physiological capabilities are translated into optimising boat speed.

Rower, blade, boat and water are in continual interaction during the rowing stroke and must be highly coordinated during a cyclical and 'closed-skill' movement in a changing external environment (wind, weather, temperature) and under internal conditions (stroke frequencies, boat velocity, mutual rower influence in a crew boat as well as progressive fatigue). Rigging is an important fundamental that is often overlooked that enables the rower and crew to realise their potential. No two rowers are exactly the same and what works for one will not necessarily work for another. Coaches need to have a good understanding of the mechanical principles of rigging in order to create the optimal rig for their crew. Even with that understanding, it will take time and trial and error to find the most comfortable and effective set-up.

Distance per stroke, power per stroke and effective work per stroke are fundamental training and performance parameters that need to be developed during training to be delivered during racing. Increasing the load through rigging or increasing the resistance to the hull of the boat will force the rowers to put down more power over a longer time per stroke and develop their length and power profile. Decreasing the span or spread, increasing the outboard of the oar, adding a strap around the boat or a sea anchor can achieve this. Increasing the length of the outboard or reducing the span or spread will have a smaller effect than adding resistance to the hull of the boat. Conversely, increasing the span or spread and reducing the length of the oars will create less load and can be used in neural training, when a race is approaching and the rowers need to be moving faster and at a higher stroke rate. It is also possible to tow or power the hull at faster speeds to help develop specific neural pathways.

It is also important to trial rigging and gearing in training, so rowers have practised the gearing they will use in extreme racing headwinds or tailwinds, as well as neutral conditions. This way, they will know what to expect and feel when the rig is deployed in racing.

Racing and Training Conditions

As rowing is an outdoor sport, open to the elements, racing and training conditions are constantly changing. This means there is the potential to adjust the boat's gearing to suit the conditions to maximise the crew's potential. As a rule of thumb, once a headwind builds to approximately 3 metres per second the coach should consider decreasing the outboard of the oars by 1cm to reduce the load on the rowers and enable them to maintain their stroke rate without shortening their stroke length. A headwind slows the boat down more than a tailwind of the same strength will speed it up. Therefore, the strength of a tailwind should be above 3.5 metres per second before a coach considers increasing the outboard to add some extra load, so the crews can maintain their distance per stroke in the faster conditions.

The speed of a boat can be affected by a number of environmental factors.

Wind

Wind direction and speed can significantly affect rowing speed by creating or reducing aerodynamic drag around the exposed elements (boat, rowers, equipment).
A tailwind is likely to help the boat move faster (because of less aerodynamic drag), whereas a headwind will slow it down, due to a greater aerodynamic drag. Crosswinds may affect steering and balance (roll on the X axis) but seem to have less effect on boat

speeds the more perpendicular the wind direction is to boat travel.

Water Conditions

Calm water typically allows for faster rowing since there is less resistance and disturbance. Rough waters or choppy conditions can slow a boat as rowers must adjust for balance and stability. They must also ensure that the height of their blades during the recovery aspect of the stroke is above any of the rough water – clipping waves on recovery will adversely affect hull speed.

Water Density/Salinity

Saltwater is denser than freshwater and generally provides a slightly higher level of buoyancy to the boat. This will cause the boat to ride higher in the water, potentially reducing drag and resistance and making it easier to achieve higher speeds.

Water Temperature

Water temperature has a significant impact on boat speed by altering the density and viscosity of the water and thus having effects on hull hydrodynamic drag. Colder water is denser and potentially more resistant or 'sticky', while warmer water might present less resistance and be more 'slick'. The faster boat times for any given distance have been recorded in warmer water. As a simple generalisation, a 1-degree change in water temperature can have the effect of a ~1-second change in the time taken to complete a 2000m race, either reducing it (warmer water) or increasing it (colder water).

Water Depth

Water depth influences the speed of a rowing boat primarily through the phenomenon of 'drag' created by interactions between the boat's hull and the water beneath it.

In shallow water, a phenomenon known as 'squatting' can occur, where the boat experiences increased hydrodynamic drag. This happens when the water flow becomes more constrained between the hull and the bottom, creating additional resistance and often causing the boat to sit lower, which slows it down.

Wave reflection and interference can also be an issue in shallower water. Waves generated by the boat can reflect off the bottom and interfere with the boat's movement. This can create additional resistance compared to rowing in deeper water, where waves have more space to dissipate.

In practice, rowing speeds are higher in water that is deep enough to avoid the drag and squatting associated with shallow conditions, but not so deep that a higher water temperature cannot be achieved.

Water Current

Rowing on a river with favourable currents will increase speed, whereas adverse currents (against the direction of the boat) will reduce it. The currents on the outside of a river bend are faster than those on the inside of it, so two boats next to each other heading in the same direction could experience differing influences on their speed, depending on where their boat is positioned on the bend relative to their competitor.

Tide

In coastal or tidal areas, the tidal flow can help or hinder a rowing boat's speed depending on whether it is moving with or against it, in much the same way as a river current will affect boat speed.

Rain and Other Precipitation

While not directly impacting the water itself, rain can influence oar handling and the thermal comfort of the rowers, indirectly affecting speed.

Air Temperature and Humidity

Extreme heat and humidity can affect the physical performance of rowers, potentially impacting endurance and speed.

Since rowing performance is influenced by numerous external environmental variables – many of which are challenging to measure accurately over a 2000m course – the governing body of rowing designates the fastest times achieved in various categories (gender, age and boat type) over 2000m as 'world's best times' rather than 'world records'. Over the past 20 years of observing and documenting these fastest times, certain consistent environmental factors have been identified. These include a direct tailwind, with wind speeds ranging from 4 to 6 metres per second, and water temperatures above 28°C. Although favourable wind directions and speeds can contribute to faster times, they would have been present only briefly during races, and rarely enough to cause significant water disturbances in the final 1000m of the course. Air temperatures typically range from 20 to 30°C.

Given that rowing is influenced by numerous variables beyond anyone's control, it is crucial to consider all these factors to accurately understand overall boat speed and assess how performances compare under different conditions.

Learning From Others

It is always useful for a coach to understand the conclusions of other coaches regarding the rig of their crews. World Rowing's periodic rigging surveys at the World Championships and some Paralympics have produced useful information that coaches can use to benchmark their own rigging standards. The data can be found at worldrowing.com/technical/coaching/info-and-links.

Rowing can also learn from other sports where gearing optimisation and power efficiency are crucial to performance. Cycling is one sport where the selective manipulation of gearing to optimise performance has been consistent through the last 50 years. In more recent times, the focus has been evolving and there is now more of an emphasis on shorter crank lengths and lower gear ratios to enhance overall performance and rider comfort. Shorter cranks, typically ranging from 165mm to 170mm instead of the

Event	Sweep/Scull	Finish Position	Country	Boat Manufacturer	Model Number	Span (cm) Scull	Spread (cm)Sweep	Overall Oar Length (cm)	Oar Inboard Length (cm)	Oar Outboard Length (cm)	Distance Through Work (cm)	Foot Stretcher Angle (deg)	Swivel above Seat (cm) starboard scull	Swivel above Seat (cm) portside scull	Swivel above Seat (cm) Sweep	Seat above Heels (cm)
LM2x	Scull	1	FRA	Filippi		159.0		289	88	201	13	41	16.5	16.3		18
						159.0		289	88	201	15	41	17.3	15.5		16
LM2x	Scull	2	ITA	Filippi		160.0		287.5	89	198.5	14	46	19.5	18.5		16
						160.0		287.5	89	198.5	20	42	20	19		16
LM2x	Scull	3	CHN	Filippi		159.0		288	88	200	18	43	17	15		15
						159.0		288	88	200	16	43	16.5	15.5		16.5
M1X		1	CZE	Empacher	X11	160.2		289	88.5	200.5	19.5	18	17.3		16.5	4.2
M1X		2	CUB	Filippi	F39	160		292	89	203	14	17	16.5		18	4.0
M1X		3	GBR	Empacher	X10			289	89	200	23	19	18		17	4.0
M2x	Scull	1	NZL	Filippi	F17	159.0		289	88.5	200.5	16	45	18.8	17.8		19.6
						159.0		289	88.5	200.5	17	45	19.2	18.2		18.7
M2x	Scull	2	POL	Filippi		158.5		289	89.5	199.5	15	43	19	17.5		16.5
						158.5		289	89.5	199.5	19	41	21	18.5		16.5
M2x	Scull	3	ITA	Filippi		159.5		289	88.5	200.5	7	42	19.5	19		19
M4x	Scull	1	LTU	Filippi	F40	159.0		289.5	88	201.5		42	19.5	18.5		19
						159.0		289.5	88	201.5		42	19	18		18.6
						159.0		289.5	88	201.5		42	19.7	18.4		18.1
						159.0		289.5	88	201.5		42	20.1	18.8		18
M4x	Scull	2	GBR	Empacher	X48	156.0		290	86	204	8	42	20	19		19
						156.0		290	86	204	16	42	20	19		18.5
						156.0		290	86	204	16.5	42	20	19		19.5
						156.0		290	86	204	15	42	20	19		19.3
M4x	Scull	3	EST	Filippi		160.0		289	88.5	200.5	15	42	21.5	20		18
						160.0		289	88.5	200.5	13	41	22.5	20.5		17
						160.0		289	88.5	200.5	11	42	22.5	21		18
						160.0		289	88.5	200.5	14	43	22	20		18
M2-		1	ITA	Filippi	F17	86.5		375.5	117.5	258	14	41.4			19	20
	Sweep					86.0		375.5	117	258.5	15	41.8			16.5	17.5
M2-	Sweep	2	CRO	Filippi	F17	86.0		374.5	114.5	260	21	44.2			17	20
						86.0		374.5	114.5	260	12.5	42.4			17	16.5
M2-	Sweep	3	NZL	Filippi	F17	86.0		375.5	116.2	259.3	14	42.5			16.2	19.5
						86.0		375.5	116.2	259.3	16.5	42.5			15.9	18
M4-	Sweep	1	AUS	Empacher	C48		85.0	377	115	262	17.0	42.0			18.0	19.0
							85.0	377	115	262	17.0	42.0			18.0	19.0

World Rowing rigging data (2017) Olympic boat class medal-winning boats (men).

Event	Sweep/Scull	Finish Position	Country	Boat Manufacturer	Model Number	Span (cm) Scull	Spread (cm)Sweep	Overall Oar Length (cm)	Oar Inboard Length (cm)	Oar Outboard Length (cm)	Distance Through Work (cm)	Foot Stretcher Angle (deg)	Swivel above Seat (cm) starboard scull	Swivel above Seat (cm) portside scull	Swivel above Seat (cm) Sweep	Seat above Heels (cm)
LW2x	Scull	1	ROU	Filippi	F36	160		287	88	199		38	13.5	12		19
	Scull					160		287	88	199		38	13.5	12		18
LW2x	Scull	2	NZL	Filippi	F36	159.5		287	87.5	199.5	23	42	16.2	15.7		18
	Scull					159.5		287	87.5	199.5	23	42	16.2	15.7		16
LW2x	Scull	3	USA	Filippi	F13	159.1		285	86	199	11.3	43	16.8	15.5		15.3
	Scull					159		285	86	199	19.2	41	16.5	15.7		15.3
W1x	Scull	1	SUI	mpache	X17	158.5		285.5	85	200.5	14.5	40	17	16		14
W1x	Scull	2	GBR	mpache	X16			286	88.5	197.5		40	18	17		
W1x	Scull	3	AUT	mpache	X17	159.5		287	87.5	199.5	19.5	44.5	14.5	13		15.5
W2x	Scull	1	NZL	Filippi	F13	160		288	87	201		42	16	15		18
	Scull					160		288	88	200		42	16	15		17
W2x	Scull	2	USA	mpache	X25	159.5		288	88	200	16	41	17.7	17		16.5
	Scull					158.5		287	87.5	199.5	10	40	15	14		17.5
W2x	Scull	3	AUS	mpache	X36	159		288	87.5	200.5	12	41	17.5	16.5		18
	Scull					159		288	88	200	12	41	17.5	16.5		19
W4x	Scull	1	NED	Filippi	F52	159		289	88.5	200.5		43	17	15.5		19
	Scull					159		289	88.5	200.5		43	17.5	16		19.5
	Scull					159		289	88.5	200.5		43	18	16.5		18
	Scull					159		288.5	88	200.5		43	17	15.5		18
W4x	Scull	2	POL	Filippi		159		288	89	199	20	43	18.5	16.5		18.5
	Scull					159		288	89	199	21	41	20	18		19
	Scull					159		288	89	199	19	42	19	17.5		18
	Scull					159		288	89	199	21	40	18	16.5		14
W4x	Scull	3	GBR	mpacher		160		289	87	202	15	46	17	16		21
	Scull					160		289	87	202	18	46	17	16		19.5
	Scull					160		289	87	202	17	46	17	16		19.5
	Scull					160		289	87	202	16	46	17	16		20
W2-	Sweep	1	NZL	Filippi			86	372	116	256	19	42			16.5	18
	Sweep						86	372	116	256	19	42			16.5	17
W2-	Sweep	2	USA	mpacher			86.5	372	116	256	12	42			18	18
	Sweep						86.5	372	116	256	12	42			18	19
W2-	Sweep	3	DEN	Filippi			85.7	373.3	115.5	257.8		44.6			18.1	19.6
	Sweep						85.7	373.3	115.5	257.8		41.4			17.5	21.5
W4-	Sweep	1	AUS	mpache	C40		85.5	373	116	257	17	42			16.5	19
	Sweep						85.5	373	116	257	17	42			17	18.5
	Sweep						85.5	373	116	257	17	42			17	20
	Sweep						85.5	373	116	257	17	42			17	20
W4-	Sweep	2	POL	Filippi	F52		85	372.5	116.5	256	17	42			17	17.5
	Sweep						85	372.5	116	256.5	17.5	42			17.5	17.5
	Sweep						85	372.5	116.5	256	19.5	42			18	20.5
	Sweep						85	371.5	116.5	255	18	42			16.5	17.5
W4-	Sweep	3	USA	Filippi	F52		85	373	115	258	15.5	42.6			16	19
	Sweep						85	373	115	258	15.5	40			16.5	19
	Sweep						85	373	115	258	17	40.2			16	20
	Sweep						85	373	115	258	15	39.5			16	17.5
W8+	Sweep	1	ROM	Filippi	F42		84.5	374	114.5	259.5						
	Sweep						84	374	114.5	259.5						
	Sweep						85	374	114.5	259.5						
	Sweep						84	374	114.5	259.5						
	Sweep						85	374	114.5	259.5						
	Sweep						84	374	114.5	259.5						
	Sweep						84	374	114.5	259.5						
	Sweep						84	374	114.5	259.5						
	Sweep						84	373	114	259	9	42			16	18
W8+	Sweep	2	CAN	Hudson			84	373	114	259	9	42			16	17
	Sweep						84	373	114	259	9	42			16	18
	Sweep						84	373	114	259	9	42			16	19
	Sweep						84	373	114	259	9	42			16	19
	Sweep						84	373	114	259	9	42			16	18
	Sweep						84	373	114	259	9	42			16	18
	Sweep						84	373	114	259	9	42			16	18
	Sweep						84	373	114	259		44			16.2	20
	Sweep						84	373	114	259		44			16.8	19.5
W8+	Sweep	3	NZL	Filippi	F42		84	373	114	259		44			17.2	19
	Sweep						84	373	114	259		45			16.4	19
	Sweep						84	373	114	259		44			18.8	20
	Sweep						84	373	114	259		44			17.5	19
	Sweep						84	373	114	259		44			17.4	20
	Sweep						84	373	114	259		40			15.8	20

World Rowing rigging 2017 Olympic class medal-winning boat rigging data (women).

traditional 175mm, help reduce knee strain and enable smoother pedalling, particularly benefiting riders with a smaller body type. At the same time, lower gear ratios allow cyclists to spin at higher cadences with less effort per revolution, which improves endurance, reduces muscular fatigue, and provides better control across various terrains. Ongoing biomechanical research suggests that such adjustments can lead to more efficient and sustainable pedalling mechanics. Overall, the shift emphasises individual rider comfort and efficiency. Is is something that rowing should be implementing at some level in high-performance crews?

Altering gearing in rowing is a choice that can only be made when the boat is stationary and most likely on land. Unfortunately, the modification of gearing from any parameter (oar length, inboard, span, rigger position) during a race is currently prohibited by the sports' governing body. A number of member federations attempted in the past to optimise the rowing movement and equipment to improve performance, dating back as far as 1872, when the first sliding rigger boat was used in competition at Henley Royal Regatta by the London Rowing Club.

The sliding rigger single scull rowing shell manipulates the rowing movement so that the seat remains fixed and the entire rigger mechanism is pressed away from the rower in order to move the oars through the drive phase and propel the boat. The mechanical advantage of the sliding rigger is that it reduces any pitching of the boat because the motion of the rower is reduced.

As it currently stands, rowing coaches and crews who want to alter the gearing of the rowing movement have the following options open to them:

- oar length
- blade shape
- rigger span
- inboard length
- relative difference in the height of the seat and feet relative to the oarlock
- slide length

While a rowing boat does not have gears like a bicycle, adjusting certain parameters can enable rowers to fine-tune their gear ratio to create a better match with their strength, technique and the specific conditions of a race. This customisation allows for a more optimal performance tailored to the individual athlete, enhancing efficiency and comfort during the race.

The concept of modifying the gearing set-up of a rowing boat to suit an individual's anthropometric and physiological characteristics, as well as prevailing race conditions and crew harmony, sounds ideal in theory. However, in practice, it is rarely trialled by coaches. Typically, the choices regarding blade shape, oar length, inboard length and oarlock span are made based on a coach's previous experience and are often heavily influenced by what other competitors are using. This approach prioritises crew cohesion and technical harmony, leading coaches to adopt fixed gear parameters across the entire crew.

Following this, decisions about blade shape and oar stiffness – usually biased towards specific manufacturers – are made, after which oar length, inboard length and oarlock span are set for the team. In contrast, cycling offers a different approach, where all gearing parameters – such as seat height, fore-aft body position, crank length, rear cassette sprocket and front chainring teeth – are individually tuned to the rider's strengths and needs for the particular race or terrain they are covering. Even in tandem cycling, where synchronisation is crucial, much like in rowing, gear settings beyond the rear cassette sprocket can be customised specifically for each rider's ability.

This comparison raises an important question: what can rowing learn from cycling regarding individualisation and the current trend of lower gearing combined with higher pedal cadence? Embracing a more personalised approach to equipment set-up for the individual athlete's needs as well as the prevailing conditions could potentially enhance performance, efficiency and comfort. This would align with broader trends in sports science and athlete-centric training.

Rowing can draw several lessons from cycling's trend of using higher cadence (higher revolutions per minute) and smaller, more manageable gears:

- Efficiency through cadence optimisation: cycling emphasises maintaining optimal cadence for energy efficiency and fatigue reduction. Rowing can benefit by training rowers to find their ideal stroke rate, which balances power output and fatigue, enhancing endurance and performance over long distances or races.
- Gear management for power and endurance: using smaller gears allows cyclists to sustain higher cadence without over-exertion. Similarly, rowers can focus on technique improvements that enable smoother, more efficient strokes at a higher stroke rate, potentially reducing energy expenditure per stroke.
- Technique and smoothness: both sports highlight the importance of technique when increasing cadence. For rowing, emphasising fluid, consistent strokes with proper sequencing can allow a higher stroke rate without sacrificing form, leading to better efficiency and injury prevention.
- Training and adaptation: cycling's trend encourages structured interval training at different gear settings to improve muscular endurance and cardiovascular capacity. Rowers can incorporate similar variable cadence training to develop adaptability and resilience at various paces.
- Power output and cadence: cycling's focus on individual athlete optimisation could be adopted in rowing to tune the crew to maintain a high but sustainable power output without causing excessive fatigue.
- Balancing start acceleration with top-end speed: 4000m Team Pursuit cyclists often use a gear ratio that balances start acceleration with top-end speed. In rowing, sacrificing a fast start to optimise mid-race power and efficiency could be a good way to trial different gearing set-ups.
- Equipment and ergonomics: cycling benefits from gear ratios tailored to rider strength and terrain; rowing equipment can be optimised by considering handle grip, seat mechanics and resistance, to support higher, more consistent stroke rates comfortably.

In essence, rowing can adopt a strategic approach to cadence and gear management – focusing on technique, efficiency and adaptability; mirroring cycling's successful trend towards higher cadence with smaller gear ratios to maximise performance and longevity.

Key Parameters for Modification in Rowing

With an athlete-centred optimisation philosophy, what parameters does rowing have that can be tailored to the individual from a gearing perspective? In cycling, gear modifications are about mechanical gear changes, but in rowing they are more about adjusting technique, boat set-up and equipment to optimise performance. Key modifications that affect the individual rower include:

- Adjusting oar length and blade design: longer or more efficient blades can improve leverage and thrust; different blade shape designs (for example, Clever or Macon) influence water catch and drive efficiency.
- Changing rowing technique and stroke rate: technique adjustments, such as to stroke length and sequencing, are essential to optimise power output and endurance.
- Working on timing and order of movements to maximise efficiency across various boat speeds.
- Setting up the boat and equipment by fine-tuning the trim (balance front/back and side to side), to influence how efficiently force is translated into boat speed.
- Adjusting the riggers, by fine-tuning the height and angle of the oarlocks as well as altering the relative position of the oarlock pin to the centreline of the hull. This will have an impact on leverage and specific gearing aspects.

Unlike cycling, which uses mechanical gears, rowing optimisation relies more on equipment tuning, technique and physiological conditioning to 'change gears' and adapt to different race segments for maximum performance.

Rowing can also learn to adapt rowing gearing to suit the conditions of a race environment, much like cyclists do for the terrain they are covering. In headwind conditions, rowing gearing and technique adjustments are crucial to maintain efficiency and speed in a 2000m race that will inevitably take longer to complete.

In headwind conditions, coaches and rowers can trial the following:

- Reducing effective 'gearing' (oar angle and power application): this can be done by using a slightly smaller oar blade or a shorter oar length to reduce leverage and power resistance. Reducing gearing will enable the rower to maintain their length. Connection and suspension are key in effective stroke length.
- Stroke rate adjustments: the stroke can be slightly lowered, to improve control and conserve energy, as higher rates can be more taxing into headwind. A steady, sustainable rhythm should be

maintained, maximising force application per stroke.
- Improvements in technique for power efficiency: the rower should focus on a strong, controlled catch and drive to make each stroke count; engage core muscles to generate more force with less wasted movement; save energy early and focus on consistent effort rather than maximal effort.

In tailwind conditions, the goal is to maximise speed while managing boat stability and energy expenditure. Performance may be optimised by the following gearing and technique adjustments:

- Increasing effective 'gearing' (oar angle and power application): this can be done by using slightly longer oars or a higher stroke rate to take advantage of the tailwind's assistance. Increasing the drive length slightly will allow for a more aggressive catch and finish since the wind will assist the boat's movement.
- Maintaining or slightly elevating the stroke rate: the stroke rate can be boosted to capitalise on the wind's push, but overloading muscles should be avoided to prevent early fatigue. The cadence should balance speed with endurance – typically, this will mean finding a higher but controlled rate.
- Refining technique for maximum power and efficiency: a smooth, powerful catch and controlled acceleration will help the rower to transition into the drive phase efficiently. More aggressive use of the legs during the drive will convert potential energy into momentum.

Boat Selection and Set-Up

If the coach has the luxury of choosing a boat for a crew, there are a few points that need to be considered, including the shape of the boat, the size of the boat in relation to the crew's size (approximate average weight) and the adjustments that can be made within the boat to accommodate the crew members. Rowing boat shapes have evolved over the centuries and have been further refined by marine architects. There are two basic shapes in rowing boats: the U shape is generally the most comfortable to the rower because it is easier to balance than the V shape, but the V shape does cut through the water more efficiently.

The displacement of the boat (wetted surface area) is composed of the mass of the rower(s) and the boat together. The boat will have been designed to sit in the water at a specific depth – the designed waterline depth – which is the calculated point where the hull reaches the minimum water resistance. This provides a platform from which the crew can row efficiently. However, the waterline depth will of course vary with the weight of the crew, which will then also influence the height of work (oarlock height). A 10kg variance in the crew's weight will affect the waterline depth of the boat by approximately 1cm. All these measurements and adjustments will need to be considered when selecting and ordering a boat. The skill level and experience of the rowers, and price points, will also be relevant when making a choice.

Once the boat has been chosen, the riggers can be secured on to it, making sure that the line of work and the face of the gate are aligned and that there is the appropriate distance between the rigger pins. This will range from 132cm to 140cm depending on the size of the rowers. This parameter effectively moves the rowers closer together or further apart and can be adjusted so that the boat pitches less and runs more horizontally. The span or spread is then set, followed by the gate to seat heights. The next stage is setting up the footstretcher angles, heights, splay and position in front of square off. Last, the slides are adjusted individually to each rower so they can slide freely without hitting either end of the slide rail.

The footstretcher set-up is important for the rower's posture, stroke length and effective foot force. The feet height and angle need to be adjusted for comfort and to allow the rower to rock over on the seat, have the weight in their feet and freely slide all the way up the slide. In the catch position the rower's knees should be no higher than their armpits and their shins should be at 90 degrees. The feet should be as wide as the boat will allow, while still being comfortable to the rower. A wider gait allows for a more comfortable position and thus more effective force application. The correct foot position will allow the rower to reach a long catch angle; to place the blade effectively (comfortably enabling them to slide through the recovery); and to initiate and execute a strong and effective leg drive.

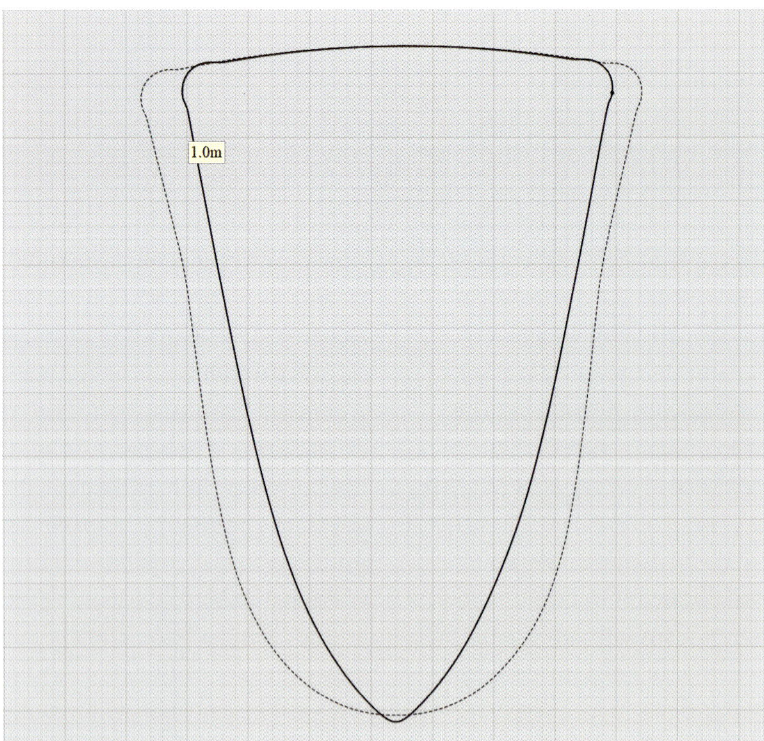

Whilst a V-shaped boat may be harder to balance, it cuts through the water more effectively and displaces less water. This figure represents a C86 (solid line) and a C87 (dotted line) Empacher eight. (Damien Carter)

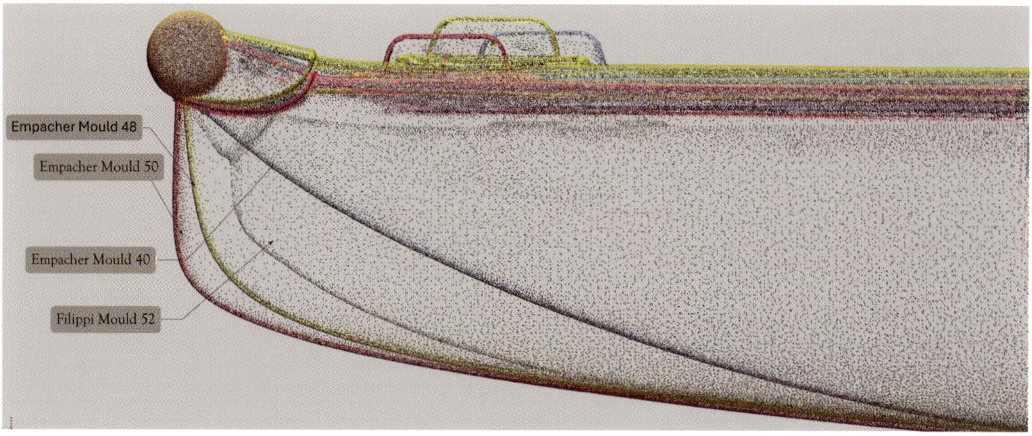

Comparison of four coxless four/quad bow shapes: the Empacher C40, C48, C50 and a Filippi F52 (Damien Carter). All four shapes will cut the water in a different hydrodynamic way.

The set-up of the footstretcher should also be individualised to take into consideration the rower's anthropometry and mobility (ankle and hip flexibility). Quite often people have a true leg length difference and an orthotic or a foot raise is used to adjust the feet so that the force is more symmetrical through both the footstretcher and the rower. This may help to avoid injury by reducing asymmetrical loading of forces through the rower.

A standard flat footboard angle is 42 degrees, but some boat builders and boat accessory companies also offer footstretchers with a bi-angle. This enables the fore foot to be steeper, providing stronger horizontal force and better connection with the heel and the foot overall with the footboard. With the feet at a steeper angle, the rower can drive more effectively through their whole foot. Driving through the heels gives better engagement through the drive with the extremely powerful gluteal muscles.

Boat manufacturers are also providing adjustments in footstretchers that allow the feet to be placed wider apart. On most boats, the toe-to-toe measurement is approximately 16cm, but this can be widened to 18–19cm, enabling more effective power to be produced. With manufacturers offering more adjustability, rowers are also able to manipulate the splay of the feet to be more comfortable and effective. In some cases, sweep rowers prefer their inside foot to be perpendicular whilst their outside foot is splayed.

The most accurate way to establish the footstretcher position is to set up the boat with biomechanical instrumentation and adjust the footstretcher until the rower is in the ideal position. A coach will need to assess this at various intensities and stroke rates as rowers tend to shorten their length as intensity increases. This sometimes happens at the front turn and sometimes at the finish, so it is important to identify which position works best for both training and racing. As a rule of thumb, the rower should be set up at two-thirds the total length in front of square off and one-third behind square off. A rower who rows

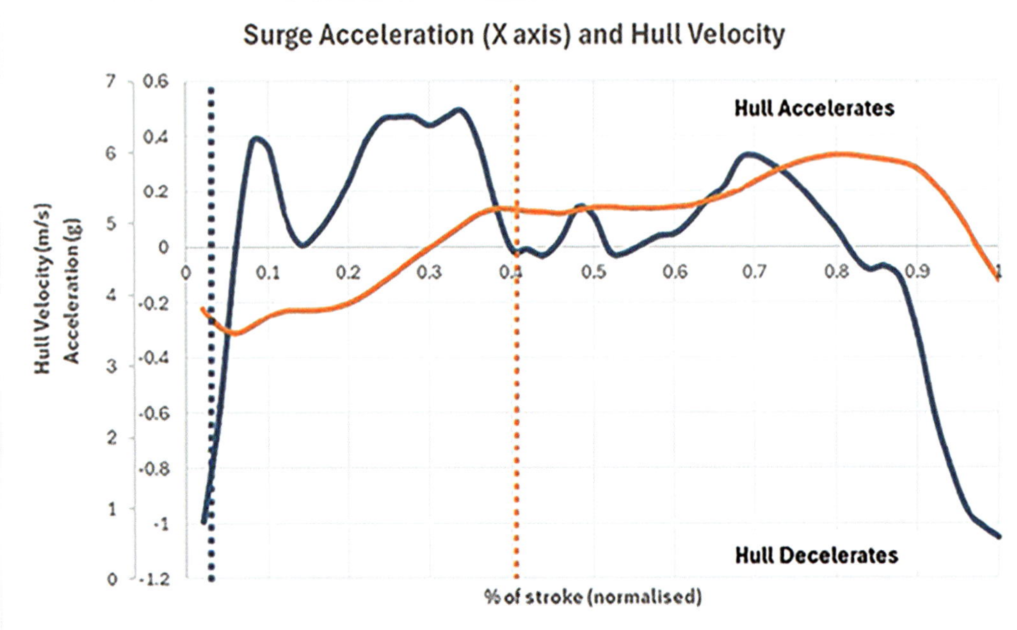
Surge Acceleration (X axis) and Hull Velocity
Hull Velocity (m/s)
Acceleration (g)
Hull Accelerates
Hull Decelerates
% of stroke (normalised)

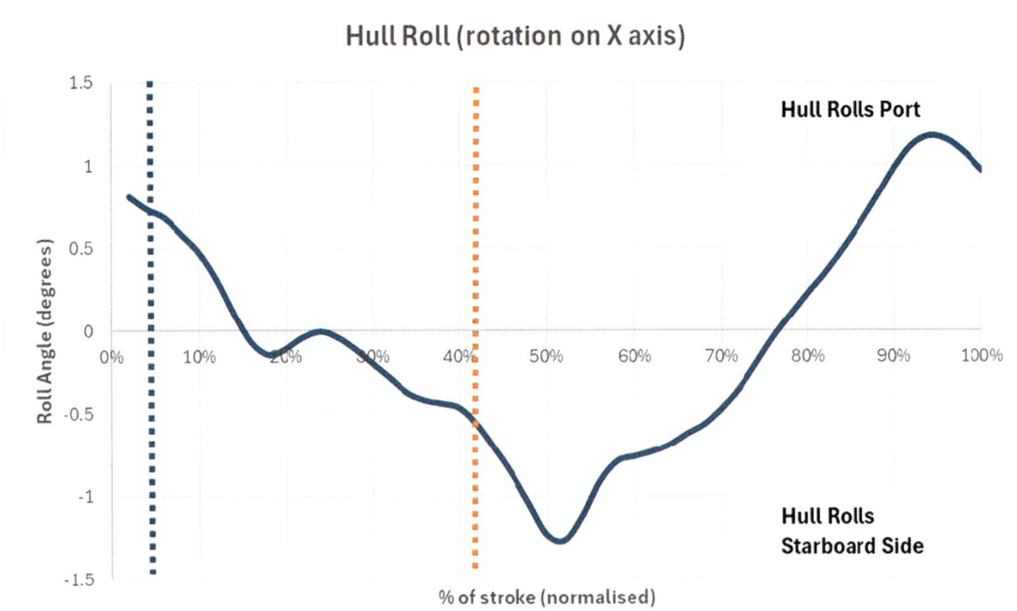
Hull Roll (rotation on X axis)
Roll Angle (degrees)
Hull Rolls Port
Hull Rolls
Starboard Side
% of stroke (normalised)

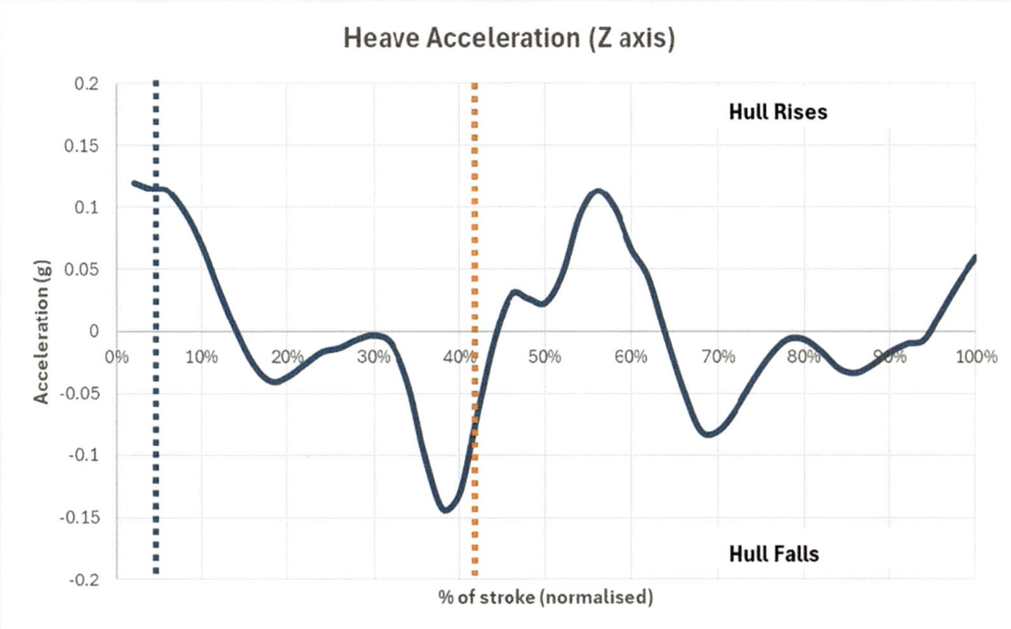
Heave Acceleration (Z axis)
Hull Rises
Hull Falls
Acceleration (g)
0.2
0.15
0.1
0.05
0
-0.05
-0.1
-0.15
-0.2
0%
10%
20%
30%
40%
50%
60%
70%
80%
90%
100%
% of stroke (normalised)

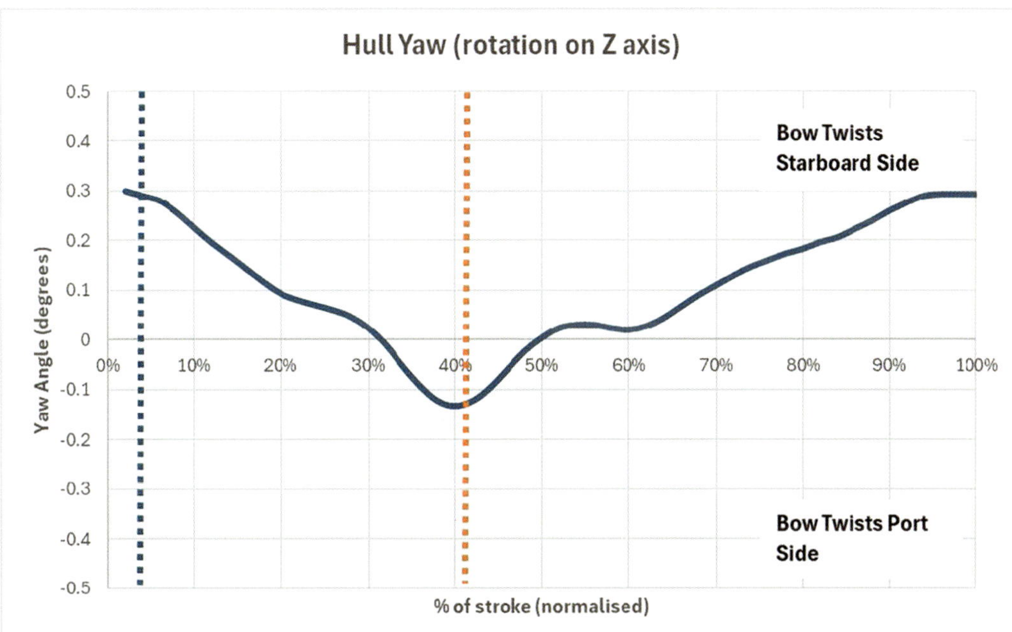
Hull Yaw (rotation on Z axis)
Bow Twists
Starboard Side
Bow Twists Port
Side
Yaw Angle (degrees)
0.5
0.4
0.3
0.2
0.1
0
-0.1
-0.2
-0.3
-0.4
-0.5
0%
10%
20%
30%
40%
50%
60%
70%
80%
90%
100%
% of stroke (normalised)

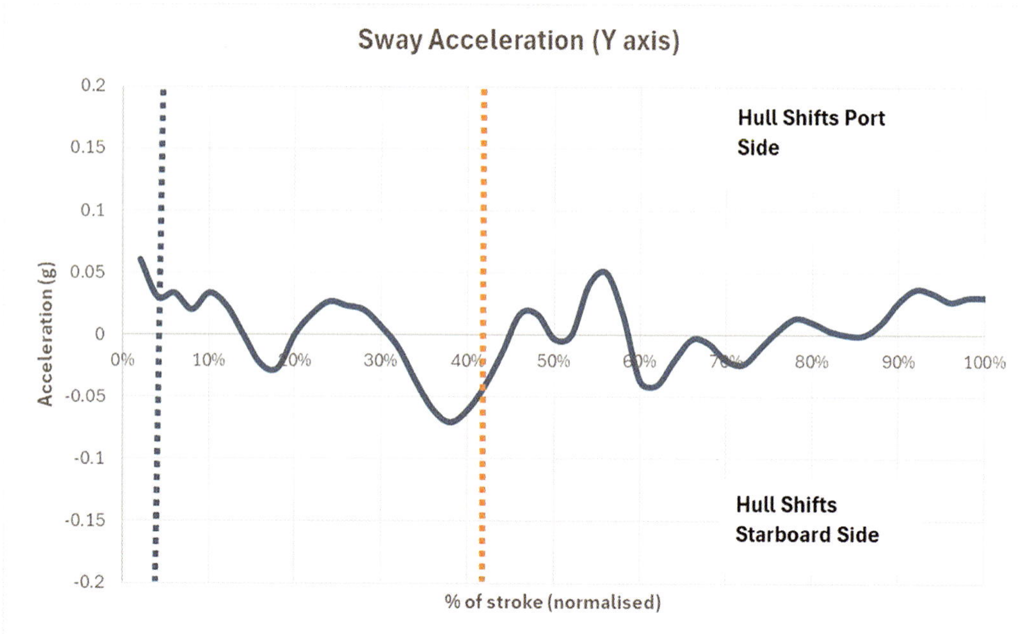

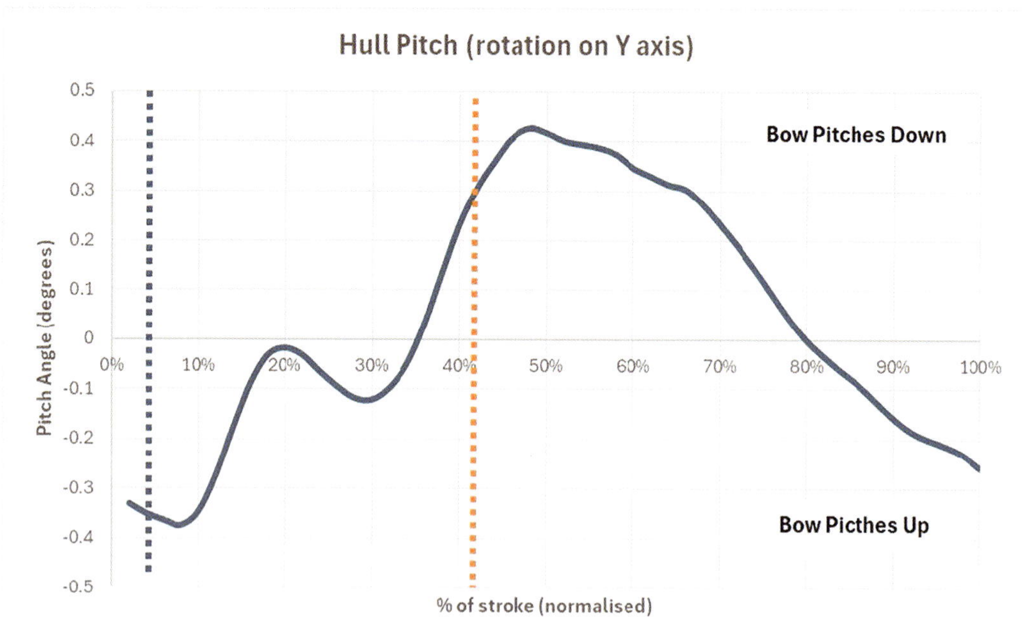

An example of a boat's pitch (movement up and down along the length of the hull), roll (side to side) and yaw (left to right). The figure is normalised single stroke traces of inertial sensors and hull velocity from an Olympic M2- training at mid race velocity with stroke rate 32 s/min. Acceleration and rotation are described above and below the horizontal axis for each of the X, Y and Z planes and axis. The blue dotted line represents the time in the stroke where blade catch occurs and the orange dotted line represents time in the stroke phase where blade release occurs.

Adjustment	Recommendation	Adjustment Requirement?	Example
Stretcher angle	40–45 degrees (42–45 ideal)	Mobility Boat type	Ankle/hip mobility
Stretcher height (Heel depth)	12–19cm	Anthropometry: Shoe size Body type Mobility	Lower/upper leg ratio Lightweight/heavyweight Ankle/hip mobility
Stretcher position	56–60cm (from pin to centre of seat in the finish position)	Catch/finish angle Leg length	
Shoe width (Toe to Toe)	12–20cm	Depending on boat category/width	1x - 13cm, 2-/2x – 14–16cm, 4-/x – 16cm, 8+ 18–20cm
Splay	Dependent on boat width	Boat type Mobility Shoes	Tight hips and gluteal muscles

Recommended stretcher and shoe set-ups. (Dr Conny Draper)

a 90-degree arc should be approximately 57 degrees at the catch and 33 degrees at the finish.

If there is no instrumentation available, the simplest method is to set the rowers up at a certain point from the back stops. Depending on the height of the rowers, the standard range is 60–65cm from the edge of the heel cups to the back stops. For a taller rower, the distance may be even greater. A coach may set the crew up at, for example, 63cm from back stops as a starting point and then make individual adjustments until the crew lengths are matched up. Video capture and feedback can help confirm whether the rowers are in the correct position.

Recently there has been a significant amount of development in terms of shoe and footstretcher set-ups in rowing boats. The aim of a coach is to individualise each rower's set-up so that they can most effectively apply their power.

Practical Guides to Rowing Equipment

Oarsman and America's Cup sailor Iain Smith is a former owner of a boat-building and repair business and a boat optimisation expert. He offers the following insights and practical guides to rowing equipment.

The sport of rowing in all forms is inherently an equipment-reliant activity and there is always debate about what percentage of overall performance can be attributed to the athlete and what percentage to the quality or suitability of the equipment. Whatever the percentage breakdown may be, the equipment aspect is vitally important at all levels of competition and an area that requires due consideration. All rowers need good, reliable and well-maintained equipment to ensure a minimum standard of performance, that is, to complete any competition safely and without breakage. Boats are expensive

Standard	BAT(Logic)/ Bont system	Shimano system
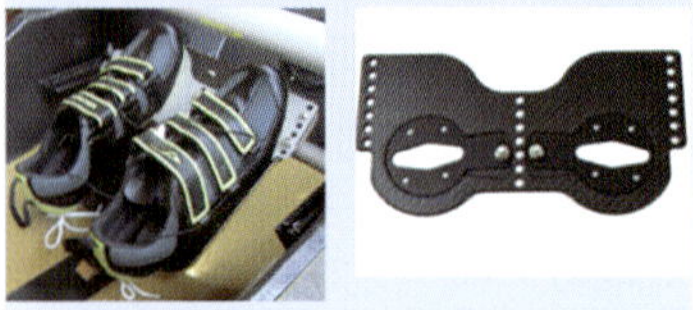	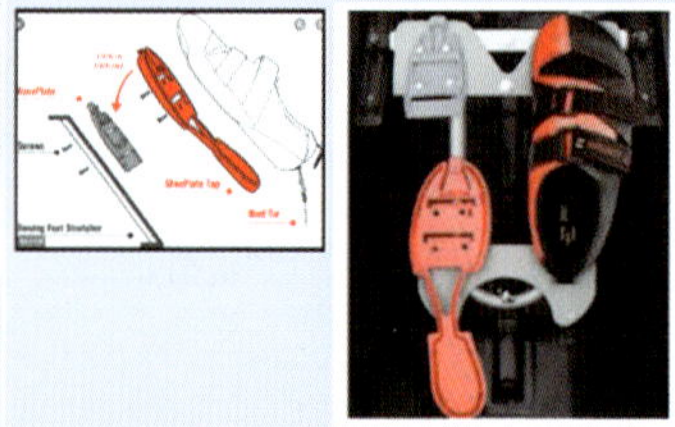	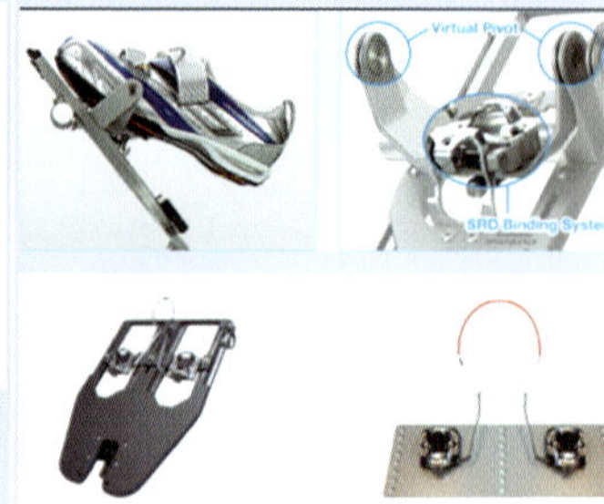
Shoe fixed to shoe plate with splay (angle) & shoe displacement width (depend on boat width/ athlete's requirement) Shoe is fixed or able to rotate slightly	Aim: the shim system allows to have an improved foot support, greater engagement and enhanced heel load through the whole stroke Hygienic (keep your own shoes)	Aim: pivot helps you get more reach at the catch Hygienic (keep your own shoes)

Different footstretcher and shoe systems for rowing.

and can last in good condition for many years if they are well looked after. If the minimum standard of boat preparation and maintenance has been achieved, it is then up to the rower(s) to determine the outcome of any competition.

Equipment requirements differ greatly depending on the level of competition. International federations competing at the Olympics, World Championships, World Cups and other international events will not have the same requirements – and budgets – as schools, clubs or individuals.

At the international and national level, those tasked with acquiring boats and managing a fleet should do the following:

- Purchase or lease the best available equipment.
- Where possible, test performance of several different manufacturers before making their final decisions.
- Roll over equipment on a regular basis to avoid a large depreciation in value.
- Be aware of what the gold standard is and what the best programmes or individuals are using.
- Do not be afraid to 'look outside the box' for suppliers and innovations from emerging manufacturers in all areas of equipment and components of equipment.
- Weigh every new boat and oar upon delivery to ensure quality of supply.

For school and club programmes, buyers should consider the following:

- Endeavour to have a minimal number of different manufacturers and models of vessels in the shed.
- Purchase vessels and oars that can be versatile and reliable across all the athletes.
- Ensure that the equipment purchased will last for ten years in a satisfactory competitive and structural manner.

- Ensure that the chosen boat manufacturer has good after-sales service and back-up along with good availability of spare parts and equipment.
- Select a supplier who uses up-to-date manufacturing processes, including pre-impregnated carbon fibre and two-pack buffable and repairable hull paint.
- Consider purchasing second-hand well-maintained equipment to match existing equipment.
- Avoid simply filtering boats and oars down from the very top to the lower levels of ability. Try to acquire a range of models that are appropriate for different levels, so that everyone has good, reliable and applicable equipment.
- Weigh every new boat and oar on delivery to ensure quality of supply.

Boat Maintenance Practical Guidelines

- Keep hulls clean by washing with mild soapy water after every row and chamois dry before racking.
- Carry out a full internal washout weekly, with disinfectant soap to remove bacteria and germs. Focus on shoes and seats.
- Lubricate bearing wheels with a dry lube after cleaning bearings in hot soapy water.
- Keep hulls out of direct sunlight.
- Regularly clean oar handles, sleeves and shafts with hot soapy water and sugar-soap handles.
- If any competition or training is on saltwater venues an anti-corrosive compound needs to be applied to all stainless-steel fasteners where they come into contact with aluminium fittings such as riggers, footstretchers, rudders, seats and rails.
- Do weekly checks of steering systems including cables and wires.
- Check fasteners regularly but do not overtighten.
- Keep internal tanks and bow/stern sections dry and air out regularly.

Boat Preparation for Racing

- Check sleeve pitches on oars and look for excessive wear on sleeves and buttons. (Buttons sit on the collar of the oar.)
- Pitch the whole boat with a pitch meter or plumb bob.
- Check oar lengths.
- Do a full fastener and fitting check, looking for loose parts. Do not overtighten. If required use medium strength (blue) Loctite on threads to stop parts from coming loose.
- Clean hull with hull cleaner and polish with non-silicone-based polish.
- Renew steering lines if any wear is evident.

Every rowing programme, no matter how big or small, amateur or high-performance, is uniquely based on many factors and may not be directly compared to any other programme.

Iain Smith's Top Tips for Coaches Regarding Boats and Equipment

- Ensure your athletes know the value of the equipment and the potential costs of repair in the case of damage. Supervise them when racking, trailer loading and launching, to ensure they know how to handle the equipment properly. Taking preventive action is better than having to pay for a repair job.

- Teach your athletes how to: measure the heights of a gate; measure the span of the pin; check the lengths of an oar and inboards; pitch a boat properly with a pitch meter or plumb bob after checking that there is no wear on the oar sleeves and that they are pitched to zero degrees; set up a pin with a level; set the feet height; measure the distance from heels to seat; understand the principles of rigging; remove and fit riggers, without overtightening rigger bolts and section bolts; section an eight using two trestles only; load a trailer and tie boats correctly; launch and retrieve the coach's boat.
- Remind your athletes that they should not change anything – such as gate heights and feet positions – without talking to you.
- Make sure the boat and oars are cleaned correctly on a weekly basis during the racing season.
- Mark pins with a white marker to show easily if a pitch changes.
- Mark footstretcher positions and rigger positions for each athlete.
- Make notes of all measurements and changes made during a season.

Oars and Sculls

With modern construction methods and materials, coaches are spoilt for choice on shapes of rowing blades. The aim of the designs is to increase the load and effectiveness of the blade, achieving a good connection at the catch and a clean release at the finish. When selecting different pieces of equipment coaches should understand the principles behind the innovation and also get a feel for the rower's engagement. Testing is difficult due to a number of variables, from water and weather conditions to rower performance, so subjectivity will always play a role in the decisions on what equipment to buy.

Darren Croker produces outstanding world-class oars, sculls and rowing accessories, and is well placed to offer advice on rowing equipment. His view is that, when considering an oar shape or brand, it is crucial that high-performance rowers have confidence in their equipment and a voice in the process. Having said that, feel does not always equate to speed, so it is important to have some objective markers to measure the impact of the change.

Equipment for club and school rowers must be right for the age and physical development of the rowers. Often, training programmes and performance equipment are passed down to less experienced and less skilful rowers, but a rower's maturational

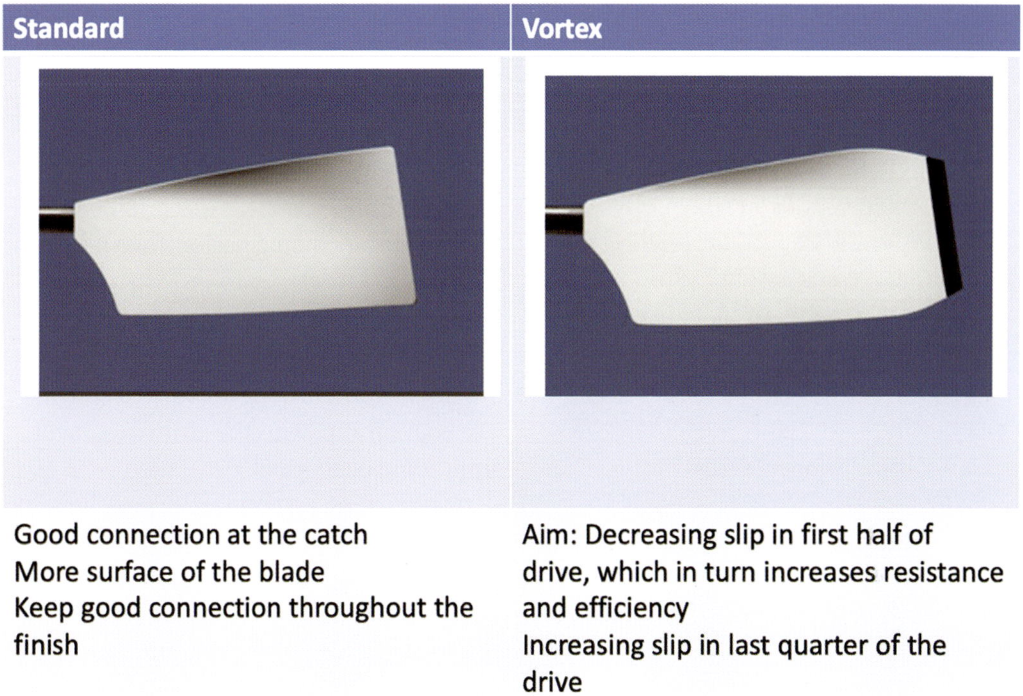

The effect of the vortex on the tip of the blade. (Dr Conny Draper)

age and strength need to be considered. Using equipment that is not sufficiently sturdy can lead to damage and a repair or replacement cost that would have been avoided if a more appropriate item had been selected. Shaft stiffness is particularly important. A stiff shaft can help transfer a rower's force more effectively, but it also puts more load through the rower's trunk, which can lead to injury. Some coaches choose to train with soft shafts and race with stiff shafts.

Grip size in both sculling and sweep is important for the rower's comfort, preventing forearm injuries and affecting the rower's technical ability to square and feather the oar. It is a simple but often overlooked part of rowing.

Maintenance of oars and sculls should involve regular cleaning of the handles and inside the shafts, and cleaning of the grips with sugar soap or a methyl ethyl ketone (MEK) thinner and an abrasive brush. Shafts should be cleaned twice a year to ensure adjustability and performance. Blades should always be checked for blade damage before any session and the oars' pitch should be checked twice a year in a jig.

Oars should be carefully cleaned, checked and prepared before any race. Coaches and rowers need to be confident that they will not be disadvantaged by their equipment on the day. When preparing for the major regatta of the season, coaches should check all oars are pitched to zero, inboard and

Top Tips for Race Preparation

- Feel does not always mean faster.
- Test and record beforehand what works for a crew or individual.
- Check the boat weight (weights can vary by up to 5kg in hot weather).
- Know the rules of racing.
- Pre-check the venue's weather and water conditions to adapt to temperature and water density.

outboard are set correctly, and the buttons are tight.

Future Trends

Applied Technology for Rowing

Thanks to the rapid growth and increased accessibility of affordable technology, miniaturised devices are now widely available to assist coaches in objectively assessing athlete and boat performance. While traditional stroke and speed coaches have long been standard tools in rowing, GPS tracking and on-water measurement systems are gaining in popularity within the community. These advanced devices have revolutionised training and performance analysis in rowing. GPS devices are routinely used to monitor a boat's speed, distance travelled, and route during both training sessions and competitions. The information is detailed and precise, enabling rowers to track their progress as well as refine their technique. Moreover, GPS technology, combined with inertial sensors and high-frequency data logging, provides coaches and rowers with multidimensional aspects of boat movement, including basic stroke rate, boat velocity, 3D acceleration and orientation (pitch, roll, yaw). This comprehensive data allows coaches to identify technical areas for adjustment in both the rowers and in the boat set-up, with the ultimate goal of improving boat speed.

The tracking systems are lightweight and non-intrusive and can provide immediate post-race analysis of highly contextual race performance data. The measurements are reliable and extremely accurate, allowing for meaningful testing of boat, blade and equipment configurations. Additional instrumentation can help assess individual technique and performance parameters, such as handle forces, oar angles, handle and seat velocity, and footstretcher forces, providing a near-complete view of an athlete's performance.

Utilising these miniaturised technologies – whether attached to the athlete or to the boat, oars or riggers – enables frequent and detailed monitoring during training and competitions. Having access to highly precise training and racing data offers a comprehensive monitoring tool that significantly enhances performance analysis. As noted by Draper (2008), measuring boat and athlete performance in real time is invaluable, emphasising the importance of careful data collection, analysis and

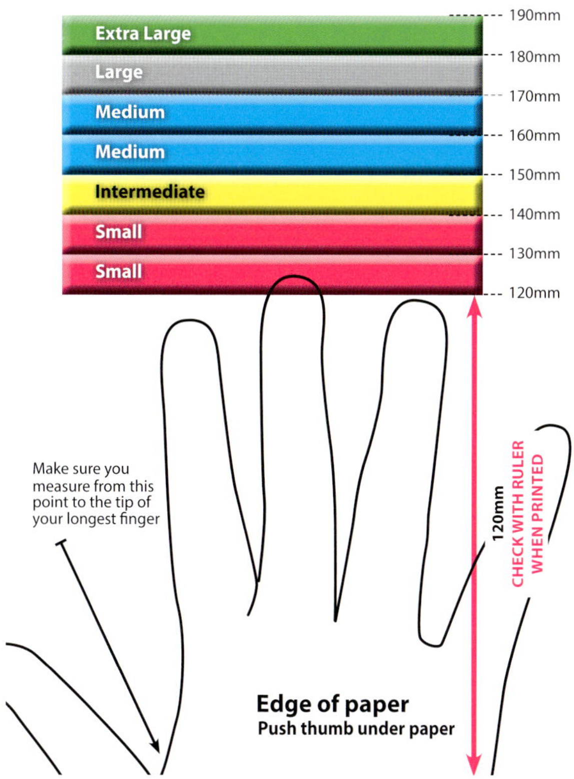

Croker grip chart.

Rigging Challenges and Opportunities (Dr Conny Draper)	
Challenges ('one size fits all')	**Opportunities (individual rigging)**
In big clubs/universities/schools, boats have mostly a standard set-up and are shared	Individual set-up improves technique and training quality
Hard to change/time issue/big squad:	Individualised set-up:
• oar gearing; • span/spread; • stretcher set-up; • shoe size (often a big problem for smaller athletes); • width of shoe displacement; • seats (height/size/type); • grip/s.	• oar load gearing depending on athlete's individual needs (anthropometry, fitness/ strength level, skill level, boat class); • grips (hand size, hand condition); • seats (gender, boat class, hip structure); • individual shoe size (very important); • stretcher (angle, height, position, splay, width of shoe displacement).

interpretation. Ultimately, this data must be meaningful and directly applicable to improving an athlete's performance, informing training strategies and refining racing approaches.

Australia has played a leading role in the development and application of GPS technology in rowing. The Australian Institute of Sport's rowing programme was among the first to utilise GPS and inertial sensor technology to collect international performance data, beginning in 2003. The practice of GPS data logging during competition events enabled them to plan, race and then measure the execution of the race strategies, as well as use the inertial sensors for fine-grain technical information on boat dynamics. Ongoing advancements in this technology, coupled with collaboration across various sports and a focus on miniaturisation, contributed to the creation of Catapult Sports.

Rowing is a sport that has evolved over hundreds of years, yet little has changed in the way the boat moves through the water and is powered by human energy. Over time, progress in boat speed has been gradual, with only small percentage improvements being recorded with each Olympic cycle. This may partly stem from the ethos of the sport's international governing body, which tends to prefer rowing to maintain its traditional appearance and resists innovations that deviate from that established image, such as the introduction of sliding rigger boats. Another major obstacle to achieving rapid increases in boat speed lies in the fundamental interface between the boat and the water, as well as the human effort that propels it. Both elements are inherently complex and resistant to significant change, making substantial and swift improvements less achievable.

Improvements in speed in other human-powered sports such as cycling, swimming and canoeing can generally be categorised into areas related to technology, tactics, environmental factors and human performance. Looking ahead, there are several potential developments across the same domains that could significantly advance rowing performance in the near future.

Advanced Materials and Boat Design

Lightweight, 3D-printed materials are being used to create items such as seats, footplates and oars, and may even be used for hulls and riggers. Hulls manufactured from composite materials are ultra-light and can be optimised for efficiency and durability. Some manufacturers are working on hydrodynamic enhancements, with adaptive hull shapes being managed via smart materials to reduce water resistance according to speed and conditions.

Smart Oars and Ergonomic Equipment

Sensor-integrated oars have embedded sensors to monitor stroke efficiency, force, angle and technique in real time, providing immediate feedback to rowers through wireless communications protocols. Oars and seats with customisable, adaptive ergonomic features powered by AI to suit individual physiologies are designed to reduce fatigue and injury rates.

Enhanced Training Tools

Virtual Reality (VR) and Augmented Reality (AR) are immersive environments for simulated races or technique correction, enabling athletes to train in diverse conditions without physical fatigue. There are also AI-powered coaching systems and machine learning algorithms that analyse performance data to give personalised training plans, technique corrections and recovery strategies. Complete prediction systems built on 'Big Data' aim to assist coaches with decision-making on equipment selection, crew formation and race environmental conditions.

Robotics

Autonomous or semi-autonomous rowing boats can be used to assist with training, provide pacing, or even compete alongside humans. Sensor network integration uses drones or buoy-based sensors to monitor water and weather conditions and boat performance metrics, to inform real-time decisions. Boats can also be equipped with sensors that adjust strategies based on wind, current and water temperature to optimise efficiency and performance.

Data Analytics and Connectivity

Cloud-based data platforms can aggregate performance, environmental and health data for detailed analysis and sharing with coaches and athletes. In real-time health monitoring, a rower's biometrics such as heart rate, oxygen levels and muscle activity can be tracked via wearable tech, ensuring optimal health management and training periodisation aimed at improving athlete availability.

6 Train to Race – Training and Racing Science

This chapter aims to explore the demands of a 2000m race, and the attributes required to compete in it. It will also look at the training and racing science and models, how training relates to racing and the successful racing strategies developed by the training.

What does it take to perform and win in racing? What are the demands of a 2000m race? These questions should be the starting point for developing a performance. Unpicking what it takes and what is important allows a coach and rower to focus on developing a successful stroke profile, race plan and training and performance plan. The principles that underpin Olympic success are just as valid to winning and performing in other rowing events.

Executing the perfect rowing race is a result of years of deliberate and dedicated practice, which is probably why most Olympic champions maintain their winning capabilities well into their late twenties or early thirties. Traditional rowing training involves conditioning the body to repeatedly perform the closed technique of a rowing stroke at near maximum effort, while maintaining perfect synchronisation with all fellow rowers (if in a crew). Immense concentration is required to flawlessly execute a race plan, demanding the deconstruction of and focused training in the core elements – technical, physical and psychological – in semi-isolation. This method allows athletes to hone each aspect without the stress of physical fatigue, before reassembling the elements cohesively under the high-pressure conditions of an actual race.

Training Science: Energy Contributions to a 2000m Race

To begin to understand the elements of human physiology that must be trained and conditioned to perform the perfect race, it is important to understand the demands of competition in their simplest form. Age, gender, boat class and training status (level, age, class) all dictate the duration of a 2000m race. For Olympic-level male athletes in the eight-oared coxed boat (M8+), the current world's best time is 5:18.68, with a velocity of 22.6km/h. This represents the fastest time to date in which a 2000m race has been finished. The slowest Olympic boat class is the single scull for women (W1X), which currently has a world's best time of 7:07.71, set in 2002 and equating to a speed of 16.8 km/h. In the Senior World

Championship regatta programme, the slowest boat class is that of the lightweight Women's Single Scull (LW1X), which has a world's best time of 7:23.36, with an average speed of 16.2km/h.

As rowing is an outdoor event, world's best times are nearly always set in very warm and deep water, with direct tailwind conditions up to ~20km/h. Once tailwind speeds get much higher than 20km/h, the water become very difficult to row in and often prevents faster boat speeds. In reality, 'world's best' rowing conditions are infrequent, and the majority of races are actually completed 2 to 10% slower than the corresponding world's best time, meaning that consistently the Olympic W1X race is completed in times ranging from 7:20.00 to 7:55.00.

Despite nearly 2:00.0 minutes separating the times to complete 2000m, rowing is predominantly an aerobic event, with up to 85% of the energy contribution for the performance coming from this fuel source. In addition, the slower the event, the more energy is supplied aerobically. Given the time to complete a 2000m race in an Olympic class M8+ is closer to the 5:30.0 domain, the aerobic energy contribution is slightly less in this event with anaerobic energy sources accounting for up to 25% and aerobic sources being ~75–77%. Quantifying the exact energy contribution is time-consuming and highly dependent on the training status of the individual and their metabolic fingerprint. As such, it is much simpler to accept that rowing at any level is primarily an aerobic event with small but highly significant contributions from anaerobic energy sources stored directly in the contracting muscles as well as being supplied rapidly through the blood.

Rowing is predominately an aerobic event with up to 85% of the energy contribution of a 2000m race coming from aerobic pathways.

The percentage of energy contributions is first dictated by the power output requirements of the event (in other words, the intensity) and then by the time the event takes to complete (*see* the graph opposite). In the case of a 5:30.0 rowing race, aerobic metabolism accounts for ~78% of the energy required for a 2000m rowing race while the anaerobic breakdown of blood-borne carbohydrates (anaerobic glycolysis) is nearly 20% and the anaerobic metabolism of stored energy directly in the muscles is ~2%. All these energy sources are constantly fuelling human movement, but at the start of a rowing race they all immediately begin mass producing energy to fuel the exceptionally high force that the rowing stroke requires. Power demands of a rowing race are exceptionally high especially from the start through to the first 250m mark and thus large amounts of energy are required immediately and must be replenished quickly. Unfortunately, the aerobic energy system can't provide energy for these demands alone for two main reasons; 1. the power requirements are simply too high and 2. the aerobic system take a number of minutes to reach full capacity and so anaerobic energy systems (anaerobic glycolysis and stored muscle phosphagens) are there to rapidly meet the needs of the first 90 secs to 2 mins of the rowing race with anaerobic

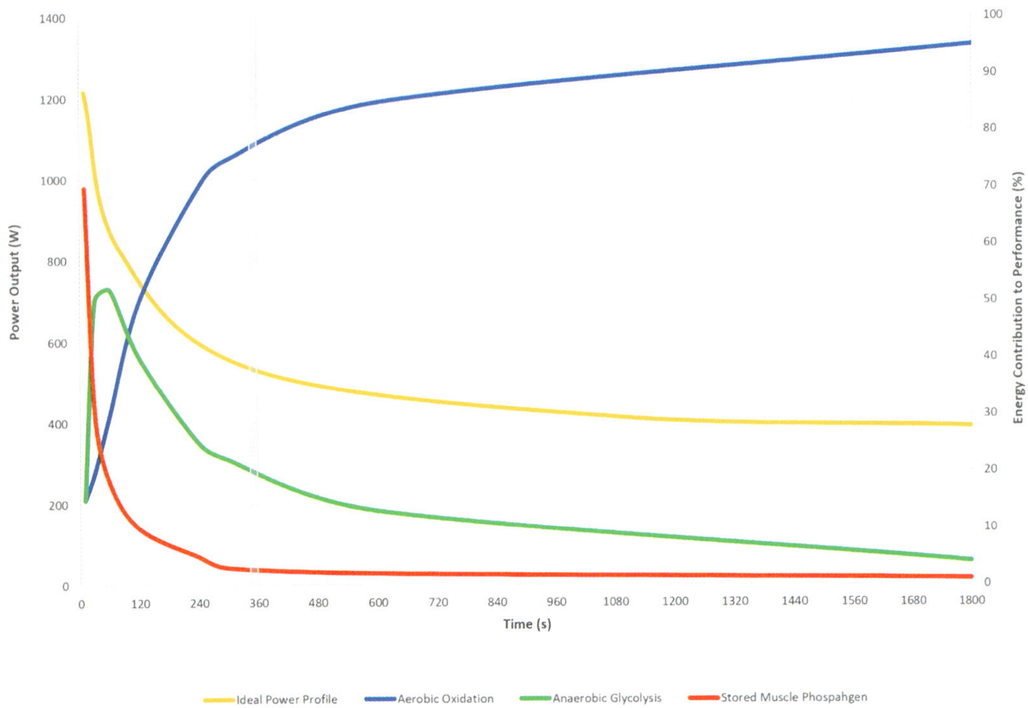

The primary energy sources for human activity against the time domain on the horizontal axis, illustrating an ideal energy characteristic of a male heavyweight oarsman. The yellow icons and line of best fit indicate the maximal power outputs for each of the grey highlighted time segments. The red, green and blue lines illustrate the theoretical energy contributions from stored muscle phosphagens, anaerobic glycolysis and aerobic glycolysis/fat oxidation, respectively. The 300–360 sec time domain illustrates the theoretical energy contributions of a 5- to 6-min rowing race.

glycolysis continuing to supplement the fuel for performance throughout the duration of the 2000m race given its ability to provide rapid and significant amounts of energy, albeit at the cost of producing high blood and muscle acidity.

Looking at the power output requirements of a M8+ completing a 2000m race in 5:26.5, despite the first and last 250m sector splits of the 2000m race being near identical, the average boat power in the first sector is almost 25% more than the last sector. This is what it takes to propel >900kg of mass (boat, oars, athletes and coxswain) from 0km/h to > 22km/h as rapidly as possible. In this phase of the race the power requirements dictate large amounts of energy supplied instantly and continuously and stored muscle phosphagens and anaerobic glycolysis intra-muscular fuels provide nearly all the energy for the first 15 to 30 seconds of the race. As this process unfolds, the aerobic oxidation of fat and glucose in the blood begins to ramp up significantly, boosting energy production to supplement the rapidly depleting anaerobic systems. By

By the time the rowers reach the 750m mark they are at or near their maximal oxygen consumption.

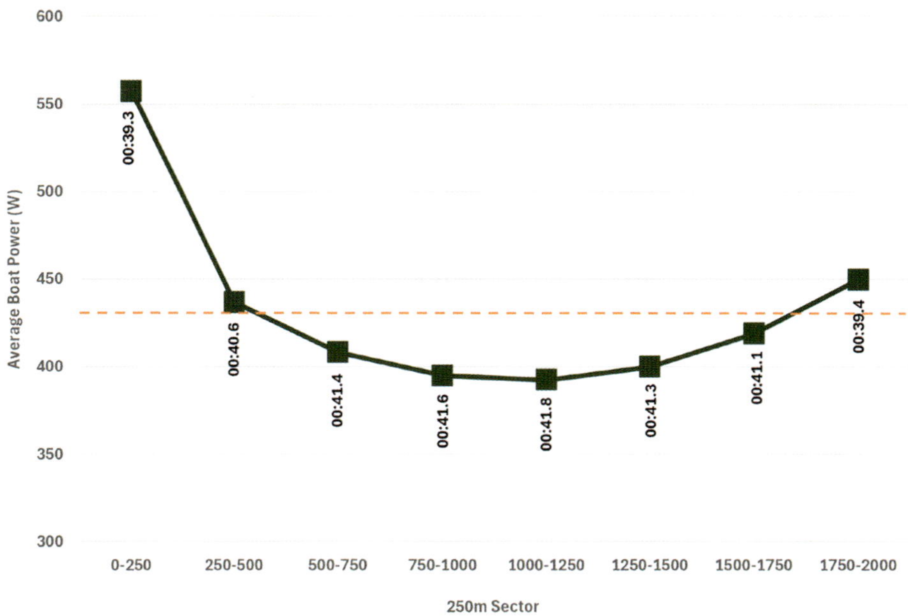

Average boat power for a M8+ completing 2000m in 5:26.5. Average boat power (shown by the dashed orange line) was 432W and the average 250m split time was 00:40.8. 250m sector times are displayed in vertical text below each marker.

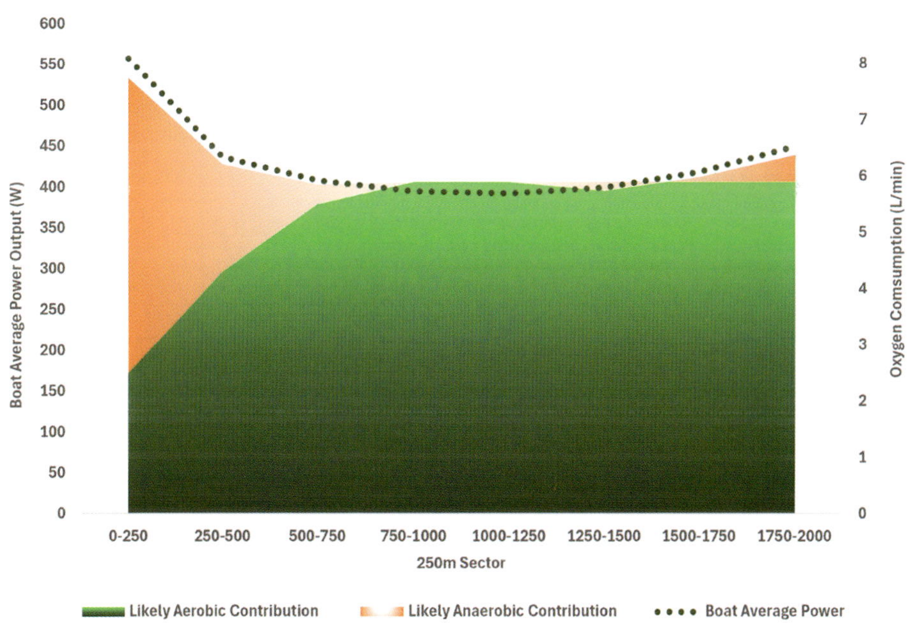

Average boat power for a M8+ completing 2000m in 5:26.5. Highlighted by the green shaded area is the theoretical energy supply for an individual with an oxygen consumption of ~6.0 l/min. Any difference between average boat power and the green shaded area requires energy to be supplied by anaerobic mechanisms. Based on race duration the orange shaded area (anaerobic energy supply) represents ~20% of the total energy production.

LT ZONE	ZONE (Session Goal/Term)	INTENSITY (% VO_2 Max/% MHR/BLa)	STROKE RATE (Lower/ Upper)	SAMPLE WORKOUT DETAILS
<LT1	Recovery (T1)	50–60% / 60–70%/~1mM/L	16/18	**Distance:** 6–10km **Total hard minutes:** 60–360' **W:R ratio:** – **Days to recovery:** – **Sample:** 10–12km easy row, skills and drills **Notes:** These are still important sessions and great for maintaining feel for the water. **Sessions per week:** 3
<LT1	Endurance (T2)	60–75%/70–80%/<2mM/L	18/22	**Distance:** 12–30km **Total hard minutes:** 60–180' **Rep duration:** 40' to 3hrs **W:R ratio:** 20:1–10:1 **Days to recovery:** 1 **Sample:** Steady rowing <LT1 HR from 40' to 3hrs; pieces of 10–30' <LT1 HR with 1–2' recovery **Notes:** Bread and butter of the programme, should account for ~80% of total on water volume, emphasis should also be on stroke mechanics at this speed. **Test set:** 2×10km at LT1 HR **Sessions per week:** 3
LT1–LT2	Tempo (T3)	70–88%/80–88%/2–4mM/L	20/24	**Distance:** 20km **Total hard minutes:** 50–90' **Rep duration:** 8–20' **W:R ratio:** 2:1–4:1 **Days to recovery:** 1–2 **Sample:** 8× 8' on 2' off, 6× 10' on 3' off, 4× 15' on 5' off **Notes:** The gains from these sessions are not as great as ones at a higher intensity so should be used wisely. Can be used effectively with resistance. **Sessions per week:** 1–2
>LT2	Threshold (T4)	85–93%/88–92%/4–6mM/L	24/28	**Distance:** 10km **Total hard minutes:** 30–60' **Rep duration:** 1–40min **W:R ratio:** 2:1–4:1 **Days to recovery:** 2–4 days **Sample:** 10× 1,000m, 2' RI; 5× 2k, 2–4' RI; 10km TT **Test set:** 5km TT **Sessions per week:** 2 (3 is possible)
	Aerobic Capacity/Race Pace (T5)	93–100%/>92%/6–12mM/L	28/36	**Distance:** 500–1,000m **Total hard minutes:** 15–30' **Rep duration:** 2–5min **W:R ratio:** 1:1 **Days to recovery:** 3–5 days **Sample:** 8× 500m on 4', 5–6× 750m on 6', 4–6× 1,000 on 8', 3× 1,250 on 10' **Notes:** Critical session for the programme, best done after a phase of Threshold work, best when done maximally, 4–5 sessions required. **Test set:** 5× 1000m **Sessions per week:** 1 (2 is possible)
	Speed–Endurance (T6)	120–150% / N/A / 8–15mM/L	36/40	**Distance:** 100m–300m **Total hard minutes:** 5–16' **Rep duration:** 20–60s **W:R ratio:** 1:1 **Days to recovery:** 2–4 days **Sample:** 4× (4× 250m on/off), 4× (300m, 200m, 100m) **Notes:** Really good for the more 'aerobic' athletes, good for understanding pace judgement. **Test set:** 4×4× 250m on/off **Sessions per week:** 1
	Anaerobic Capacity (Speed Maintenance) (T6)	150–175%/N/A/8–20mM/L	>40	**Distance:** 100m–300m **Total hard minutes:** 6' **Rep duration:** 20–60s **W:R ratio:** 1:5–1:10 **Days to recovery:** 4–6 days **Sample:** 5–8× 150–250m rolling/standing; 5' RI, 6× 300–400m rolling/standing, 10' RI **Notes:** Use carefully as it is brutal. Understand if your athlete is aerobically or anaerobically inclined prior to undertaking this work. **Test set:** 5× 250m standing **Sessions per week:** 1
	Alactic (Speed Production/ Starts) (T7)	N/A / N/A / N/A	–	**Distance:** up to 100m **Total hard minutes:** 1' **Rep duration:** 5–12s **W:R ratio:** 1:10 **Days to recovery:** 2–4 days **Sample:** 6× 100m standing, 8× 75m standing, 4× 20s w/ resistance then 4× 20s no resistance **Sessions per week:** 1 (2 is possible)

Australian Rowing categorises training into seven distinct zones, along with their associated metabolic and physiological references. Typically, only the first six are used to prescribe training sessions and their corresponding intensities. Each zone includes specific stroke rate ranges and sample workouts to help with planning. The six zones are: LT (lactate threshold); VO_2 max (maximal oxygen consumption); MHR (maximal heart rate); BLa (blood lactate, in mmol/l; re duration (repetition duration); and W:R ratio (work to rest ratio).

The rating of perceived exertion (RPE) linear scale, which is utilised to offer guidance and feedback on exercise intensity.

the time the rowers reach the 750m mark in the race, they are at or nearing their VO_2 max. Consequently, the power output for the remaining three minutes or so of the race must primarily rely on aerobic mechanisms. If the power output exceeds what aerobic energy production can supply, the body will need to resort to anaerobic energy production. This switch leads to an increased production of hydrogen ions, which can cause muscular fatigue and inhibit muscle contraction.

The final 250 metres of the race demand a power output exceeding what aerobic energy systems can supply (*see* above). At this stage, most athletes in the boat will have reached their VO_2 max, so the additional energy needed to boost power output and possibly increase boat speed must come from their remaining anaerobic reserves. For some rowers, these reserves may be nearly depleted, while others may still have significant stores. Those with sufficient anaerobic reserves, who can also maintain technical precision, will find themselves capable of increasing their power output, thereby enhancing the boat's speed.

Different Types of Race Training

Foundational Rowing Training

Rowing performance over 2000m can be improved through deliberate and purposeful training of the right energy systems.

Outside experts in other sports have often questioned why rowers undertake copious volumes of training at boat speeds for an event that only lasts somewhere between 5:20.0 and 7:45.0. As numerous researchers (Billat; Padilla; Murray; Smith) have shown, there is a direct relationship between a rower's performance on the water or on the ergometer and their maximal aerobic power (VO_2 max). Clearly, a rower who can improve their aerobic efficiency and capacity will improve their 2000m rowing times (with all other extraneous factors being equal).

One of the fundamental training sessions to improve aerobic efficiency and power is termed 'long slow distance' (LSD) training. LSD training is a foundational

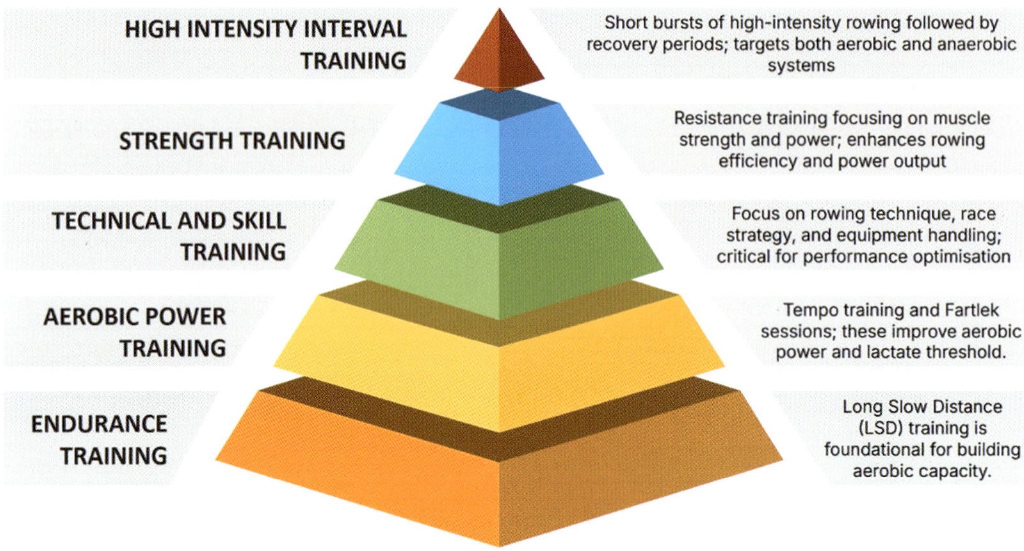

Depiction of a rower's training pyramid. This example indicates ATL and CTL for an individual over a three-month period at the recommencement of training.

aspect of endurance training for rowers, focusing on building aerobic capacity and endurance while minimising the risk of injury, especially when recommencing training after illness, injury or detraining. The purpose of LSD training is to enhance the body's ability to utilise oxygen more efficiently, build muscular and cardiovascular endurance, increase capillary density in muscles and ultimately train the body to utilise fat as a fuel source. In the long term this fat oxidation adaptation ensures more carbohydrate is saved for fuel when training intensity increases.

LSD should generally be performed in the <LT1 training zone (*see* the table above) with a rating of perceived exertion (RPE) level of 2–4/10. A good rule of thumb for LSD training is that the athlete should be able to hold a conversation while working. If it becomes difficult for them to complete a full sentence because they need to take frequent breaths, then the intensity of the session is too high and can no longer be considered LSD training. One of the real benefits of LSD training for rowers is that they can focus on proper rowing technique throughout the entire session without fatigue impacting the ability to execute perfect strokes consistently.

Regardless of the training periodisation there should always be at least one session per week of this style of training, and in the base training phase there may be up to six sessions per week. As the crew approaches the racing season and the specificity of training targets race-like intensities, the frequency of these sessions will reduce. However, it is important to keep some LSD training in the weekly plan to ensure base aerobic capabilities, metabolic efficiency and low-intensity technique refinement are continually addressed.

Race-Specific Intensity Training

Despite rowing being a primarily aerobic event, the typical low-intensity high-volume methods (known as LSD) are not always the most appropriate when dealing with athletes who largely have a well-developed and efficient aerobic system and/or have a very large training history (more than ten years at national or international level). In these cases, the coach and well-trained athlete need to focus on stimulating gains through higher, more specific mechanisms in both cross-training and rowing-specific sessions. There are a number of training methods that the coach of a high-performance athlete can consider, to further develop their aerobic capabilities and maintain or increase motivation (*see* above).

Much of the training needed to shift rowing fitness in well-trained and elite rowers focuses on intensities bordering the theoretical aerobic and anaerobic threshold transition point. There are various terms for this band of intensity, but here it is referred to as Lactate Threshold 2 (LT2). Training at or around LT2 intensity has been proven to enhance athletic performance, endurance and fatigue management. Importantly, LT2 is a very strong predictor of endurance performance, with athletes with a higher anaerobic threshold often achieving more success in endurance events of a short to medium duration (Coyle, E.F., 'Substrate utilisation during exercise in active people', *Journal of Sports Sciences*, 13(S1), S35–S44, 1995). Testing and establishing a rower's LT2 allows for a more individualised training programme, with training intensities being tailored to each crew member (Capostagno, B., & Lambert, M.I., 'The importance of the anaerobic threshold in cycling performance', *Journal of Sports Sciences*, 34(3), 274–280, 2016).

Heart-rate threshold refers to the heart rate at which the body transitions from primarily using aerobic energy production (with oxygen) to anaerobic energy production (without oxygen). This transition point is crucial for training because it indicates the maximum intensity that an athlete can sustain for an extended period without quickly fatiguing. This allows workout intensity to be guided, and training to be optimised, for improved endurance and performance. Typically expressed as a percentage of an individual's maximum heart rate, it can be determined through various fitness assessments.

Heart-rate threshold and lactate threshold are related, although they refer to slightly different physiological events. Specifically, heart-rate threshold corresponds to the point during exercise when the body's metabolic shift occurs, making it useful for setting training zones. On the other hand, lactate threshold is the precise exercise intensity at which lactate starts to accumulate in the bloodstream faster than it can be cleared. This accumulation, a byproduct of anaerobic metabolism, leads to quicker fatigue beyond this point. While both thresholds signal the shift from aerobic to anaerobic exercise, the lactate threshold offers a more precise measure of when significant lactate build-up begins. The heart rate at this juncture can differ slightly from the general heart-rate threshold but normally by only a few beats per minute, so the measures are often interchangeable.

Once the aerobic to anaerobic threshold intensity has been determined, this transition point needs to be targeted in training. This needs to be done regularly and for varying durations to stimulate adaptation and subsequent performance improvement.

Certain styles of training anchor their intensity around the LT2 transition power/ intensity:

- Lactate threshold training (LT training) is crucial for rowers aiming to optimise their performance by increasing their capacity to sustain high efforts without accumulating excessive lactate. Sessions should focus on training at or just below LT2 (Lactate Threshold 2; historically referred to as anaerobic threshold), to improve the body's ability to clear lactate and to sustain higher intensities for longer, through improved metabolic efficiency. Up to two sessions per week of this type of training will accelerate aerobic adaptations for the well-trained rower. Simple examples include the following:

    3 × 15 minutes at LT2 intensity (~28 strokes per minute; RPE 7/10) with 5–10 minutes of easy rowing recovery between intervals;

    2 minutes performed at an intensity >LT2 (28–30 strokes per minute; RPE 8/10), followed by a 2-minute light paddle recovery; then 4 minutes at >LT2 intensity (28–30 strokes per minute; RPE 8/10), followed by a 4-minute light paddle recovery; then 6 minutes at >LT2 intensity (28–30 strokes per minute; RPE 8/10), followed by another 4-minute light paddle recovery. Move on to 4 minutes at >LT2 intensity (28–30 strokes per minute; RPE 8/10), followed by a 2-minute light paddle recovery. Finish with 2 minutes at the same intensity (28–30 strokes per minute; RPE 8/10); shorter, higher-intensity efforts (for example, 1 to 3 minutes) at or above LT2 with brief recoveries (1 to 2 minutes).
- Tempo or 'sweet spot' training refers to sustained efforts at a moderate to high intensity, generally between 75 and 85% of an athlete's LT2 power, pace or heart-rate threshold. This area is often called the 'sweet spot' and is the point where improvements in both aerobic and anaerobic capacities can be achieved. The intensity should be higher than that normally held for a long steady-state row, but it should be constantly sustainable for 60 minutes with a perceived exertion of 5–6/10. As fitness and capability improve, the duration can be stretched out towards 90 minutes, all the while maintaining a constant speed and perceived exertion level. For on-water specific sessions this would be a stroke rate of 22–24 strokes per minute and 82–84% of projected gold medal speed for the chosen boat class specific to gender age and training. As the intensity and boat speed of these sessions increases, it is vital to maintain proper technique to avoid injury and ensure the motor patterning of the stroke nearing race intensity is correct. Effective form becomes even more important as fatigue sets in.
- High-intensity interval training (HIIT) incorporated into a regime can lead to

significant and rapid improvements in aerobic and anaerobic capacities, enhance race performance, and allow athletes to reach peak conditioning levels more rapidly. HIIT involves short bursts of intense rowing (on-water or on the ergometer) followed by periods of lower-intensity rowing for recovery. This training approach enhances cardiovascular fitness, increases VO_2 max, and improves metabolic efficiency. In HIIT, the body is required to operate at a near race-like intensity. The periods of effort are shorter than for a full race but in combination they enable the athlete to complete two to three full race distances at or near race pace in a single training session. The body adapts to this stress in a variety of ways but, when managed correctly with adequate rest and alternate LSD training sessions, the HIIT stimulus can provide the right dose for rapid improvements in rowing performance. A classic example of a HIIT session aimed at improving lactic acid tolerance and aerobic capacity would be 4 to 6 repetitions of 4 minutes of high-intensity rowing (95% average race speed or >95% average 2000m power) with 3 to 4 minutes of active recovery in between. HIIT can also target anaerobic mechanisms by adopting intervals that are even shorter in duration but higher in intensity. An example of a session that would specifically target the anaerobic capacity and high boat speed would be 10 x 1 minute at 95–98% intensity with 1 to 2 minutes of easy rowing for recovery between intervals.

Fartlek Training

Fartlek training – from the Swedish term meaning 'speed play' – is an effective method for rowers to enhance both speed and endurance by integrating varied pacing within a session. Much like HIIT, it involves alternating between higher and lower intensities, but the sessions are typically much less structured than in traditional HIIT. Fartlek training helps develop both aerobic endurance and anaerobic power, making it suitable for race preparation. By mimicking the varying intensities experienced during competitive races it helps rowers to adapt to the changing speeds and tempos that often occur during a rowing race.

Examples of Fartlek training for rowing include the following:

- Mixed intervals: alternate between a series of fast-paced rows (for example, 30 seconds to 3 minutes) followed by similar durations of lower intensity, such as 3 × 2 minutes at high intensity (90–95% average race speed) followed by 2 minutes of easy rowing to recover; or 5 × 1-minute all-out efforts with 2 minutes of slow rowing in between.
- Variable pacing: row at a steady moderate pace for a specific duration, then mix in randomly timed bursts of speed throughout the session. For example, row for 30 minutes at a moderate pace (80% projected gold medal speed) while incorporating 4-5 short bursts of several seconds to 1 minute at maximum effort spread throughout the session.
- Landmark intervals: landmarks or markers (buoys, trees, or distances

on a rowing machine) are used for pacing changes. For example, row at a sustainable pace (72–75% projected gold-medal speed) to the first landmark, then sprint to the next one, then return to the sustainable pace.

Polarised Training

The polarised training model emphasises a combination of high-intensity sessions and low-intensity sessions, minimising time spent in moderate-intensity training zones. It is not a specific training type but is more akin to a training philosophy, as it incorporates the idea that training for high-intensity aerobic endurance events is best undertaken through a combination of LSD-style sessions and higher-intensity sessions targeting LT2 intensity or above (that is to say, Fartlek, HIIT or LT training). Under this philosophy, 'sweet spot' training would not be used, as this clearly and deliberately operates in the moderate-intensity training zones.

Polarised training was a popular methodology for over a decade but regained some renewed enthusiasm and focus following the success at the Paris 2024 Olympics of the Dutch team, who had reportedly shifted back towards this style of training. Despite their success, though, polarised training may not be the best approach for all athletes or crews. It is important to consider all the positives and negatives of the style when evaluating the best method of training for a particular individual or crew. The positive aspects include the following:

- Improved aerobic capacity: low-intensity training enhances the aerobic system, allowing rowers to perform better over longer distances.
- Enhanced recovery: the majority of training at low intensities allows for adequate recovery, reducing the risk of burn-out and injuries.
- Increased performance in high-intensity efforts: the focus on maximal effort during a smaller percentage of training can lead to improved performance during sprinting or race conditions.
- Mental freshness: lower-intensity workouts can reduce mental fatigue, making training more enjoyable and sustainable.
- Skill development: slower, low-intensity sessions allow rowers to focus on technique and form, enhancing skill acquisition.
- Reduced risk of over-training: by balancing training intensities, rowers may be less prone to over-training syndrome.

On the negative side, the coach and their athlete(s) should consider the following issues:

- Spending significant time at low intensity can be less efficient for those with limited training time, making it challenging to fit into a busy schedule.
- Potential lack of specificity: some may find that too little time spent at moderate intensities (if applicable) could hinder performance in certain race situations that require sustained efforts.

- It can be challenging consistently to monitor and adjust training intensities to meet polarised training standards.
- If not carefully managed, insufficient high-intensity sessions may lead to a lack in the adaptation needed for peak performance in competitive settings.
- Not all athletes respond equally to polarised training; some may benefit more from different training models.
- Deviating from the basics, and over-emphasising low and high intensities, may lead to a neglect of functional endurance training at moderate intensities, which can be important for race pace development.

Managing Training Loads in a Rowing Programme

Rowers typically undertake a significant volume of training relating to the duration of the 2000m event. The reasons for this large training volume are clear, but the physical and mental effects of the training load have not been addressed.

Rowing training aims to improve a rower's performance in a 2000m race by enabling the body to adapt to the training stress that is applied during regular and appropriately periodised sessions. The term 'training stress' refers to the physiological and psychological load imposed on an athlete. It encompasses various factors, including the intensity, duration and frequency of workouts, as well as the overall impact those workouts have on the body and mind.

The concept of training stress can be broken down into a number of key components:

- Physical stress includes the strain on muscles, energy systems and cardiovascular function during exercise. It can lead to fatigue and adaptations that improve fitness over time and is often the most widely understood stress of training.
- Mechanical stress is the load that is placed on the joints, bones and muscles as a result of training, which will influence muscle soreness, recovery, and the risk of chronic injury.
- Psychological stress is the mental strain associated with training. It includes the factors of motivation, focus and mental fatigue, and the emotional response to training loads.
- Cumulative training stress is the total impact over time from all training sessions, which can influence an athlete's physical adaptations, recovery needs and risk of long-term fatigue.
- Recovery stress refers to the body's response to recovery periods after training, which are essential for adaptations to occur. Inadequate recovery can lead to increased training stress and a higher risk for injury, illness and long-term fatigue.

Proper management of all types of training stress is vital for optimising performance. Monitoring training stress can help a coach to balance the workload, recovery and performance improvement, ensuring that the athlete benefits from their training while minimising the risks of injury and long-term fatigue.

It is common practice now for individuals and training programmes to use sophisticated software to track and predict training stress through theoretical indices such as acute and chronic training load (ATL and CTL) (*see* Chapter 7). These measures can be calculated after every session, and future loads in upcoming planned sessions can also be predicted. By using this information an athlete and/or their coach can individualise training to optimise the balance between fitness and fatigue, to gain the best outcomes from a block of work.

The variables of acute training load (ATL) and chronic training load (CTL), and their integration, are described below. For a more through exploration, *see* https://help.trainingpeaks.com/hc/en-us/articles/204071944-Training-Stress-Scores-TSS-Explained, and the associated links within the article.

Acute Training Load (ATL)

Acute training load refers to the total training stress from recent training sessions, typically measured over a short time period (for example, one week). It is analogous to the 'fatigue' that is a result of recent training. ATL can assist with microcycle (weekly) periodisation as it focuses on short-term monitoring and recovery management. Short-term monitoring allows athletes and coaches to assess immediate training impacts and adjust workloads rapidly. Intensity and recovery management helps ensure that the athlete is not over-reached or under-recovered in the short term by balancing high-intensity sessions with lighter recovery days.

Chronic Training Load (CTL)

Chronic training load refers to the athlete's average training load over a longer duration (for example, several weeks or months). It reflects the cumulative training stress absorbed by the athlete and is analogous to the changes in 'fitness' that they are likely to demonstrate. CTL is the key parameter on which training periodisation is based and could be viewed as the training 'dose' given to the athlete. Periodisation is then achieved through understanding and prescribing the correct volume and duration of the dose to get the best balance between training stress and fatigue accumulation. CTL influences training periodisation in micro, meso (monthly) and macro (yearly) cycle planning, as it aids with the quantification of gradual and progressive overload, tapering and recovery phases. For instance, building CTL before a competition peak and having a value to the training stress that has occurred can then help with prescribing the best tapering workloads for optimal performance.

Integration of Acute and Chronic Training Load

There are a number of software tools that enable daily tracking of ATL and CTL parameters. The most precise measures of training stress come from monitoring power for all endurance sessions that are undertaken by the athlete and relating it to the functional threshold power (analogous to power at LT2) of that athlete. When it comes a rower cycling, this can be done simply through the use of stationary trainers or power meter interfaces connected to the bike cranks. For a rower on the ergometer, it can be achieved by recording the stroke-to-stroke power measures from the various rowing ergometers and their accompanying or third-party-connected software. Although tracking on-water rower power is possible, undertaking it on a session-by-session stroke-to-stroke basis and passing that to software to calculate ATL and CTL is very cumbersome, time-consuming and expensive. Two of the most common alternative variables used to calculate on-water ATL and CTL are sessional RPE and heart rate, but both measures are imprecise and subject to several internal and external influences, making comparisons between individuals difficult. However, measures of ATL and CTL from heart rate or sessional RPE within a single individual can compensate for a number of these imperfections and do a good job of reflecting the 'dose' of training absorbed by the rower.

The measures can be represented by a pyramid diagram (*see* below). The base of the pyramid represents the largest component of the rower's training time, each column represents the dose of training, and the total training stress is represented by the height of the daily column. If more than a single session is completed in a day, but all the sessions are of the same modality, the height of the column increases. If the rower completes multiple sessions of different modalities in a day, the height of the column increases, and different colours are used to indicate the different modalities. Each day of training completed contributes to training fatigue or ATL (7-day weighted average) as well as endurance fitness or CTL (28-day weighted average).

The higher the level of training stress, the more the body will have the drive to adapt and improve performance, but this must be balanced with the fatigue that will accumulate as a result. Prolonged excessive fatigue will lead to non-functional over-reaching, which exists on the over-training continuum (*see* below). However, when it is managed correctly in a well-periodised plan, it can lead to the greatest improvements in performance. The colours of the over-training continuum and the training stress ratio (ATL/CTL) graph are consistent. When the ratio is in the green and orange zone, training is being managed well. If the ratio remains consistently in the red zone the body extends into the non-functional over-reaching stage of the continuum; if unchecked, this may become over-training and, quite often, rowers will become sick, injured or demotivated.

By effectively integrating acute and chronic training loads into their periodisation strategy, rowers can optimise their training stress, enhance recovery protocols, and ultimately improve performance outcomes. This structured approach enables better management of fatigue and adaptation, allowing athletes to peak at the right time while minimising the risk of excessive and long-term fatigue.

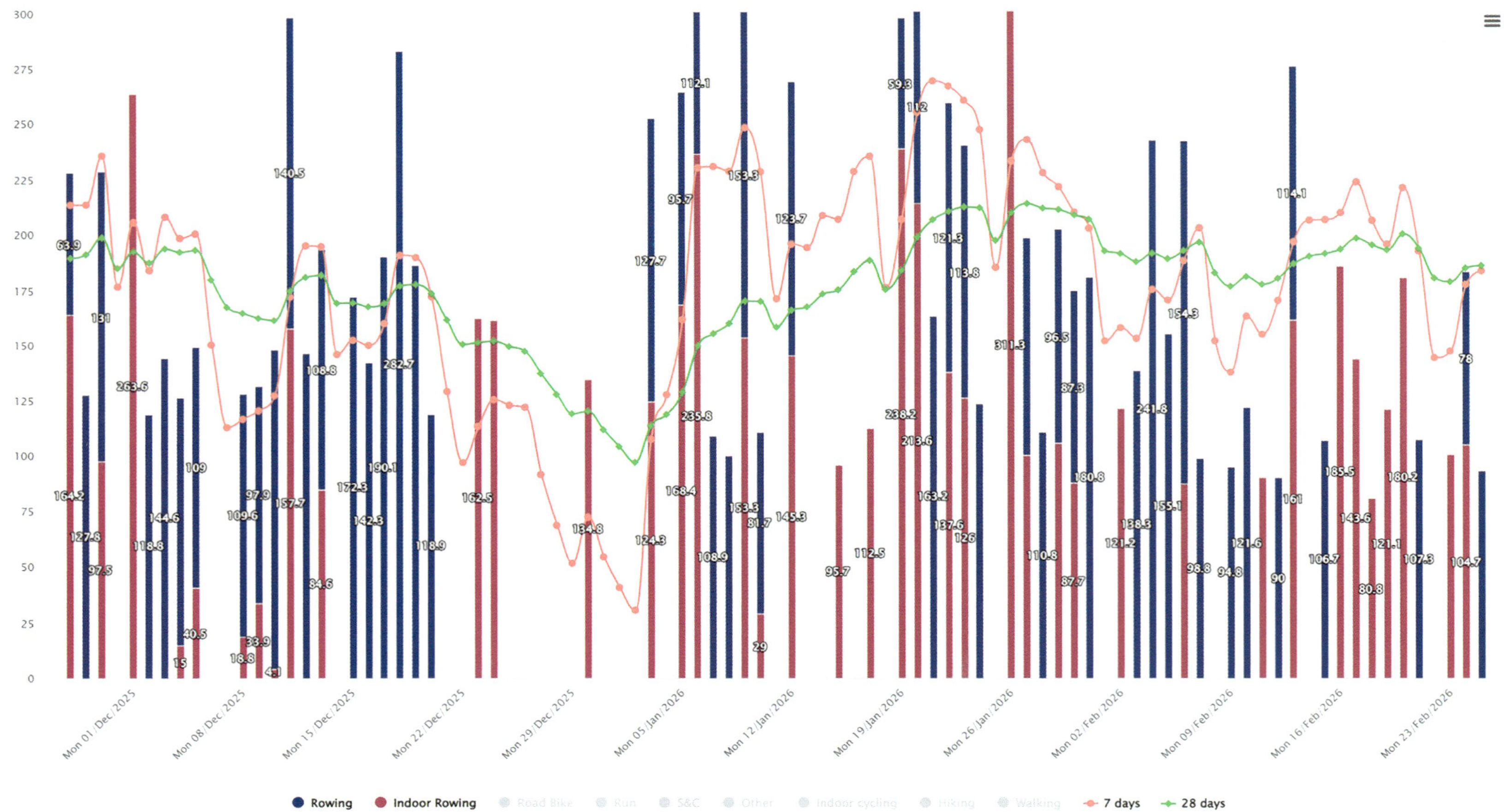

Training stress (individual columns), acute training load (ATL; akin to fatigue; orange line) and chronic training load (CTL; akin to fitness; green line) for a well-trained rower recommencing training after a break period. This chart shows a very well-managed training load with periods of low training stress interspersed with 3- to 5-day blocks of high training stress, allowing for a steady increase in CTL. With ATL > CTL for the majority of the 3-month period the saw-tooth nature of ATL ensures a manageable stress and recovery cycle that produces and then maintains excellent rowing fitness in this individual.

Progression of training-induced fatigue, which exists on a continuum (adapted from Halson et al. and Herzog et al.). It begins from the Ideal Training State, where daily training stress induces Acute Fatigue, which is characterised by rapid recovery within 24 to 48 hours. Prolonged Acute Fatigue will escalate to over-reaching and eventually can lead to over-training. Over-reaching can be divided into functional over-reaching (FOR) and non-functional over-reaching (NFOR). FOR is an intentionally induced short-term dip in performance due to training overload, such as during training camps, and typically requires about two weeks for recovery. It is a component of strategic periodisation. In contrast, NFOR may take several weeks or even months to overcome, with no supercompensation benefits, making the downsides more significant than the advantages. The most severe form, over-training syndrome (OTS), is extremely rare and involves a substantial decline in performance. Recovery can take months to years and often signifies the conclusion of an athletic career.

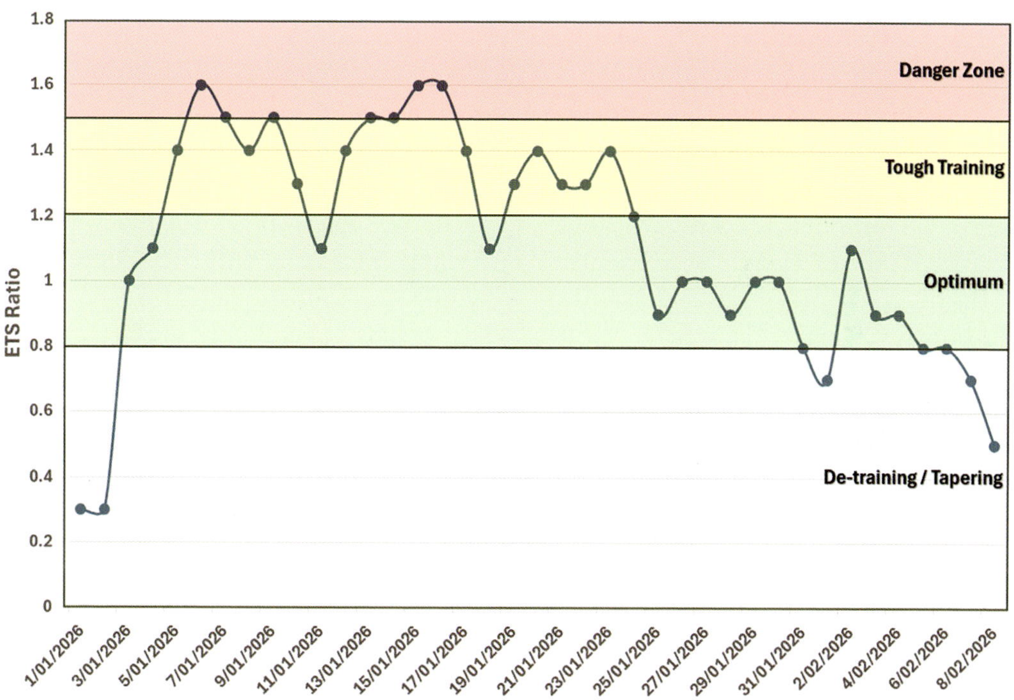

Data from earlier figure represented as ATL:CTL ratio. The colourisation of the ATL:CTL ratio can be directly applied to the over-training continuum (*see* above). [Figure 6.7] Maintaining ATL:CTL within a range of approximately 0.8 to 1.2 is optimal for maximising training volume and maintaining the Ideal Training State. Ratios above 1.5 indicate a sharp increase in workload and movement into a Functional Over-Reaching state, which must be managed effectively with structured recovery and a lower dose of training stress. Ratios over 1.5 are possible for very short durations but place the rower at risk of Non-Functional Over-Reaching indicating greater chance for illness, injury and lack of compensation to the training stress.

Racing Science

Analysing Data from Three Olympic Games

Renowned rowing biomechanist Valery Kleshnev has done extensive research into racing speed and performance trends at World Rowing events from 1993 until present. His research is relevant to understanding speed prognostication, race profiles and the relationship between stroke rate and work per stroke. It is insightful to look back at three Olympic Games – Rio, Tokyo and Paris. Events at Rio and Tokyo were both were held on saltwater but in very different conditions – Rio in crosswinds and headwinds and Tokyo in strong tailwinds and crosswinds. The Paris Olympic Games were held on freshwater in Vaires-sur-Marne Nautical Stadium. The conditions varied considerably throughout the regatta but in general there were mild cross tailwinds. The last day of the finals was the fastest and the second day of the finals was the slowest of the four finals days.

Utilising GPS data from World Rowing, Kleshnev assessed the racing stroke rates and boat speeds, and the effectiveness of the crews' work per stroke (the distance/power per stroke that the crew would travel at a given stroke rate). He compared the winner and medal winners against finalists and then compared and contrasted the difference between the finish placings for these variables. He deduced that the Olympic regatta in Rio was 'the second-slowest over the last 24 years (since 1993), only being led by the Worlds in 1995 in Tampere'. The Games in Paris were the eleventh-fastest since 1993 and almost identical to the winners' speed of Beijing in 2008 and London in 2012.

As in previous world-level regattas Kleshnev found 'no statistically significant difference was found in average stroke rates between finalists...the races were won by means of longer distance per stroke and a higher effectiveness of work per stroke, not by higher stroke rate'. From the data relating to A Finals, he calculated that a crew that had 1.4% higher effective work per stroke on average would finish one place higher. Out of the fourteen Olympic events there were four exceptions to this rule. These winners were successful due to a higher stroke rate.

In Tokyo the conditions were predominantly a strong cross tailwind. There were six world's best times set and Kleshnev's work showed that the event 'was the second fastest World Regatta since 1993, only 0.3% slower than Worlds-2014 Amsterdam'. He concluded that the faster conditions enabled a faster boat speed, creating higher racing stroke rates:

> *The average stroke rate in the 12 Olympic boat classes (GPS data of two boat classes weren't available) was 39.0spm, which is 0.6spm higher than in previous Worlds – 2019 in Linz and similar to Worlds – 2018 in Plovdiv.... The differences in the rate between finalists was insignificant: only +/-0.2spm within the first four place takers, though 8 out of 12 winners showed lower average stroke rate than their silver competitors.*

This analysis demonstrates the balance and relationship between distance per stroke and stroke rate during racing but also shows that the most successful crew gets more distance travelled each stroke at a given stroke rate than their opposition. Length of stroke, power per stroke and distance per stroke are key components to focus on technically and as part of the training programme.

Pacing Strategies

Kleshnev further emphasised the critical nature of the body of the race: 'The winners were among the slowest at the first 100–150m after the start, but significantly faster than their competitors during the middle of the race.' This suggests that appropriate race-start pacing could allow winners to sustain higher mid-race boat speed, which has the net effect of surpassing any margin that is sacrificed in the first 150m. Obviously the balance between race-start and mid-race pace for individual crews must be developed through training, simulated racing and high-value competitive racing.

Winning pacing strategies may be based on simple 500m split data from World Rowing. In competitive international rowing, the boats that are among the first to reach the 1000m and/or 1500m marks of the race are most likely to win. Typically, medal winners tend to come from the top three boats at the 1000m point; a boat that is outside this group by the 1500m mark is very unlikely to secure a medal. To maximise its chance of success, a boat needs to position itself efficiently within the top three early on (first 500m of the race) and especially by the 1000m mark, since the outcome is often decided in this phase. Gold medals are usually secured during the third 500m segment, with strong evidence to suggest that, barring any anomalies, the boat with the fastest middle 1000m boat speed is likely to lead at the 1500m mark and maintain its position through to the finish. Only in rare cases do significant changes in placement occur in the final 500m.

Fast boats, particularly those competing for gold medals, tend to be aggressive from the outset, consistently winning heats and semi-finals. This early pace and dominance tends to carry through to the final. Evidence from several Olympic boat classes supports this trend. In the 2023 World Rowing Championships in Belgrade, four boat classes – Lightweight Women's Double Scull, Women's Single Scull, Women's Pair and Women's Double Scull – consistently led from the first 500m to the end, with the top three positions at 1000m generally remaining unchanged through the race. Moreover, in six out of seven female Olympic boat classes, the top three at 1500m also finished as the medallists, illustrating the importance of early positioning. The only exception was the Women's Eight, where a boat outside the top three at 1000m, specifically the USA, managed to medal in the last 500m.

Similar patterns are observed in male heavyweight sculling boat classes such as the

Men's Single Scull, Men's Double Scull and Men's Quad Scull, where the leading boat maintained a commanding lead from the first 500m all the way to the finish. Most often, the top three boats at 1500m went on to claim the medals, a trend evident across the majority of male Olympic classes. Some races saw minor lead changes, such as between Romania and Great Britain in the Men's Eight in the second 500m, but the overall pattern remained consistent. The A Final in Belgrade 2023 of the Lightweight Men's Double Scull was an exception, with the lead changing hands in the last 500m, demonstrating that late shifts can occur if there is enough determination on the part of the crew. Despite these rare anomalies, the prevailing racing style over recent years indicates that success at the senior international level is achieved by establishing a top three position – often first – by the 500m mark and then maintaining or expanding this lead through the middle 1000m. The final 500m then become a task of sustaining or managing the winning margin, completing a strategic race focused on early dominance and strong middle-section performance.

Delivering the Perfect Race

These observations are critical in the building of a training programme and performance plan to achieve rowing success. The technical principles (stroke development and correction to achieve a long stroke with good power and distance per stroke), the training programme, and the racing strategy and plan all need to be aligned in order to deliver the perfect race.

The principle of sport specificity means that adaptations are directly related to the specific stimulus of the rower's exercise modality, training intensity and training volume. The nature of rowing and the spoon of the oar interacting with water, and the properties of water, mean that, once a rower is rowing hard at approximately stroke rate 24 the time the spoon is in the water is similar to racing and that the differences are that force application is earlier and there is less time on the slide during recovery. This means that with 20 to 24 stroke rate training rowers can be close to race-specific forces and timing without full race intensity. Ultimately, this will enable the crew to develop technically and rhythmically at sub racing rates. By building up to race rates they can spend time developing their length, work per stroke and distance per stroke. Once at their racing stroke range they can use trial and error to determine what is their optimal race stroke rate and pace.

Monitoring and testing the development and progress of training in rowing are essential for ensuring that both the crew and the coach are focusing on key components to maximise the speed of the boat and its athletes. While the stopwatch is an impartial tool for measuring performance, external factors in the rowing environment can significantly impact speed and consistency. Elements such as stream strength, water temperature, wind direction and intensity, and water depth all play a role in determining how fast a boat can go.

To enhance comparability of times, it is crucial to maintain consistency in the training location and to measure performance under similar conditions. For instance, headwinds can slow a boat down substantially, while a tailwind can create a more stable environment for evaluation. Utilising tailwinds allows for more reliable comparisons of times and provides an opportunity to measure performance against World or other championship benchmarks, inspiring crews to reach for elite levels of achievement.

Boat speed and the times recorded during measured pieces and races result from a complex interplay of biomechanical, technical, physiological and psychological factors. Effective coaching hinges on identifying and focusing on the key elements that influence boat speed. Fundamental to a powerful drive phase are stroke length, the power (in Watts) produced by each rower, and the timing of the drive movement. One of the primary factors that can hinder a boat's speed is the drag created by the hull in the water.

Equally vital is the efficiency of the rower and crew's recovery phase, as it enables the boat to glide horizontally and smoothly, maximising its run. The interplay between these two phases – drive and recovery – creates a rhythm and consistent stroke rate essential for performance.

By employing biomechanical analysis to evaluate these critical parameters, coaches can manipulate and track progress over time. This enables them to objectively assess a crew's performance development and training status. Understanding the key biomechanical parameters – stroke length, effective work per stroke and distance per stroke – will help both the rower and the coach to recognise the types and magnitude of change that can be anticipated as they transition from training sessions at sub-maximal loads and stroke rates to competitive racing.

7 Use of Technology in Understanding Training and Performance

This chapter aims to explore the various software platforms that are available to rowers, coaches and support staff to help log, analyse and plan training. The strengths and weaknesses of the software will be addressed in detail, but this is not a comprehensive review of each platform. The aim is for you to understand what each platform can do to assist you in progressing your fitness and performance.

Background

The sport of rowing demands a unique combination of endurance, strength and technique, requiring athletes to engage in highly specialised training programmes with large training volumes. As the sport evolves, so too does the approach to coaching and athlete management. The integration of training software has become increasingly prevalent in the rowing community, providing significant advantages for both rowers and coaches.

Traditionally, rowing training has relied on manual methods of recording performance and tracking workouts, which could be time-consuming and prone to human error. Coaches have often depended on their intuition and experience to design training programmes, leading to variability in quality and effectiveness. With advancements in sports science and technology, there has been a shift toward data-driven methodologies that emphasise precise measurement and analysis of athletic performance.

Training load software for rowers helps athletes and coaches monitor and optimise training schedules, track performance, and prevent over-training by analysing data from various sources such as heart rate monitors, GPS devices, rowing machines and bicycle power meters or indoor/stationary trainers. Some of the software suites allow communication between users and the transfer of live data from athlete devices back to a central location for viewing in real time. The list of features offered by a software platform will nearly always be more than the user needs or accesses routinely. However, experience has shown that some users are typically accessing two to three different suites to investigate metrics from the same session, as a complete software suite that has everything a rower or coach would ever need does not appear to exist.

Core Components of a Software Suite

Among the most commonly used platforms, some also provide the ability to plan training as well as analyse. They may also include components for recording daily wellness from self-reported measures and wearable technology and plan and record strength and conditioning sessions.

It is difficult to create the perfect software suite that meets all the needs of all its users, but there are some core components and methods of organisation that have proven to be successful for the long-standing players in the market. Listed below are 'must-haves' to be aware of when trialling software for integration into a programme:

- **Data tracking and management**: ability to log and store data from various sources, including workouts, nutrition, sleep and recovery metrics.
- **Performance metrics**: comprehensive tracking of factors such as heart rate, pace, distance, power output, body mass, training stress balance and/or ratio, blood lactate and perceived exertion measures.
- **Workout planning and scheduling**: tools for planning, scheduling and modifying training workouts, allowing for periodisation across micro, meso and macro cycles, and the ability to then provide customisation.
- **Analysis tools**: advanced analytics that provide insights into performance trends such as modality specific power profiles, strengths and weaknesses over time, helping to identify areas for improvement.
- **Integration with devices**: compatibility with various fitness devices (such as GPS watches, heart rate monitors and cycling power meters) for seamless data import/export.
- **Integration with third-party sources**: compatibility and exchange of data with other providers, to assist with providing a broader range of features. Data aggregation and consolidation enable a more comprehensive overview of performance and health metrics.
- **Visualisation and reporting**: progress is summarised in clear visual representations of data through graphs and charts, and there are comprehensive reporting features.
- **Goal setting and tracking**: functionality for setting specific performance goals and tracking progress towards those goals over time.
- **Recovery and nutrition insights**: modules to track recovery metrics (such as sleep quality, muscle soreness and heart rate variability, or HRV) and nutrition information, emphasising the importance of recovery in an endurance training programme.
- **Community features**: social aspects such as forums or leaderboards to engage with other athletes for motivation and support as well as communication between users (coach to athlete, athlete to coach and athlete to athlete).

- **User-friendly interface**: intuitive navigation and an easy-to-use interface to ensure that athletes can access and interpret their data without a steep learning curve.
- **Mobile-specific interface**: optimisation of information using all available screens, regardless of the OS or screen size, whilst ensuring easy navigation and accessibility to key components of the platform with consistent web to mobile transition.

By incorporating these core components into the platform, a rower and their coach can be methodical and have a structured approach towards goal setting, training periodisation and performance improvement. Experience has shown that the sport of rowing is rather slow to adopt new training paradigms and technologies that support understanding of an athlete's development. Often, individuals and coaches choose to rely on traditional programming and coach/athlete 'feel' to gauge the progress of training rather than use a more evidence-based approach.

Logging rowing training data is crucial for several reasons. It allows athletes to track their progress over time, identify patterns in performance, and set achievable goals. By maintaining detailed records, rowers can pinpoint specific areas that need improvement, whether that is technique, endurance or strength. Moreover, when issues arise, such as a decline in performance, or an increase in illness or injuries, reference to a comprehensive log can help coaches and athletes analyse potential causes and adjust training regimens accordingly. This data driven evidence-based approach not only enhances training efficiency but also fosters a better understanding of each individual's unique response to training stimuli, ultimately leading to more effective and personalised rowing strategies.

The software also enables engagement with the athlete, helping them to maintain motivation by using certain incentives – inviting them to participate in challenges and share their workouts, giving them updates on their training status or ranking their training and racing efforts on a leaderboard. The social features of the software play a significant role in engaging rowers and fostering a sense of community within the sport. Many platforms incorporate social networking, competition leaderboards and team challenges, which encourage interaction among athletes. By allowing rowers to share their achievements, progress updates and training tips, a supportive environment is created, motivating individuals to stay committed to their training goals. Virtual races or team events cultivate camaraderie and healthy competition, enhancing the overall experience for the athletes. Engaging with others through these platforms not only makes training more enjoyable but also helps rowers to build connections that can lead to valuable friendships, improving retention and participation in the sport.

Popular Training Load Software

TrainingPeaks

Launched in 2022, TrainingPeaks (TP, trainingpeaks.com) is one of the first, and probably the most popular and comprehensive online software suite available to endurance athletes. It has an online and offline/local computer (WKO) module. Although it is primarily designed for use by an individual, it has a very complete capability for a coach to deploy training plans across a number of athletes at one time and then individualise the global plan to suit the needs of each group member. It has excellent load monitoring metrics including ATL, CTL, TSB and graphically displays this information on a customised performance management chart (PMC). Reports and summaries are easily generated through predefined variables and periods. Unfortunately, TP does not handle crew boat information such as boat GPS and inertial sensors, nor does it allow for single data streams to be spread across multiple athletes, which would be useful in a crew.

TP's greatest feature is its PMC, which uses power-based and HR-based training load scores to be exponentially weighted across time constants to elicit fitness (CTL) and fatigue (ATL) estimates. This allows users to visualise changes in these parameters as a result of training, taper, rest, injury or illness.

Strava

Strava (strava.com) is primarily known for its social networking features for athletes, but also offers GPS tracking, workout analysis and heart rate data. It helps to foster athlete motivation through engaging a community of like-minded individuals, who may or may not be local. The software has a specific set of metrics for analysing training but does not provide specific planning or coaching capability. There are a number of features that appeal to rowers. First, it handles modality reporting very well and will easily provide a summary of training completed, on a week, month or yearly basis and broken down across exercise modality. Within each training session a user can use pre-determined 'segments' that Strava saves and it then analyses previous and future activities based on geolocation. Rowers can create a geo-fenced segment for each lane on a rowing course and then simply row the course and have lap times automatically created each time it crosses into or out of it. This is exceptionally handy for coaches, who cannot be at the start line and finish lines at the same time, or for rowers who are training as individuals. The geo-location segment feature is useful when cycling and running as part of a training programme.

It is not always strategic to have all the training statistics accessible immediately at the completion of a session, but Strava can facilitate this, with automatic sharing of segments between those with permission – athletes, coaches and fellow rowers. Although premium Strava accounts have a number of metrics that are similar to those in TrainingPeaks and LUDUM,

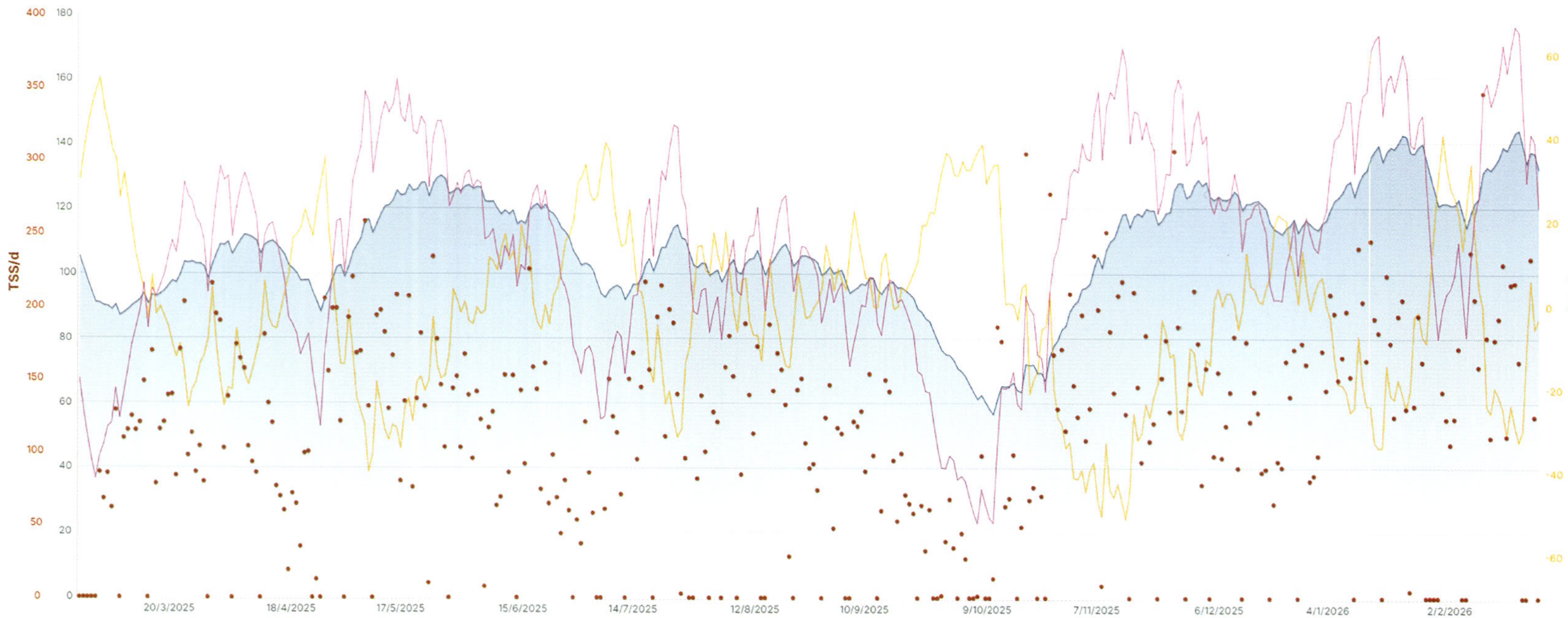

An example of a 365-day training log with shaded blue representing chronic training load, purple line representing acute training load and training stress balance shown in yellow. This performance management chart helps athletes optimise their training strategy by balancing periods of intense training with recovery, ultimately aiming to enhance performance while minimising the risk of injury or burn-out.

the platform is built on training analysis and not coaching and planning tools.

Garmin Connect

Launched in 2008, Garmin Connect (connect.garmin.com) is a web-based platform to support users of Garmin fitness devices in tracking and analysing their workout data. It has continued to evolve since then, with new features and integrations added to enhance the user experience for athletes and fitness enthusiasts across various sports, including running, cycling, swimming and rowing. The strength of the Garmin Connect website is the tight integration with its proprietary hardware devices – fitness watches, bike computers and GPS loggers. The Connect IQ store has thousands of free and paid-for widgets, apps and data fields that can be loaded on to the devices, providing near limitless scope for measurement and display of data. Importantly, the Connect website natively recognises these IQ 'add-ins' and displays the data streams accordingly. Garmin fitness watches now all have 'Rowing' and 'Indoor Rowing' as pre-set modalities, which then trigger the accelerometer in the device to pick stroke rate both indoors and outdoors.

The Garmin Connect mobile app offers a seamless experience with its desktop web-based version, however, it is designed to work by downloading data directly from its own proprietary devices. These accept third-party peripheral data (power pedal, cadence sensors, other HR monitors and so on) into their data stream to time align with other data, prior to uploading to Garmin Connect at the completion of each session.

Garmin Connect uses a calendar-based interface with colourisation and icons to indicate sessions and modality. Basic weekly totals are displayed in the right-hand column and further reports can be accessed via a dedicated menu option. Garmin Connect and Garmin devices are excellent partners for the rower and coach; daily use adds significant value to evidence-based decision-making.

Polar Flow

Polar Electro (flow.polar.com) was first established in 1977 and is well known for its innovations in heart rate monitoring and related technologies for sports and fitness. Its Polar Flow software suite began

The traditional calendar interface is a great landing point for accessing a training session through Garmin Connect.

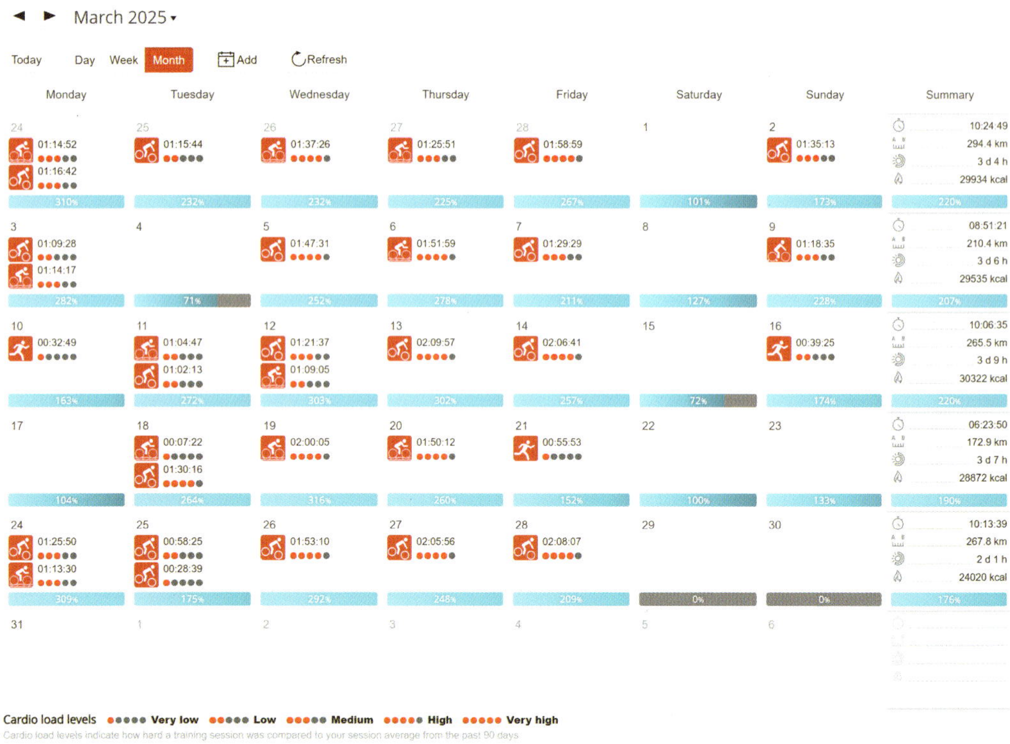

Polar Flow's calendar interface has weekly metrics on the right-hand side of the calendar, updated at the conclusion of each day or each session. The five-dot indicator provides a visual cue as to the 'cardio load' of each particular session.

in 2014 and, paired with its proprietary fitness devices, provides an exceptionally comprehensive platform for planning and logging rowing training. Polar devices are renowned for their accurate heart rate monitoring, which is vital for optimal training intensity, resting heart rate variability measures and accurate HR-based training load measures. Polar Flow offers customisable training plans that will help individual rowers plan and track their training, but it does not offer a coach-focused account, which means that the process typically involves accessing each athlete's account separately.

The software provides detailed performance analysis, including metrics such as stroke rate, distance, speed and heart rate zones, allowing rowers to fine-tune their training whilst providing valuable insights into performance changes. Similar to Garmin Connect, Polar Flow uses a calendar-based navigation with sessions detailed using icons and some simple duration metrics. Polar's own 'Cardio Load' measure is shown after each session indicating in a simple 1–5 system how hard the session has been compared to the session average from the past 90 days.

Ludum's widget-based landing page, highlighting the company's effort to offer a simplified and accessible approach to training planning and assessment. It features important data such as the ATL:CTL ratio, upcoming squad training sessions, and the most recent completed sessions. A menu system provides access to the calendar and other useful tools.

LUDUM

LUDUM (ludum.com) is a comprehensive training management platform originally designed specifically for on-water paddling sports (rowing, canoeing and kayaking). The platform has now expanded to incorporate many other training modalities and assists teams and individual athletes in high-performance sports. It helps rowing coaches and athletes to plan, monitor and analyse training effectively by allowing single data streams to be spread across crew members in the same boat. Key data analysis that is relevant to rowing performance includes stroke rate, stroke efficiency, boat speed (relative to world's best times or prognostics) and ergometer performance. Coaches can create personalised training plans based on individual rower profiles, strengths and weaknesses, while real-time data and feedback during both indoor and outdoor rowing can be undertaken using LUDUM LIVE. The portal provides ample space for posting on-water video from training that can be viewed by the individual or crew at their convenience once the session has completed.

LUDUM aims to improve training and racing outcomes for coaches and rowers by providing detailed metrics and insights, which in turn leads to a greater evidence database on which to make more informed decisions. The LUDUM coach and athlete landing pages provide a simple dashboard of critical and relevant information, providing the user with a better understanding of an athlete's current training status.

Concept2 Logbook and ErgData

Concept2 have been building ergometers since 1981. They are known particularly for rowing ergometers, but now also offer indoor bike ergometers (BikeErg) and a double hand pull ergometer that simulates the upper-body movement of cross-country skiing (the SkiErg). Originally, data from the Concept2 work monitor (now at iteration PM5) was stored on a specific smart card for each individual rower. Now, however, with the addition of ANT+ and BLE, real-time data is transferred to their own proprietary mobile app (ErgData), as well as to a number of third-party sites, including LUDUM, RowNation and RowPro (all live data) and Strava, TrainingPeaks, FitBit, Apple Health and Google Fit (all post-session data).

The Concept2 web portal and ErgData app are neither sophisticated nor difficult to master but they do offer all the features that most individual rowers need from their ergometer sessions, including weekly, monthly and yearly totals, challenges, leaderboards and social connection, as well as the important connections to other software platforms where more in-depth analysis can occur. Concept2 LogBook and ErgData work well and do exactly what they are designed for and nothing else.

RowPro

RowPro (digitalrowing.com) is stand-alone rowing software designed specifically for Concept2 indoor rowers. It offers an immersive training and racing experience that leverages the Concept2 PM4 or 5 work monitor to provide data streams to PC- and Mac-based software via USB. What makes RowPro special for rowers is its ability to 3D-render training and racing scenes based on input variables and real-time data from the Concept2 monitor. It provides basic performance analysis during sessions by allowing users to track their progress over time with metrics such as stroke rate, split times and distance. Rowers are able to compete against each other or against their past performances in a virtual environment, which fosters motivation and engagement.

Additionally, RowPro supports customisable training plans and workouts tailored to individual goals, making it ideal for both recreational and competitive rowers. Its community features encourage interaction among users, enhancing the overall training experience, but it offers no third-party connections. Instead, it allows individual rows to be exported to Concept2 LogBook and from there connections can be made to TrainingPeaks, Strava and so on. As such, RowPro is primarily built for the individual rower and aimed at improvements in performance through engagement in a lifelike environment whilst providing the consistency and flexibility that indoor rowing offers. It is exceptionally useful for rowers returning to training after injury or illness or for those who are away from their daily training environment for an extended period of time, to keep them on track and motivated.

RowNation

Row Nation (rownation.co) intentionally broadens the scope of rowing, integrating it into the wider fitness and wellness markets. Traditionally, ergometer rowing was limited to rowing clubs and elite training centres, but rowing machines have now gained popularity in gyms and homes worldwide, recognised for their effective and comprehensive fitness benefits. However, despite the rise in usage across various markets, access to structured and in-depth rowing fitness content has been limited. Row Nation addresses this gap with an innovative, user-friendly digital platform designed to make rowing-based fitness accessible to all.

The Row Nation app harnesses technology to offer inclusive, structured rowing workouts that are accessible to everyone, regardless of their prior rowing experience or fitness level. Through a thoughtfully designed digital experience, the platform provides scientifically crafted sessions that cater to individual users at home as well as group classes at community facilities, thereby actively expanding participation in indoor rowing.

The app offers structured workout content consisting of professionally designed training sessions with guided video instructions, pacing strategies, and clear workout structures tailored to various fitness levels – beginner, intermediate and advanced. It is compatible with all rowing machines and can be integrated with the Concept2 PM5 monitor, allowing widespread use without the need for specialised hardware. Interactive metrics displayed live during workouts include heart rate, stroke rate (with a traffic-light system to indicate adherence to targeted zones) and drive length (shown in metres).

For group facilitation, the app includes an integrated dashboard that allows administrators and coaches to create and publish workouts and structured programmes. This feature supports posts, event promotion, and direct engagement with club members. In terms of progress tracking and motivation, the app tracks personal achievements in-app to encourage sustained engagement and community-building through friendly competition, shared experiences and event participation. The events integration section is specifically designed to enable clubs or administrators to promote events, encourage direct sign-ups, and foster greater community participation.

The platform actively expands participation by targeting audiences beyond traditional rowing demographics, making the sport appealing and approachable for general fitness enthusiasts and novices alike. Designed to be scalable and community-oriented, it facilitates efficient implementation across multiple venues and diverse user groups, supporting community-building, club management and sustained engagement in indoor rowing. Its inclusive and intuitive approach offers user-friendly pathways into structured rowing fitness by reducing entry barriers through adaptive technology, approachable session designs and clear visual feedback. However, as a relatively new platform, it currently has limitations, including a lack of detailed analytical features such as physiological metrics or training load management, focusing instead on participation, motivation and community health outcomes. Additionally, more advanced functionalities like saving and sharing custom workouts, direct integration with third-party apps such as Strava or Garmin, and deeper community-building tools are still in active development.

Row Nation represents a purposeful response to the evolving role of the rowing machine within the wider health and fitness landscape. By embracing technology-driven accessibility and strategically positioning rowing as a mainstream fitness option, Row Nation actively contributes to the growth and diversification of rowing's participant base.

As technology continues to advance, the role of training software in the rowing community is expected to grow. Innovations in data analytics, wearable technology and artificial intelligence may further enhance the capabilities of the existing platforms, enabling even more precise monitoring and tailored training programmes for individuals as well as those within a training group. The adoption of training software represents a significant shift in rowing training methodologies, providing both athletes and coaches with tools to improve performance, enhance communication, and streamline the training process. By leveraging data, AI and hardware technology, the rowing community can optimise training outcomes and foster continued excellence in the sport.

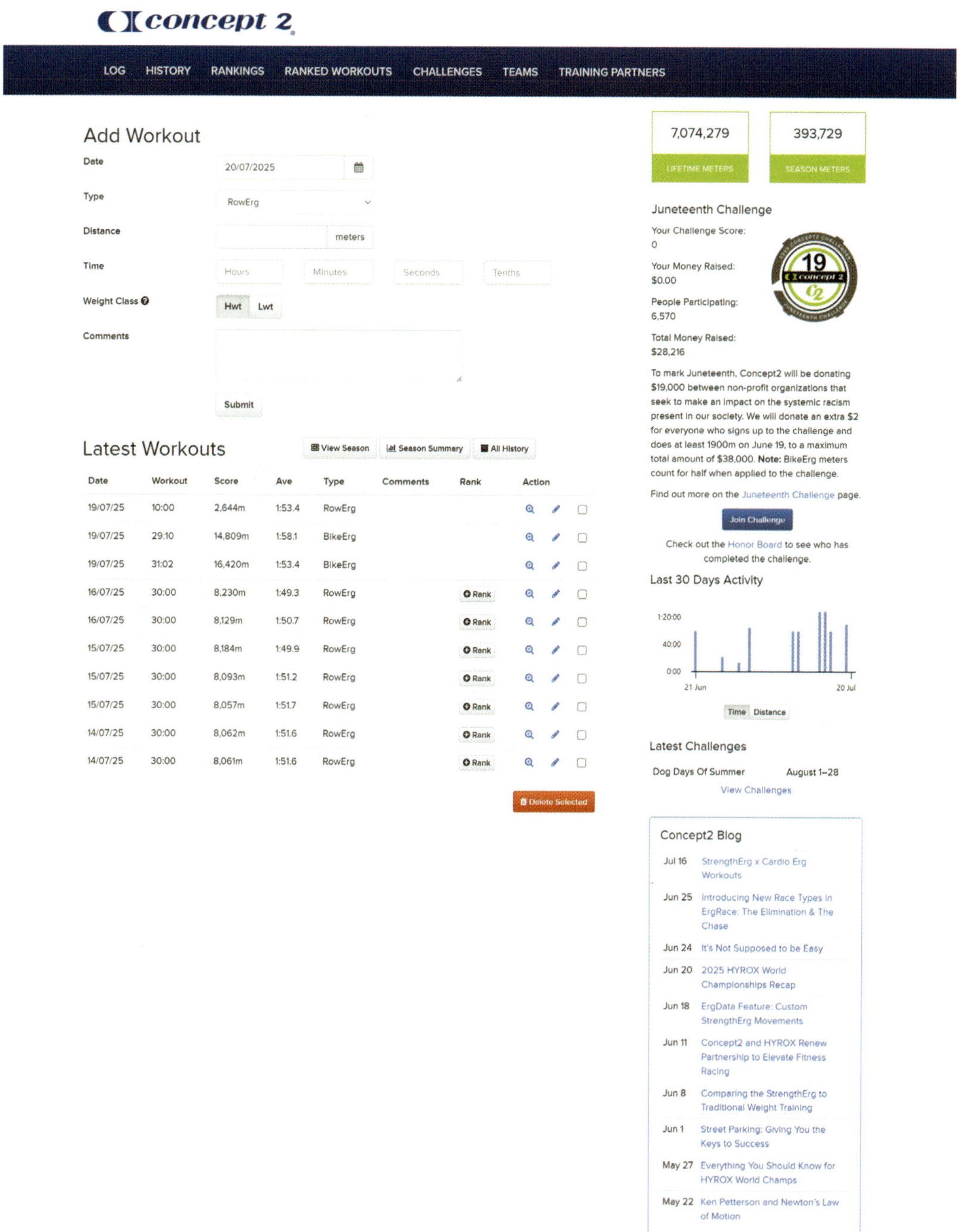

The Concept2 LogBook is a centralised platform where all recorded sessions from RowErg, BikeErg and SkiErg can be accessed. Users simply need to log their ergometer workouts using the ErgData mobile app, which collects data from the PM5 monitor via Bluetooth. This ensures seamless synchronisation and easy tracking of training progress.

The following section highlights each platform's strengths and functions and also provides a comparison and a best-case guide.

TrainingPeaks

TrainingPeaks provides comprehensive **activity tracking**, capturing sessions from a wide range of third-party devices. It offers strong **general data analysis** and moderate **rowing-specific analysis** through integration rather than native metrics. The platform supports robust **file import** from external devices and strong **export capability** in common performance formats. It is highly effective for structured **training plans**, delivering detailed **performance insights** over time, though **real-time data collection** is limited.

TrainingPeaks enables **custom workouts** and integrates well through extensive **syncing with other apps**. It does not rely on **proprietary hardware** and has limited **community features** beyond coach–athlete interaction. **Nutrition tracking** is available via integrations. The **dashboard** is comprehensive but requires some familiarity. A strong **mobile app** supports remote access.

It is a **cloud-based platform** with desktop compatibility and operates under a **tiered subscription model**, with free and premium options.

Strava

Strava supports strong **activity tracking** across numerous devices and delivers moderate **general data analysis**, though **rowing-specific analysis** is limited. It allows **file import** from most tracking systems and supports basic **export functionality**.

Structured **training plans** are not a primary function, but it offers useful **performance insights** through trends and comparisons. **Real-time data collection** is limited. **Custom workouts** are not native, but it excels in **syncing with other apps**.

Strava does not depend on **proprietary hardware** and has very strong **community features**, which are central to its value. **Nutrition tracking** is not native. The **dashboard** is highly user-friendly, supported by a strong **mobile app**.

It operates as a **cloud-based platform** with free and paid subscription tiers.

Garmin Connect

Garmin Connect offers strong **activity tracking** via proprietary devices and provides solid **general data analysis**, though **rowing-specific insights** are limited. It supports **file import** and good **export capability**.

The platform allows structured **training plans** and delivers useful **performance insights**, supported by effective **real-time data collection** through Garmin hardware. **Custom workouts** are supported.

It integrates through moderate **syncing with other apps** but is centred on **proprietary hardware**. **Community**

features exist but are limited. **Nutrition tracking** is minimal.

The **dashboard** is clear and functional, with a well-developed **mobile app**. It operates as a **cloud-based ecosystem** included with Garmin devices, with no additional licensing cost.

Polar Flow

Polar Flow supports reliable **activity tracking** through Polar devices and provides moderate **general data analysis**. It offers limited **rowing-specific insights**.

It allows **file import** and basic **export functionality**. Structured **training plans** are supported and contribute to individual **performance insights. Real-time data collection** is enabled via Polar hardware.

Custom workouts are supported and syncing is moderate. The system is built around **proprietary hardware**. **Community features** and **nutrition tracking** are limited.

The **dashboard** is user-friendly and supported by a capable **mobile app**. It is a **cloud-based platform** included within the Polar ecosystem.

LUDUM

LUDUM delivers strong **activity tracking** across internal and external sources and provides advanced **general data analysis**. It offers meaningful **rowing-specific insights** where integrated.

It supports both **file import** and strong **export capability**. Structured **training plans**, wellness monitoring, and squad oversight provide significant **performance insights**.

Real-time data collection is limited but monitoring inputs are strong. **Custom workouts** are supported and the platform integrates well through **syncing**.

LUDUM does not rely on **proprietary hardware** and has moderate **community features** within teams. **Nutrition tracking** can be integrated.

It offers a clear **dashboard** and strong **mobile app**, operating as a **cloud-based platform** with tiered **licensing options**.

Concept2 Logbook/ErgData

Concept2 Logbook provides dedicated **activity tracking** for indoor rowing and moderate **general data analysis**. It offers strong **rowing-specific analysis** based on machine outputs.

It supports **file import** from Concept2 devices and limited **export capability** (CSV). It does not support structured **training plans**, but provides useful **performance insights**.

It enables strong **real-time data collection** through connected ergs but offers no **custom workouts**. **Syncing** is limited to Concept2 ecosystem tools.

It relies on **proprietary hardware** and has minimal **community features**. No **nutrition tracking** is included.

The **dashboard** is simple and supported by a strong **mobile app**. It is a **cloud-based platform** and is **free to use**.

RowPro

RowPro provides strong **activity tracking** for indoor rowing and moderate **general data analysis**, with strong **rowing-specific functionality**.

It supports limited **file import** and export capability. It does not provide structured **training plans**, though it supports performance tracking and delivers useful **performance insights**.

Real-time data collection is strong when connected to ergometers. **Custom workouts** are supported. **Syncing** is limited.

RowPro relies on **Concept2 hardware**, has minimal **community features** and no **nutrition tracking**.

It operates via a locally installed **platform** with a simple interface and no mobile app. It is available via **subscription licensing**.

Comparison Summary

Across the platforms reviewed, there is a clear distinction between **performance management systems**, **device ecosystems**, **rowing-specific tools** and **social tracking platforms**.

TrainingPeaks and **LUDUM** sit at the performance management end of the spectrum, offering the strongest capability in structured planning, performance insights and integration across multiple data sources. These platforms are best suited to coached environments where monitoring and training prescription are central.

Garmin Connect and **Polar Flow** operate primarily as proprietary ecosystems built around hardware. They provide reliable activity tracking, real-time data capture and solid general analysis, but are less effective as standalone coaching or team monitoring tools.

Concept2 Logbook/ErgData and **RowPro** are rowing-specific solutions. They offer the strongest rowing-relevant insights and real-time ergometer data but are limited in broader performance management functionality.

Strava stands apart as a participation and engagement platform. While not designed for structured training oversight, its strength lies in visibility, motivation and community interaction.

Overall, the ecosystem spans from:

Rowing-specific performance capture → Device-led monitoring → Integrated coaching systems → Social engagement tools.

No single platform delivers complete functionality across all dimensions; rather, they serve complementary roles within modern rowing programmes.

Rating-Based Positioning Table

Platform	Overall Rating	Performance Planning	Data Depth	Rowing Specific	Integration	Real-Time Capability	Ecosystem Dependence
TrainingPeaks	★★★★★ (5)	Excellent	Advanced	Moderate	Excellent	Limited	Independent
LUDUM	★★★★★ (5)	Excellent	Advanced	Moderate	Strong	Limited	Independent
Strava	★★★★ (4)	Limited	Basic	Low	Excellent	Limited	Independent
Garmin Connect	★★★★ (4)	Moderate	Moderate	Low	Moderate	Strong	Garmin
Polar Flow	★★★★ (4)	Moderate	Moderate	Low	Moderate	Strong	Polar
RowPro	★★★ (3)	Limited	Moderate	Strong	Limited	Strong	Concept2
Concept2 Logbook	★★★ (3)	Limited	Basic	Strong	Limited	Strong	Concept2

Best Use Case Guide

Platform	Best Use Case
TrainingPeaks	High-performance programmes requiring structured planning, coach oversight and longitudinal monitoring
LUDUM	Team environments needing centralised athlete monitoring and readiness tracking
Strava	Athlete engagement, motivation and visibility of training activity
Garmin Connect	Individual athletes operating within Garmin hardware ecosystems
Polar Flow	Individual monitoring with structured training support via Polar devices
Concept2 Logbook/ErgData	Accurate indoor rowing performance tracking and benchmarking
RowPro	Structured indoor rowing training and simulation

Epilogue: The Endless Pursuit of Speed

Rowing is a sport of paradoxes – simple in its essence, yet infinitely complex in its execution. It is a discipline where the pursuit of speed is never truly finished, and where mastery is measured not only in medals, but in moments of clarity, connection and progress.

High-performance rowing is defined by an intricate interplay between art and science. From biomechanics to mindset, from rigging to rhythm, from physiology to feedback, there are scientific principles that underpin speed and the practices that sustain excellence. This book aims to be a resource that empowers rowers, coaches and practitioners to think critically, train purposefully, and coach with intent. The lessons within its pages are not static. They are meant to evolve – just as the sport does. Technology will continue to advance, training methods will refine, and new generations of athletes will bring fresh perspectives and challenges. What will remain constant is the need for curiosity, reflection and collaboration.

The novice being guided through their first strokes, the crew preparing for an Olympic final, the individual who is simply seeking to understand the sport more deeply – all need to remember that rowing is a journey that rewards patience, demands precision and celebrates unity. The boat moves fastest when everything – and everyone – works together.

The aim of this book has been to help you find new ways to make the boat go faster. But more importantly, it has sought to inspire you to keep asking questions, keep seeking better, and keep rowing forwards.

Paul Thompson MBE & Dr Anthony Rice.

Glossary

Rowing Terms

Button/Collar The oars button or collar sits on the sleeve of the oar and determining the oars inboard/outboard.

Catch The moment the blade enters the water at the beginning of the drive phase.

Drag Factor Resistance setting on an ergometer influencing load.

Drive Phase The segment of the stroke where force is applied through legs, trunk and arms to accelerate the boat.

Effective Stroke Length Arc where meaningful force is applied to the water.

Ergometer (Ergo) Indoor rowing machine used for training and testing.

Feathering Rotating the oar so the blade is parallel to the water during recovery.

Finish End of the drive phase when the blade exits the water.

Foot Stretcher Adjustable plate where rowers secure their feet.

Gearing Ratio of oar length and spread/span determining load.

Gearing Ratio Mathematical ratio describing mechanical load based on oar length and spread/span.

Inboard/Outboard Measurements of the oar from handle to the oars button (inboard) and collar to blade tip (outboard).

Para-Rowing Classes (PR1, PR2, PR3) Categories based on functional ability for adaptive rowing.

Pitch Angle of the oar blade relative to the water during the stroke.

Pitch Meter Instrument used to measure the oar's pitch. A builder's plumb-bob can also be used to measure pitch.

Rating Strokes per minute (spm).

Recovery Phase The segment of the stroke from the finish of the stroke back to catch, where the boat runs.

Rigging Adjusting boat setup (span, pitch, foot stretcher) for optimal performance.

Roll-ups Drill to improve timing and blade placement.

Span/Spread Distance between the rigger gates pin (sculling = span; sweep = spread).

Square Blades Rowing without feathering; used as a drill for bladework.

Suspension Hanging body weight between handle and foot stretcher during drive.

Science and Biomechanics Terms

Angular Velocity Speed of rotation; relevant for oar movement.

Biomechanics Study of movement and forces.

Conservation of Momentum Principle explaining boat movement when rowers shift mass.

Eccentric Contraction Muscle lengthens under load; common in recovery phase.

Force Curve Graph showing force applied during stroke; used for technique analysis.

Hydrodynamic Drag Resistance of water against the hull.

Intrinsic vs Extrinsic Feedback Internal sensory feedback vs external (coach, technology).

Isometric Contraction Muscle contraction without movement; stabilises trunk during drive.

Kinetic Energy Energy of motion; in rowing, stored in hull, rower and oars.

Lactate Threshold Intensity where lactate accumulates faster than it clears.

Momentum Product of mass and velocity; explains boat acceleration and deceleration.

Pitch, Roll, Yaw Rotational movements of the boat around its axes.

Potential Energy Stored energy due to position (e.g. trunk position at catch).

Power Rate of doing work (Watts); critical for rowing performance.

Rate of Force Development (RFD) Speed at which force is applied; key for a fast catch.

Self-Determination Theory Psychological model emphasising autonomy, competence, and relatedness for motivation.

VO_2 Max Maximum oxygen uptake; indicator of aerobic capacity.

Work Energy transferred when force moves an object (Work = Force × Distance).

Recommended Reading

1. Joyce, D. and Lewindon, D. (eds). (2014). *High-performance training for sports.* Human Kinetics.
2. Kleshnev, V. (2016). *Biomechanics of Rowing.* The Crowood Press.
3. Mallory, P. (2011). *The Sport of Rowing: Two centuries of competition.* River & Rowing Museum.
4. Mallory, P. (2016). *The Rowing Stroke.* Self-published.
5. Nolte, V. (ed.) (2011). *Rowing Faster* (2nd edn). Human Kinetics.
6. Nilsen, T. (ed.) (2014). *Advanced rowing: International perspectives on high performance rowing.* Bloomsbury Publishing.
7. Thompson, P. and Wolf, A. (2012). *Training for the Complete Rower: A guide to improving performance.* The Crowood Press.
8. Thompson, P. (2005). *Sculling: Training, Technique and Performance.* The Crowood Press
9. Australian Institute of Sport. (2012). *Physiological Tests for Elite Athletes* (2nd edn; Rebecca Tanner & Christopher Gore, Contributors). Human Kinetics.
10. Billat, V.L. (2001). Interval training for performance: A scientific and empirical practice: Special recommendations for middle- and long-distance running, cycling, and rowing. *Sports Medicine*, 31(1), 13–31.
11. Joyner, M.J. and Coyle, E.F. (2008). Endurance exercise performance: The physiology of champions. *The Journal of Physiology*, 586(1), 35–44.
12. Laursen, P.B. and Jenkins, D.G. (2002). The scientific basis for high-intensity interval training: Optimising training programmes and maximising performance in highly trained endurance athletes. *Sports Medicine*, 32(1), 53–73.
13. Mujika, I. (2011). Tapering for competition: A review. *Science in Sports and Exercise*, 43(1), 205–219.
14. Pyne, D.B., Trewin, C.B. and Hopkins, W. G. (2004). Progression and variability of competitive performance of Olympic swimmers. *Journal of Sports Sciences*, 22(7), 613–620.
15. Seiler, S. (2010). What is best practice for training intensity and duration distribution in endurance athletes? *International Journal of Sports Physiology and Performance*, 5(3), 276–291.

16. Tanaka, H. and Swensen, T. (1998). Impact of resistance training on endurance performance: A new form of cross-training? *Sports Medicine*, 25(3), 191–200.
17. Tønnessen, E., Sylta, Ø., Haugen, T. A., Hem, E. and Seiler, S. (2014). The road to Gold: Training and peaking characteristics in the year prior to a gold medal endurance performance. *PLOS ONE*, 9(7), e101796.
18. Bompa, T.O. and Haff, G.G. (2009). *Periodisation: Theory and methodology of training* (5th edn). Human Kinetics.
19. Fleck, S.J. and Kraemer, W.J. (2014). *Designing resistance training programs* (4th edn). Human Kinetics. (Contains relevant principles for endurance training periodisation.)
20. Issurin, V. (2016). New horizons for the methodology and logic of training periodisation. *Sports Medicine*, 46(3), 329–338.
21. Rønnestad, B.R. and Mujika, I. (2014). Labeling a training program as a 'tap or peak': An important concept for understanding training periodisation. *Scandinavian Journal of Medicine & Science in Sports*, 24(4), 607–611.
22. Taylor, K.L. and Wood, I.G. (2017). Endurance training periodisation: A review of concepts and applications. *Sports Medicine*, 47(8), 1575–1586.
23. Vervoorn, C. and Hartgens, F. (2017). Periodisation and peaking in endurance sports. *International Journal of Sports Physiology and Performance*, 12(Suppl 2), S227–S232.
24. Zatsiorsky, V.M. and Kraemer, W.J. (2006). *Science and Practice of Strength Training*. Human Kinetics. (Includes foundational concepts applicable to endurance periodisation.)

Bibliography

Abbott, A.E. and Hannafin, J.A. (2001) Rowing injuries. *Sports Medicine*, 31(7), pp.537–555.

Arumugam, A. et al. (2020) Rowing injuries and musculoskeletal adaptations in elite rowers. *Journal of Sports Medicine.*

Attenborough, A., Smith, R. and Sinclair, J. (2012) Influence of technique on rowing performance. *Journal of Sports Sciences.*

Bernstein, N. (2002) *The Co-ordination and Regulation of Movements.* Oxford: Pergamon Press.

Billat, V. (Various publications) Research on physiological determinants of endurance performance.

Boland, A.L. and Hosea, T.M. (1994) Rowing and sculling injuries. *Sports Medicine*, 17(6), pp.417–426.

Bompa, T., Hebbelinck, M. and Van Gheluwe, B. (1985) Physiological and biomechanical factors in rowing performance. *International Journal of Sports Medicine.*

Buchmann, G. et al. (1974) Biomechanics of rowing technique. *International Journal of Sport Biomechanics.*

Buckeridge, E. (2013) Biomechanical asymmetries and joint loading in elite rowers. PhD thesis, University of Western Australia.

Buckeridge, E. (2014) Biomechanical determinants of elite rowing technique and performance.

Buckeridge, E. et al. (2015) Understanding technique and performance in rowing. *Sports Biomechanics.*

Capostagno, B. and Lambert, M.I. (2016) The importance of the anaerobic threshold in cycling performance. *Journal of Sports Sciences*, 34(3), pp.274–280.

Carl, D. and Mechling, H. (1992) Rowing biomechanics and performance analysis. *Sportwissenschaft.*

Cookson, A. and Nolte, V. (2017) *Rowing Faster.* Champaign, IL: Human Kinetics.

Deci, E.L. and Ryan, R.M. (1985) *Intrinsic Motivation and Self-Determination in Human Behaviour.* New York: Plenum.

Draper, N. (2008) Sport science applications in rowing. *Journal of Sports Sciences.*

Gorman, S. (2012) Applied biomechanics in rowing. *Journal of Sports Science and Coaching.*

Green, S. and Wilson, R. (2000) Rowing physiology and performance. *Journal of Sports Sciences.*

Hislop, H., Avers, D. and Brown, M. (2010) *Daniels and Worthingham's Muscle Testing: Techniques of Manual Examination.* St Louis: Elsevier.

Hochmuth, G. (1981) *Biomechanics of Athletic Movement*. Berlin: Sportverlag.

Ingham, S.A. et al. (2002) Determinants of rowing performance. *Medicine & Science in Sports & Exercise*.

Jowett, S. (2020) Coach–athlete relationships in sport. *International Journal of Sport Psychology*.

Jowett, S. (2022) *Interpersonal Relationships in Sport and Exercise*. London: Routledge.

Karlson, K.A. (2000) Rowing injuries: identifying risk factors. *Sports Medicine*.

Keenan, K., Senefeld, J. and Hunter, S. (2018) Sex differences in fatigue mechanisms. *Sports Medicine*.

Kibler, W.B., McMullen, J. and Uhl, T. (2002) Shoulder rehabilitation strategies for the overhead athlete. *American Journal of Sports Medicine*.

Kleshnev, V. (2006) Rowing biomechanics and performance analysis. *BioRow Technical Reports*.

Kleshnev, V. (2010) *Biomechanics of Rowing*. BioRow Ltd.

Lewin, K., Lippitt, R. and White, R.K. (1939) Patterns of aggressive behaviour in experimentally created social climates. *Journal of Social Psychology*, 10, pp.271–299.

Lieber, R.L. and Fridén, J. (1993) Muscle damage mechanisms after eccentric contraction. *Journal of Applied Physiology*.

Ludewig, P.M. and Reynolds, J.F. (2009) The association of scapular kinematics and shoulder pathology. *Journal of Orthopaedic & Sports Physical Therapy*.

MacKenzie, B. (2003) *101 Performance Evaluation Tests*. London: Electric Word.

Mason, B. (1988) Biomechanical analysis of rowing technique. *AIS Biomechanics Reports*.

Mattes, K. (2006) Biomechanical analysis of rowing stroke technique. *Sport Biomechanics*.

McGregor, A.H., Patankar, Z. and Bull, A.M.J. (2008) Spinal kinematics in rowing. *Clinical Biomechanics*.

McGregor, A.H. et al. (2016) Spinal loads and rowing performance. *Journal of Sports Sciences*.

Noguchi, T. et al. (2013) Scapular dyskinesis and shoulder dysfunction. *Journal of Orthopaedic Science*.

Nugent, F. et al. (2020) Shoulder injury risk in rowing athletes. *Sports Medicine*.

Page, P., Frank, C. and Lardner, R. (2010) *Assessment and Treatment of Muscle Imbalance*. Champaign, IL: Human Kinetics.

Persad, R. (2016) Rowing biomechanics and injury mechanisms. *Journal of Sports Medicine*.

Prinold, J. (2012) Scapular mechanics and shoulder stability in rowing. Imperial College London.

Proske, U. and Morgan, D.L. (2001) Muscle damage from eccentric exercise. *Journal of Physiology*.

Rumball, J.S. et al. (2005) Injury patterns in elite rowing. *Sports Medicine*.

Seiler, S., Waneen, T. and Martin, J.C. (1997) Physiology of rowing performance. *Medicine & Science in Sports & Exercise*.

Soper, C. and Hume, P. (2004) Rowing injury risk factors. *Sports Medicine*.

Spencer, M. (2016) Spinal-exercise prescription in sport: classifying physical training and rehabilitation by intention and outcome. *Journal of Strength and Conditioning Research.*

Teunis, T. et al. (2014) Shoulder injury epidemiology in athletes. *British Journal of Sports Medicine.*

Thompson, P. and Wolf, A. (2016) Strength and conditioning approaches for rowing. *Journal of Strength and Conditioning Research.*

Thornton, J. et al. (2017) Scapular mechanics in overhead athletes. *Journal of Shoulder and Elbow Surgery.*

Turpin, N. et al. (2011) Rowing biomechanics and efficiency. *European Journal of Applied Physiology.*

Urbanczyk, C. et al. (2020) Biomechanical modelling of rowing technique. *Sports Biomechanics.*

Urbanczyk, C. et al. (2022) Rowing performance modelling. *Journal of Sports Engineering.*

Vinther, A. et al. (2006) Rowing performance determinants. *Medicine & Science in Sports & Exercise.*

Volianitis, S., Yoshiga, C.C. and Secher, N.H. (2020) Physiology of rowing. *Comprehensive Physiology.*

Warden, S.J. et al. (2002) Serratus anterior function in athletic performance. *Journal of Orthopaedic Research.*

Wolf, A. (2020) *Strength and Conditioning for Rowing.* Ramsbury: Crowood Press.

Index

First published in 2026 by
The Crowood Press Ltd
Ramsbury, Marlborough
Wiltshire SN8 2HR

enquiries@crowood.com
www.crowood.com

British Library Cataloguing-in-Publication Data
A catalogue record for this book is available from the British Library.

For product safety-related questions, contact: productsafety@crowood.com

ISBN 978 0 7198 4602 1

Typeset by: Simon and Sons

Cover design by Sergey Tsvetkov

Printed and bound in India by Parksons Graphics

Acknowledgements

Paul and Tony are extremely grateful and thankful for the collaboration of so many people on this project. Dr Conny Draper's contribution has been instrumental in the development of this book, and her insights, knowledge and deep understanding of rowing and biomechanics permeate the text. Considerable input has come from Nico Furlan, with his understanding of athletic development and performance rowing; Paul Haines, with his deep engineering and biomechanical experience; and Professor Alison McGregor and Dr Caryn Urbancyk, with the rowing research they have done at the biodynamic lab at Imperial College, London. The expert insight into Para Rowing from Tom Dyson and James Loveday has been enlightening, so we are grateful to them. Thank you also to Ellen Randell, Tufe Sele, Dr Andrew Griffin, Tristan Shipsides, Jan Legg and Eva Nates, for your contributions, and to Darren Croker and Iain Smith, who were valuable collaborators and contributors regarding equipment and boat optimisation.

Thanks to all the wonderful rowers who appear throughout this book – their skill, dedication and prowess are truly inspirational. A special thank you to the late Peter Spurrier and to Karon Phillips for the cover photo.

Image credit